P9-AFK-847

"When I wrote *Secrets of a Freelance Writer*, it was th[...] [...]gures as a commercial freelancer. Of the dozen-plus books written on the subject since then, this book is by far the most comprehensive, useful and valuable."

Bob Bly, Author (50+ books)
Secrets of a Freelance Writer, The Copywriter's Handbook

"Peter Bowerman has done it again! *Back for Seconds* is packed with useful tips and resources, along with advice from top professionals in the field. If you've been afraid to tackle corporate writing because you think you don't know enough about "business," this book has everything you need to get you started."

Moira Allen, Author
Starting Your Career as a Freelance Writer
Editor, **www.Writing-World.com**

"Over the years, I've urged dozens of people to buy *The Well-Fed Writer* for ideas on building a writing business from scratch with no experience and no contacts. Now, I'll be recommending the sequel as well. Its case studies, small-market business building tips, cold-calling script and myriad resources are unbeatable."

Marcia Yudkin, Author
6 Steps to Free Publicity (and 10 other books)
www.yudkin.com

"The writing community has been eagerly awaiting Bowerman's next book. They won't be disappointed. This second helping of advice tackles the psychological roadblocks of the business beautifully, and the specific examples of what works (and doesn't) are excellent."

Jenna Glatzer, Author
Make a Real Living as a Freelance Writer
Editor-in-chief, **www.AbsoluteWrite.com**

"This book is enormously needed. As a publisher who hires freelancers, I've learned most writers absolutely stink at marketing themselves. The real-life stories and practical checklists will inspire you and keep you moving in the right direction."

Anne Holland, Publisher
MarketingSherpa Newsletter
www.marketingsherpa.com

"I absolutely loved this book and couldn't put it down. If you want to PROFIT handsomely from your writing, get it. Bowerman drives home the point that selling anything—including writing services—is all about relationship building and as such, nothing to fear."

Joan Stewart, *The Publicity Hound*
www.PublicityHound.com

"Presenting a smorgasbord of information on how to snag new writing clients, squelch your marketing fears, supercharge your networking plan and further sharpen your professional image, Bowerman offers a tried-and-true recipe for freelance success!"

Bev Walton-Porter, Editor/Publisher, *Scribe & Quill*
www.scribequill.com

"If you want to succeed as a freelance writer, buy this book and read it cover to cover. Then read it again. This is the real stuff, told by a great writer and a relentless marketer."

John Clausen, Editor, **www.writingformoney.com**; Author
Too Lazy to Work, Too Nervous to Steal:
How to Have a Great Life as a Freelance Writer

"A feast of practical, down-to-earth advice on running your own writing business—from building your portfolio and getting clients to say 'Yes' to transitioning from journalism and academia and running the business in smaller markets. Highly recommended!"

Gary McLaren, Author
The Freelancer's Guide To Finding Writer's Markets
Editor, **www.WorldwideFreelance.com**

"This is the smartest, most useful guide to freelance writing I've ever read. If you want to turn your words into income, get this book and follow its savvy advice."

Daniel H. Pink, Author
Free Agent Nation: The Future of Working For Yourself
www.freeagentnation.com

"Peter Bowerman's books have what other "how-to-write-for-a-living books" sadly lack—practical, real-world advice on how you can really make it happen."

Cameron Foote, Author
The Business Side of Creativity
Editor, *Creative Business newsletter*—**www.creativebusiness.com**

"I'm a huge fan of *The Well-Fed Writer*. That's why I'm back for seconds! I love the way Bowerman demystifies sales, marketing and prospecting. This book is just what writers today need to get more and better clients."

Steve Slaunwhite, Copywriter & Author,
Start & Run a Copywriting Business

"Marketing skills are as important as good writing skills to today's aspiring freelancer. This book helps writers change their attitudes about selling themselves and their work while providing plenty of specific strategies to crack the lucrative business writing market."

Kelly James-Enger, Author
Ready, Aim, Specialize! Create your own Writing Specialty and Make More Money
www.kellyjamesenger.com

"Most self-employed writers work at home and thus we've come to share their needs. Peter Bowerman's books offer easily digested insights and techniques for making it in today's changing markets."

Paul and Sarah Edwards, Authors (16 books)
Working From Home:
Everything You Need to Know About Living and Working Under the Same Roof

"Ideas and solutions galore to overcome the most common freelance obstacle: marketing, marketing, marketing! And by helpfully demystifying 'hidden' opportunities, this great resource can help both beginners and veterans earn more with better-targeted efforts."

Lucy V. Parker, Author
How to Start a Home-Based Writing Business

"Bowerman packs a powerful punch with clear step-by-step methods for earning a six-figure income as a copywriter, even if it's new territory for you. Jam-packed with valuable tips and insider techniques, it's an interactive seminar disguised a book."

Marisa D'Vari, Author
Building Buzz (and four others), **www.BuildingBuzz.com**

"If writing is a piece of cake but selling gives you indigestion, this is the book for you."

Jennie L. Phipps, Editor/Publisher
www.FreelanceSuccess.com

"A superb companion to *The Well-Fed Writer*—especially for moms who want to work from home. As an entrepreneur and at-home mom, I found invaluable information and resources in both books. Thanks for continuing to ease the path to home-employment for moms!"

Tammy Harrison, Independent Creative Representative
Home-Based Working Moms (**www.HBWM.com**)

"Offers dozens of proven, easy-to-follow strategies for anyone interesting in thriving as a freelance writer. Bowerman shows exactly how you too can have the same success so many of the readers of *The Well-Fed Writer* are enjoying."

Katie Yeakle, Executive Director
American Writers & Artists Institute

"Bowerman's book isn't the usual pie-in-the-sky, 'tap your inner creative guru' junk. It's simple nuts and bolts stuff on how to make money as a writer and keep the 'free' out of freelancer."

Luke Sullivan, Author
Hey Whipple, Squeeeze This: A Guide to Creating Great Ads

"With more companies outsourcing and more people starting freelance careers, this is the essential resource for newbies and pros to be successful and profitable as freelance writers."

Brian Konradt, Freelancer & Founder
www.FreelanceWriting.com

"Delightful, engaging, humorous and filled with inspiring success stories from readers of *The Well-Fed Writer*. If you want to have a successful writing business, you need this book."

Cheryl Demas, Editor, **www.WAHM.com**—The Online Magazine for Work-at-Home Moms
Author, *It's a Jungle Out There and a Zoo in Here:
Run Your Home Business Without Letting it Overrun You*

The Well-Fed Writer— A Well-Praised Book!

"This book is the best information on how to make more money with corporate clients I have ever read. It answers everything you want to know. Highly recommended."

Bob Bly, Author (50+ titles),
Secrets of a Freelance Writer, The Copywriter's Handbook

"Bowerman shows…how almost anyone can forge ahead as an independent writer. His advice is good, couched in brassy prose…He anticipates every conceivable question…great common-sense tips…"

Booklist

"…truly rewarding reading for aspiring freelance writers, copywriters, scriptwriters, columnists, journalists, and anyone else wanting to earn from what they write."

The Midwest Book Review

"Engaging, motivating, and comprehensive—but above all, powerfully useful. An encyclopedic collection of freelancing fundamentals suffused throughout with the spirit of freedom and possibility all would-be freelancers crave."

Michael Perry, Author, Speaker
Handbook for Freelance Writing

"As a former communications manager and employer of freelance writers, I believe The Well-Fed Writer does a great job describing the depth of opportunity in this lucrative field. The information and direction are right on the money."

Marsha Hawkins, (Former) Employee Communications Manager, *BellSouth*

"Large companies often outsource their copywriting to proven freelancers. This book provides the who, what, when, where and how of getting into these companies' doors and becoming one of their 'go-to' writers. If you're serious about freelancing, this book is the single best investment you can make."

Michael J. Baker, Senior Writer/Editor/Marketing Communications, *MCI*

"Smart, informative and funny! As a 'client' in the marketing industry, I highly recommend The Well-Fed Writer to demystify the often intimidating dream of becoming a successful freelance writer. Good, smart writers are crucial to the success of business communications."

Kristi Sumner, (Former) Marketing Director/Creative Development, *Mercedes-Benz Credit Corporation*

"We have a school that teaches people to make a career out of writing—a fun well-paid career. *The Well-Fed Writer* is now on our recommended reading list. And even though I've been teaching people how to make a living as advertising copywriters for over 20 years, I'm amazed at how much this book has taught me in a couple of hours."

Norm Grey
(Former) President, *The Creative Circus, Inc.*—Atlanta, GA
(School for Copywriting, Art Direction, Photography, Design/Illustration)
Former Sr.VP/Group Creative Director, *J. Walter Thompson*

The Well-Fed Writer:

Back for Seconds

*A Second Helping of "How-To" For
Any Writer Dreaming of Great Bucks
and Exceptional Quality of Life*

Peter Bowerman

Fanove Publishing—Atlanta, Georgia
2005

This book includes information from many sources and gathered from many personal experiences. It is published for general reference and is not intended to be a substitute for independent verification by readers when necessary and appropriate. The book is sold with the understanding that the neither the author nor publisher is engaged in rendering any legal, psychological or accounting advice. The publisher and author disclaim any personal liability, directly or indirectly, for advice or information presented within. Although the author and publisher have prepared this manuscript with utmost care and diligence and have made every effort to ensure the accuracy and completeness of the information contained within, we assume no responsibility for errors, inaccuracies, omissions or inconsistencies.

Publisher's Cataloging In Publication

Bowerman, Peter

The well-fed writer: back for seconds/a second helping of "how-to" for any writer dreaming of great bucks and exceptional quality of life / Peter Bowerman

– 1st ed.

p.   cm.

Includes index.

LCCN: 2004095588

ISBN: 0-9670598-5-2

1. Authorship—Marketing.   2. Authorship.   I. Title

PN161.B69 2005   808.02

**ATTN: QUANTITY DISCOUNTS ARE AVAILABLE TO YOUR
COMPANY, EDUCATIONAL INSTITUTION OR WRITING ORGANIZATION**

for reselling, educational purposes, subscription incentives,
gifts or fundraising campaigns.

For more information, please contact the publisher at
Fanove Publishing, 3713 Stonewall Circle, Atlanta, Georgia 30339
770/438-7200—peter@wellfedwriter.com

Dedication

To my contributors.
Without you, this book would never have happened.

Table of Contents

Acknowledgements

My sincere thanks to:

"The Copy Hos"—Paul, Kathy, Steve, Georgia, and Barbara, my writing "homies"—for your wit, wisdom and unspoken support. Your quiet competence, unassailable integrity and unwavering professionalism have contributed to this journey far more than you'll ever know.

Chris DiNatale for being my grand graphic guru—brilliant book covers, fab flyers and other miscellaneous magnificence that makes me look good…AND for being my professional cohort in crime for the last 10 years (**www.dinataledesign.com**).

Chris Papas for being the constant maestro of my Web presence—with me right from the beginning of this grand adventure. **www.mm-ltd.com**

Shelley, Beth, Sylvia, Susan and the whole BookMasters gang for doing such an absolutely bang-up job of making my life exponentially easier (printing, fulfillment and more: **www.bookmasters.com**).

David and Richard—my intermittently ornery but consistently brilliant computer gurus

Buddy for refusing to let all this go to my head (and occasionally succeeding) by never missing an opportunity to remind me of what a dork I really am. You're a good friend.

Mom and Sis for relishing all this with me every step of the way.

Hilda—fellow scribe, dear friend, adopted sister, guerilla editor and favorite straight-shooter—I'm glad you're in my life.

Shawn Morningstar—my delightful new typesetter (interior book layout) extraordinaire. Her creativity, professionalism, reliability and eternally upbeat attitude made her an absolute joy to work with. **www.mstarbookdesign.com**

Mim "Eagle-Eye" Eisenberg for her wonderfully unsolicited (and heretofore unforgivably unacknowledged) proofreading of my first book. This woman is good. (**www.wordcraftservices.com**—editing, proofreading, tape transcription and more).

Joyce Dierschke (Hollywood, Florida) and Rich Silver (Scappoose, Oregon) for coming up with the killer title, *Back For Seconds*.

Bob Bly for being the enduring example of how it's done. You're the real deal. **www.bly.com**.

All of my contributors—too numerous to name—for generously sharing your triumphs and defeats. Your courage, creativity and resourcefulness are humbling.

Finally, all my readers, around the globe—thanks for your support. May all your writing be well-fed.

Peter Bowerman
September 2004

Introduction

There's no scarcity of opportunity to make a living at what you love. There is only a scarcity of resolve to make it happen.

Wayne Dyer

Welcome back. A lot has happened in the four years since *The Well-Fed Writer* came out. Little did I know what I'd unleash. In that time, most importantly, I've learned that there are a lot of roads to well-fed writing. And that's the key. I've never been interested in ways to simply eke out a living as a freelance writer. You can find that anywhere.

My ongoing goal is to show that you can be a writer for a living *and* pay all your bills, buy a house, amply fund a retirement account and take a few nice vacations a year. And in the process, have a quality of life most of the world can only imagine—one where you call the shots, determine your schedule and live life on *your* terms.

And all that's possible because you're earning more. In Well-Fed World, you won't find lists of new markets paying five cents a word. Or the latest online job site where you can bid with dozens of other writers fighting over *The Amazing Shrinking Fee* (Watch It Get Smaller Before Your Very Eyes!). My approach has always been to give you the tools and ideas you need to make a handsome full-time living as a commercial writer.

By definition, my experience was limited: big city location, sales background, full-time startup (*and* by cold calling), a generalist, etc. Over the past few years, however, I've heard from thousands of people with vastly different stories, circumstances, strategies, backgrounds and geographic settings. Many had questions I couldn't answer:

How can I build this in a remote area or small town?

Given that I work 9 to 5, Monday through Friday, how can I make the transition to this part-time?

Have you used e-mail marketing to build a business and if so, how does it work?

What other arenas of commercial writing are there besides the ones in your book?

Is cold calling the only way to build the business?

Different Situations, Different Answers

To these inquiries, I could offer a reasonably educated opinion, but in most cases, not much more than that. But then, to the rescue, came writers from all over with answers—or evolving answers—to these questions and many more.

In May 2002, I launched THE WELL-FED E-PUB, my monthly e-zine, which accelerated the process of sharing new ideas, often told through some pretty cool and inspirational success stories. When I had enough good stories, I decided to write another book.

An All-Star Parade

You'll find dozens of accounts and reflections from well-fed writers of every description. There's the guy—married, children, active in his church and community—who built a nicely profitable side business in Kansas City in less than six months, doing it *very* part-time while continuing to hold down a full-time job.

There's the ex-publishing company employee, who moved to Austin, Texas, not knowing a soul and in the midst of a high-tech recession. Surrounded by armies of gloomy out-of-work technical writers, she began cold calling on September 11, 2001. In six months, she'd doubled her past income, doing mostly high-tech work—a subject she knew nothing about when she started.

You'll meet a 29 year-old African-American woman, who moved from Philadelphia back home to small market—and predominantly white—Ft. Myers, Florida. With a combination of aggressive marketing, resourceful ingenuity and an unbeatably optimistic attitude, she's got lessons for folks twice her age.

You'll hear from a single mom in California who gradually made the transition from journalism to commercial writing, leaving behind a ton of stress, a long commute, guilt over endless daycare and a far lower quality of life.

Many Paths, Common Goal

You'll hear from people building the business in small towns and rural areas. Doing it part-time. Working in interesting niches. Like the woman in Santa Fe who focuses exclusively on company case studies. Or the guy who serves the death care industry, writing for funeral homes across the country. Or the gentleman who works primarily with school districts. And so many more.

They all have one thing in common: they're quietly exploding the stereotype of the starving writer and making handsome livings with their words in this vast and profitable zone between poverty and seven-figure novel advances. And their accounts are filled with great ideas for *anyone, anywhere*, in *any* situation.

Just because you're a fearless cold caller doesn't mean there's nothing worth reading in the cold-calling chapter. Just because you built or can build your business full-time doesn't mean you should skip the chapter on part-time start-up. Just because you're building the business in a major metro doesn't mean the chapter on small town/remote area startup won't hold any value for you. Trust me, the part-timers and smaller market/rural area folks are tough, smart and resourceful.

Much More Marketing

And speaking of cold calling, I'm offering up dramatically expanded marketing and cold calling chapters. If your many e-mails are any indication, you creative types just fear and loathe *sales* and *marketing*. Well, we'll demystify (and declaw) the whole marketing process. Cold calling may never make it onto your *My Favorite Things* list, but I'm guessing it won't be quite so dark and scary anymore. We'll cover some cornerstone principles of sales, which for many of you will prove to be revelations *and* gateways to more effective marketing of your own and your clients' businesses.

We'll look at direct mail, e-mail prospecting, fax marketing and creating Web sites. We'll explore starting, building and running a writers group, while maximizing its potential. I've even got a chapter called, *"Let Me Clarify…"* where I set the record straight on a variety of questions, myths and preconceptions about this business.

The Well-Fed Writer Revisited

I've devoted Appendix A to summarizing *The Well-Fed Writer*. This will serve as a quick review for most of you. For those who never got around to reading the first book, it'll get you up to speed, so read it first. Appendix B serves up a dozen profiles of successful commercial freelancers of all descriptions, backgrounds, specialties and circumstances. Appendix C delivers a detailed case study of a one particular project, and in response to many requests, Appendix D covers business structures, taxes, investing and insurance for the self-employed.

Appendix E offers a tasty array of writing resources and in Appendix F, I discuss another arena of "well-fed writing" near and dear to my heart: self-publishing. You'll hear a bit about my successful journey as a preface for my next effort, *The Well-Fed Self-Publisher*, due in the 2005/2006 timeframe.

My books are, at best, a few chapters in the big juicy story of "well-fed" writing. While this book will reveal even more new, different and exciting writing directions, I want you to keep asking, *What other writing opportunities might be right under my nose?* Like the first book, this one doesn't have all the answers. But, I think it's got a lot of good ideas. We writers like good ideas—especially ones that can make us a lot of money.

A Looser Structure

Think of this book as one big potluck dinner party—and you know how potlucks are. Some dishes are meatier than others. Maybe there are two or three pasta salads. Some dishes are "quick prep," others more involved. But, put it all together and you won't leave hungry.

Compared to its predecessor, *Back for Seconds* is much looser. And because it's full of information that fleshes out and supports the overarching processes and systems laid out in the first book, it's less structured and less sequential. But, in many ways, it's a much richer and juicier book precisely because there are so many more voices chiming in. You'll realize that there are no hard and fast rules about how to approach the business, just a lot of different strategies worth exploring.

Okay, since marketing and sales are such foreign and frightening concepts to many, I think that's a wonderful place to start. So, grab a plate and let's dig in…

•   •   •

NOTE: *Throughout the book, you'll see several abbreviated references:*

TWFW: The Well-Fed Writer

FLCW: Freelance Commercial Writer (how I refer to those in our field)

E-PUB: THE WELL-FED-E-PUB (my monthly e-zine)
(Subscribe at **www.wellfedwriter.com**, *then "Free Ezine Signup")*

Chapter 1

THIS THING CALLED SALES

(Sung to the tune of "Crazy Little Thing Called Love"
—Queen, 1979)

This thing called sales
I just can't handle it.
This thing called sales
I must get round to it.
I ain't ready...
Crazy little thing called sales.

This thing called sales
makes me cry, like a babe at night.
I think, of sales
And I shake all over like a jellyfish.
I can't hack it...
Crazy little thing called sales.

There goes my sanity,
I don't know what to do.
It drives me crazy,
It gives me hot and cold fever,
And leaves me in a cool cool sweat.

I gotta be cool, relax, get hip.
Hit the phones and fax,
Maybe network, pass out my card.
Convince myself that it ain't that hard.
Until I'm ready...
Crazy little thing called sales.

Let's start this new journey with something I'm guessing most of us can relate to. I received this e-mail from a reader some time back—one of many in the same vein:

> *You're succeeding in a business I've sort of ambled through for the past five years. Like many writers and other types of artists, I have the skills and the talent—but HATE MARKETING MYSELF. [Caps his, not mine.]*

Hence the song adaptation above. While I could have used the word "marketing" just as easily as "sales" in the song, sales *did* fit the rhythm better. But both *marketing* and *sales* engender the same panic in creative types.

As I received more and more correspondence like the above, I began to realize that SALES and MARKETING are indeed *The Boogeymen* for many creative types. It's the thing that wakes people up at night, gasping and sweating, and makes them chew their fingernails to the quick. More importantly, it keeps them from actively chasing their dream, from pursuing the freelance writing life that really calls to them. As this became clearer to me, I knew I had to flesh out the discussion of marketing I started in my first book—not only to give you tips on how to market your writing skills and business, but to start a richer discussion about developing a marketing *mindset*, so you can write ever better marketing copy for your clients.

Sales & Marketing—Different Things

For the record, sales and marketing are different things. Both involve making connections with prospective customers. Sales generally refers to *direct contact*—whether in person or on the phone. Marketing refers more to efforts to build awareness in less personal ways (e-mail, direct mail, advertising) among your target audience—about who you are, what you're selling and why they should do business with you. But when you're building a small business (as we are here, with freelance writing), I think it's safe to say that the two activities become a lot closer in function and the two terms much more interchangeable than would be the case with, say, a large corporation. So, if I use one in the context of a small business, I could just as easily be using the other.

The good news: Despite the fear they inspire, sales and marketing as concepts really aren't that hard to grasp and implement successfully. Let me share a story that should provide a little comfort…

Operative Word: Feasible

A few winters back, I gave a talk to an Atlanta-based group of freelancers I belong to. While it includes a healthy number of graphic designers, photographers, Web designers, illustrators, etc., about 50 percent of its members are writers. On the night I spoke, there were about 75 people in the audience and I asked how many of them had been successfully freelancing for at least three years. I figured if folks had been able to stay in business for three years, they must be doing something right. Probably 50 to 60 percent of the crowd raised their hands. My second question: *Of those who just raised their hands, how many of you market yourselves on a regular, consistent basis?* Care to guess how many hands went up? Exactly two.

Here was a group of successful freelancers, people who had been paying their bills by way of the freelance life for three or more years, and less than five percent of them conduct any ongoing continuous marketing campaign. Okay, for you statistical purists out there, yes, this is indeed anecdotal evidence and not a representative sample. Still, my personal experience has borne this out as well—once you've got the machine up and running and have gotten into some good promotional habits, it's not some endless grueling battle to scratch out a tiny bit of market share. In competence there really *is* security. If you're good at what you do *and* you're willing to let the world know you're out there on a consistent enough basis, you'll always eat well.

What Marketing IS

Let's establish what marketing is, and just as importantly, what it isn't. For many, marketing looms as a shadowy, elusive, overly complicated beast. With teeth. Let's muzzle it, shall we? I humbly offer up my simple definition of marketing:

> *Successful marketing of a freelance commercial writing business is simply letting prospective clients know you're out there—on a consistent basis, in a variety of ways and with a message they can hear through the clutter.*

If you can effectively reach enough of the people who can hire you, and you do that until you have as much work as you want, and then repeat the process (with good results) whenever you don't have work, I say you're a successful marketer.

More good news: Once you're in the game, it's simply a matter of employing the same proven strategies over and over again. Simple. Not necessarily easy, but simple. And none of it is beyond the capability of any reasonably intelligent human. Now, add in the power of the Internet. This single technological marvel can so dramatically streamline and simplify your marketing efforts, it'll take your breath away.

What Marketing ISN'T

Marketing on this level isn't some arcane, wildly esoteric and obscure puzzle that only reveals itself to Harvard or Wharton graduates after exhaustive, mind-numbing research and analysis. Sure, that kind of marketing does exist, replete with all the vernacular: demographics, psychographics, market share, etc. And for all intents and purposes, it only comes into play with much larger companies, not one-person writing shops. That's that. This is this. And ne'er the twain need ever meet. So relax.

Even if you have zero experience in marketing or marketing writing, you can probably gain all the knowledge you need to succeed in this business by reading some books on the subject. Check out the reading list in Appendix E.

You're Driving

National catastrophes notwithstanding, sales and marketing aren't things that are out of your control. In fact, there are enough components of the marketing process that you have complete control over, and they're more than sufficient to ensure your success. This is important to get, so let's say it again:

> *There are enough components of the marketing process*
> *that you have complete control over, and they're more*
> *than sufficient to ensure your success.*

Do a few simple things, and do them enough, and you'll have plenty of work. And once you master the process, you can put it into action anytime and anywhere, with predictable results. You control the number of calls you make (both initial and follow-up), the number of e-mails you send and the number of postcards you mail. Provided you're targeting the right audiences, if you do all those things regularly and consistently, you'll be successful. That's powerful stuff. *Teaching-yourself-to-fish* stuff. And here's some good news to ponder: For the most part, your prospects already know their lines. You just have to learn yours. Let me explain.

A Game Already in Progress

A few years back, I discovered the culinary adventure known as Dim Sum: the unusual, ultra-tasty and oh-so-very-reasonably priced Cantonese feast usually served on weekends in authentic Chinese restaurants. My first time was a revelation. Not just because it was this new and wonderful epicurean experience, but more importantly, because the place was packed. Here was something that I didn't even know existed and zillions of other people had been enjoying it for years!

In a way, it'll be the same kind of feeling when you start your business and begin making your marketing inroads. For many of you, here's something you've never done and you have all these fears about the process—fear of failing, of not being good enough, of making an idiot of yourself, of going broke (left any out?). Those are understandable, but if you're calling large corporations and middlemen clients, there's one fear you shouldn't have: that the person on the other end of the line isn't going to have any idea who you are and what you're offering. Just as Dim Sum was already known by the masses before I encountered it, marketing calls are commonplace to the folks you'll be calling.

I guarantee it: You'll be all freaked out making the calls and they'll be so matter-of-fact on the other end, because they expect to hear from copy-writers in the course of doing business. True, you may be pursuing smaller companies in the beginning, and the folks you talk to there may need more educating about what you have to offer, but any company that wants to grow and prosper will understand the value of good writing. And frankly, I've been pleasantly surprised at how savvy many small firms are about the need for professional assistance with their writing.

Dare to Be Seen

As a single guy, I occasionally surf over to one of the online dating sites. The clichés there are rampant. Here are zillions of people, looking for the most important relationship of their lives, and barely one in a hundred takes the time to craft a message that is even remotely creative and original.

Virtually every ad lists such unique gems as *I love moonlight walks on the beach*…(FYI, that's "moonlit") *romantic, candlelight dinners*…(FYI, that's "candlelit"), *snuggling in front of a fire*…and, my favorite one to hate, *a man who's as comfortable in a tux as blue jeans*…just like EVERYONE else's.

I always want to ask: Do you think you'll attract the opposite sex by blending in with everything around you? That's called camouflage. People in the armed forces do this very thing when their lives depend on not being noticed or standing out in any way. If you want to be seen, you have to draw attention to yourself. As commercial writers, precious few do regular mailing, phoning or networking campaigns to elevate themselves above the din. Getting noticed isn't all that hard if you're one of the few who make the effort to stand out.

Business-Building is NOT Immodesty

I know—you hate drawing attention to yourself. That's…immodest. Listen. There's not a darned thing immodest about drawing attention to yourself when you have a legitimate, high-quality contribution to make to the marketplace—a professional offering that's in demand by every successful business under the sun. You're living in a certain place, driving a certain car, wearing certain clothes, dining at certain restaurants and vacationing in certain places because some company successfully marketed something to you. Or to the friend who made the recommendation to you. And you're probably glad it did.

By the same token, there are a lot of companies in Atlanta that are glad I made it my business to let them know I was out there in the marketplace. And they acknowledge the difference I've made every time they pick up the phone and call me for another job.

I hate to say it, but you'd better be willing to draw some attention to yourself or you'll need to find another line of work. You're not selling some Veg-o-Muncher on late-night TV. You're not some smarmy car salesman. You're a professional writer marketing a service for which there is a huge need.

Keep Showing Up

Want to know the simple key to success in this business? Keep showing up. Assuming you're a competent, creative and reliable writer, it's all about multiple impressions. The writers who build thriving businesses have just kept showing up in front of their clients and prospects in a variety of ways. And kept knocking on new doors. A *Last Man Standing* sort of thing. It's that simple.

And sometimes that process can literally take years. My friend and colleague Erick Dittus, an Atlanta-based speechwriter, echoed this sentiment:

> In my business, on the first few calls [to prospective clients]
> I almost always hear 'there's no work here' or 'it's very rare
> that we hire outside.' It's the tone of how they say that—or
> the power of the brand—that makes me call them on a
> cycle (about every 2-5 months). Delta, Coke, McDonald's
> all [became clients] after a couple years of calling.

And while the speechwriting gestation period from contact to hiring may be longer than for straight copywriting work, the point is nonetheless sound.

That Icky "Sales" Thing

When combined with marketing, sales comprises, for many FLCWs, the "Panic Pair." In *TWFW*, when I wrote, "This business is, first and foremost, a sales and marketing venture," oh, the e-mail I received: *I'm terrible at sales… I could never sell anything to anyone… The thought of selling something to somebody is downright frightening to me…* and on and on. Alas. All so unnecessary. So, let's talk about what sales really does—and doesn't—mean.

Bad Associations

Somewhere along the line, for many of us, "sales" of anything got wired to high-pressure techniques, pushy salespeople, slick sales practices, etc. Why did this happen? Because, at some point, we've been the target of salespeople who embodied all the negative stereotypes about sales. Maybe it was someone selling cars. Time-share vacations. Encyclopedias. Aluminum siding. Perhaps enough obnoxious telemarketers got thrown into that broad "sales" bin as well. However, wherever, whenever, and at whoever's hands it happened, it happened.

Sales: Meeting Needs

Well, guess what? That's not what sales is. Sales is nothing more than matching your product or service with a prospect's needs. With this definition in mind, we can start seeing the potential for "sales" to morph into a more *consultative* function. If you build a commercial writing business, one thing's for certain: Whether or not you thought of yourself as selling something, you *did*. That client *bought* you and your service because of who you are, how you presented yourself and what you had to offer. And he or she had a need for that product or service. Over time, as we're about to discuss, you dismantled the barriers standing in the way of that client doing business with you.

And, it's funny—sales can mean different things to different people. Be sure to check out the end of this chapter, where I share the definition of sales from a variety of successful writers—an eye-opener, for sure.

Now, I'm going to make a few generalizations here. Maybe not true in all cases (so please don't e-mail me with your exception), but certainly valid enough to serve the purpose of underscoring a few key points.

B2B vs. B2C

Sales takes place in two main arenas: **business-to-business** (**B2B**) and **business-to-consumer** (**B2C**). A B2B sale (what we as FLCWs do, in case you're unsure) is generally a "problem-solving" type of sale. You're a professional selling a product or service to other professionals. Examples include: mainframe computers, medical equipment, software, billing systems, pharmaceuticals, copywriting services, marketing consulting, graphic design and about ten gazillion other things. You're helping a business address its challenges and your "solution" will enhance its position in the marketplace by making it more efficient, profitable, reputable, competitive, etc. So far, so good.

Business-to-consumer is the other big arena and, as consumers, many of the bad sales experiences we've had in our lifetimes fall into this category. By definition, all door-to-door, in-home and telemarketing sales are B2C sales. Why are B2C sales usually the ones that bring out the "dark side" of sales and salespeople and turn us off to sales? Well, for a few inter-related reasons.

Discretionary vs. Non-Discretionary

Many sales in the B2C realm are discretionary, meaning they involve items you don't actually *need*. For example, you don't need a time-share, encyclopedias, aluminum siding, etc. And yes, you may need a car, but you don't need that $50K car. And when you don't need something, emotions play a much bigger role in your buying decision. Playing on those emotions becomes a B2C salesperson's big role. He or she has to resort to pressure and manipulation until you can sometimes feel—well, pressured and manipulated. And so you may walk away from those sales experiences with an icky taste in your mouth about sales in general.

In the B2B arena, sales are generally more non-discretionary. Sure, an organization makes a choice to buy a product or service. But, instead of some ephemeral want or desire being the catalyst—as in many B2C scenarios—it's much more prosaic but crucial considerations like profitability, operational efficiency and competitive edge that carry the day. In today's cutthroat climate, if a business wants to thrive, it doesn't often have a lot of choice about investing in certain things.

Emotional vs. Unemotional

Yes, emotion can play a slight role in B2B sales—that is, from the standpoint of planting the idea that a product carries with it the promise of success (or conversely, the fear of business failure through non-action), enhanced competitive advantage and the professional rewards that might logically come to a wise decision-maker. But we're still dealing with the primacy of business considerations.

Translation? B2B sales are much more unemotional than B2C. And when emotion isn't ruling the proceedings, pressure and manipulation become non-issues. Not that they're ever appropriate in any sales arena, but in the B2C realm, when a juicy commission is on the line, many salespeople see the consumer as a sitting duck to be exploited for his discretionary desires. In our business, high-pressure sales tactics—what many think of as the "sales model"—aren't just inappropriate; they're irrelevant.

An Apropos Analogy

Let's bring these discussions of marketing and sales together in an entertaining way—with an example that illustrates the idea of multiple marketing impressions and the overall sales cycle. As you may recall from

TWFW, the last job I held before starting my writing business was in the sales department of a video dating service.

This company's whole marketing approach nicely demonstrates what I'm talking about here regarding the sales cycle: the idea of multiple impressions, an understanding of the limitations of each step of the process, and how everything works together to lead you to the final desired result.

Here's how the sales process worked: The company's telemarketing department would book appointments for people to come in and meet with a "member representative" (i.e., salesperson; my job). The member rep would explain how the program worked, give them a tour and then attempt to "close" them on buying one of the memberships, which ranged in price from roughly one to three thousand dollars.

When these folks came in, one of the first questions we'd ask is, *What made you come in today?* Invariably, they'd answer with minor variations of *Oh, I was just curious.* Ri-ight. Of course, we never really expected anyone to say, *Well frankly, my social life sucks*, or *I haven't had a date in two years.* But we'd ask anyway. And when they answered thusly, we always smiled to ourselves, because we knew things they didn't know we knew. Lots of things.

For starters, we knew they were much more than curious. In fact, they were very serious about making a change in their social lives. The mere act of entering our doors proved that beyond a doubt. We knew that by the time they walked in and spoke to us, they'd jumped through multiple psychological hoops. Let me explain.

Hoop One

This company was big on making multiple impressions. They'd repeatedly send out direct mail questionnaires, knowing that most people would throw away the first eight to ten they'd receive. But then, one day, for whatever reason—the recipient just broke up with someone, had a string of bad dates, was feeling lonely—a prospect would actually fill out a response card and send it in. That in itself was a huge long shot—and a compelling testimonial to the power of multiple impressions.

Those people decided to fill out the questionnaire precisely because they had received many others in the past. Those past surveys had slowly but inexorably built credibility in their minds, most likely unconsciously. By the time they actually sent one in, they were quite familiar with this outfit, had probably read through several past flyers before tossing them, and knew the company was a reputable, nationwide organization. Chances are good they even knew someone who had joined and spoke well of the place. All bricks in the wall.

Not only that. Each time they received another flyer, it confirmed the solidity of the organization (They're still around…). Ergo, there was a crucial trust level established. Same with any ongoing direct mail or e-mail marketing campaign you decide to undertake. The mere repetition of it will boost your credibility in your market.

And yes, in the case of this dating service, there would always be a percentage of people who would never consider pursuing this approach to meeting someone, just like there will always be some folks who will never consider using a freelancer, for any number of reasons.

HOOP TWO

Okay, after sending the flyer in, our prospects would get a call from someone in the telemarketing department to go over the questionnaire, with the goal being to book them for an in-office appointment. Not surprisingly, at that point, many dropped out. They'd realize that by taking it to the next level, they were serious about this part of their lives and many just weren't prepared to admit that to themselves. Or, they'd explain to the telemarketer that they'd filled out the survey in a moment of frustration or despair, which had since passed. Maybe since sending it in, they'd met someone and were now excited again about their romantic prospects.

But even if they did drop out at that point—and the organization counted on a huge percentage doing just that—these prospects were gathering still more information about the process (*Okay, so they call you when you send one in*) and, by extension, becoming more comfortable with it. And unless they did indeed suddenly meet the mate of their dreams, chances were good that the emotions that had caused them to fill out the survey in the first place would quite likely resurface soon enough. Which, in fact, was precisely the reason why, at this stage of the sales cycle, a certain percentage of people did indeed choose to take the next step and agree to come into our offices and talk with someone about the club.

You'll likely communicate with prospects many times before you get work from them. And each time you do, if you're professional and you share a bit more about yourself and your skills, you'll build a bit more rapport, credibility and legitimacy in the prospect's mind. And as you do, you'll be making it that much easier for that prospect to do business with you.

HOOP THREE

Oh, you thought that was it? They just show up for their appointment and we're done? Hah! Stop reading for a moment and take a guess as to what percentage of people who booked appointments actually showed up…

Try 15 to 20 percent. Roughly one out of six who booked a meeting would actually follow through on it. The sales managers would literally book six to seven times as many appointments as they could handle because they knew, from years of doing this, that the average no-show rate was 80 to 85 percent. A rate you could set your watch by. But every day, that 15 to 20 percent showed up like clockwork and when they did, we knew, intimately, what the odds were of that happening (exquisitely slim). And so, whenever we heard, "Oh, just curious," it was hard not to chuckle.

So, what can we take away from this? Know the limits of any one contact. Think long-term. Keep showing up. Stay in the game and you can't help but win, eventually. Know it's all a cumulative effect. *No* doesn't mean *not ever*—sometimes it means *maybe*, or more specifically, *I need more information*. Now, in this case, I *am* talking about prospects who say they hire freelancers but haven't hired *you* yet, *not* prospects who say they're not in the market for freelance writing services at all. There's usually little point in continuing to beat your head against the wall trying to convert the second group. But, it's usually very prudent to stay in touch with the first.

Dismantling Barriers

Think of landing work with new clients as a process of gradually removing the barriers that stand in the way of their doing business with you. And before you start lamenting that all this "sales" stuff is just too much for your non-sales brain, remember, the ideas I'm discussing here are just part and parcel of any human interaction, whether it be finding a mate, landing a job, getting a promotion, etc. Same goes for you when you're buying some big-ticket item—a house, car, boat, expensive artwork, or the like.

When you walk into that car dealership, you've got lots of barriers erected. And if anyone asks, you're *Just looking*. If you walk out two hours or two weeks later with the keys to a new car, then clearly those barriers got dismantled one by one.

When you call prospective clients for the first time, assuming you've determined they have a need for your services, you're at Ground Zero with them. They know nothing about you. They have their barriers up. They're *Just looking*. You talk a bit, and they learn a bit about your background and experience. A few barriers start coming down. You steer them to your Web site, where they can quickly see your work. If they like what they see and can see your skills meshing with their ongoing needs, a few more barriers come down. And if they like your personality, they get rid of another.

If you then go to meet them and show them your portfolio and all that goes well, a few more fall. Maybe they absolutely love what they see, and even have an immediately pending project that's a perfect match for what you can offer. *Voila!* You're in business. If not, maybe what they've seen is enough to have them try you out on a small project. If that turns out well, you're in a good place.

Make it Easy For Them to Say Yes

Assuming these prospects don't have any work for you at that point, or they're working with another writer, you may decide, at their suggestion, to keep in touch with them. And if they continue to get regular check-in correspondence from you in the form of an e-mail, postcard, mailed sample or periodic phone call, they're continually reminded of you *and* they know you're still around, still a viable business entity. More barriers come down, until it's not even about you anymore; it's about them and finding the opportunity to work with you.

8 Sales Tips For Non-Salespeople (from CEO of Sales Training Firm)

I picked up a new client some months back (through a graphic design firm...) and the company's probably helped me as much as I've helped them. This Atlanta-based firm of 21 employees, Aslan Training and Development, is a sales training enterprise specializing in Inside Sales. Translation: phone sales. A few of their clients? BellSouth, Xerox, FedEx, Apple Computer, Oracle, GE, HP and Russell Athletic.

As I worked with them, an idea bubbled up: to have CEO Tom Stanfill contribute something to this book. After all, Aslan specializes in transforming non-sales people into effective phone marketers. Are your ears burning?

Unlearning Bad Habits

In the course of working with Tom, many of the things I'd learned from my past sales background—i.e., "ABC - Always Be Closing," asking for the order, making a strong call-to-action, and others—ran contrary to what this guy—running a highly successful sales training organization—was saying.

At the same time, many ideas he was espousing were exactly what I've been saying about "sales" for a long time: that it's not about being slick, pushy or aggressive. It's not about "closing" hard. It's about taking the time to understand a client's needs and exploring whether your product/service meets those needs. It's really about service, not sales. I asked Tom to offer up some tips for this book, keeping in mind that he was talking, largely, to creative people deathly afraid of "sales." Here are the gems he served up ...

THE TIPS

1. **Clients Don't Want To Be Sold.** They want a partner, so adopt the voice of a partner. And what's a partner? Someone who knows he or she can't be successful unless their client is successful.

2. **Asking For The Order Doesn't Motivate People To Buy.** What motivates people to buy is when they get that you "get" them— that you understand their world and have shown how your product/service will impact their company in the ways that are important to them. In most cases, the salesperson who wins the deal isn't the one with the best product or lowest price, but the one who can best articulate the customer's point of view.

3. **"Drop The Rope."** While it's unlikely that people already fearful of the sales process would actually "lean on" a prospect, it's still worthwhile to grasp the concept of "Drop the Rope." Take the analogy of a tug-of-war. If two people are holding a rope and one pulls, the other will pull back. If prospects sense you have your sales hat on, they'll resist. They're not rejecting your solution, service, or product; they're rejecting you.

   In the course of prospecting, if you get resistance from a prospect, regardless of your approach, "drop the rope" by saying, *Mr. Prospect, I'm not even sure my service is a fit for your company, but I'd certainly love the opportunity to learn more about what you do and see if there is some common ground.* Speaking of which…

4. **Sell the Meeting, Not the Service.** Don't try to sell people writing services. Sell them on getting together—by phone or in person—for a "discovery meeting" and exploring, together, what they do, what you do and whether there's a fit between the two. In a discovery meeting, you can evaluate the client's needs and determine how to position your services. Most importantly, you've built a relationship that will ensure, at the very least, your recommendation gets heard.

5. **Sell the Process, Not the Service.** Often sales people rely too much on the client to determine the next steps. Make sure that every interaction with a customer ends with a specific event the customer agrees to (i.e., another meeting, a follow-up call at a set time, etc.). And the agreement is crucial. A planned action is much more likely to happen than one left to chance. Just as importantly, you stay in your customer's field of vision.

6. **Stop Trying To Be a Salesperson.** Every day, we teach non-salespeople to be effective salespeople, not aggressive, pushy closers. Those attributes are self-centered, and self-centered doesn't sell. *Motive is ultimately transparent.* If your motive is to truly do what's in the best interest of the customer, the customer will sense it and pursue a potential partnership. If it's to sell the customer something, regardless of need, the customer will avoid you. You don't need to be a salesperson; you need to be a passionate, competent copywriter who is unafraid to share your talents—not because you need the money but because *they* need the help.

7. **Calculate The Value Of Your Prospecting Time.** Once you're established, figure out how much you've made up to a certain point divided by the number of hours you've "prospected" for that business. If you figured out that you put in 100 hours prospecting which netted you $10,000 in work, then your prospecting time was worth $100/hour. You might just get a bit more motivated knowing this.

8. **Answer the Question, "Why You?"** What's different about you? How are you going to differentiate your services from the competition? Don't assume the client will figure this out. There always exist multiple solutions: doing nothing, hiring a competitor or doing it themselves. Once you have determined your unique offering, make sure the client "gets" that difference, either by just telling them (or validating it through success stories), or, better yet, ensuring the customer experiences the difference through your actions—reliability, professionalism, creativity, etc.

Pretty healthy philosophy, no? So, if you run across a company that mentions the need for sales training, I'm not sure they could do better than Aslan. And I'm not just saying this to pay Tom back for his generosity (though there is that…) but also because, frankly, if more companies operated according to these principles, the "customer experience" couldn't help but improve. **www.aslantraining.com** (770/690-9616). And ask for Tom. He'll leave the voice mail on for you (sorry, couldn't resist).

Sales Redefined

Some time back, I was mentoring a budding L.A. FLCW named Rob Rutkowski, who was leveraging his 15 years in high-end software sales. He shared this great example from his selling days of an exceptionally strong sales approach. I'm sharing Rob's story here to give you a particularly good example of a very different take on sales from how you may be accustomed to considering it. Keep the ideas in mind (not the specifics as much as the creativity) as you consider how to approach your clients. And yes, Rob knows he's good. Another lesson worth internalizing...

Three years ago, my sales team was put through some outstanding sales training by one of the top sales training firms in the country led by a Zig Zigler type with amazing credentials. Now, in this room of 50 folks were the best salespeople in the company, 10- to 20-year veterans who were used to making $500K and up. And me. The new guy. Who showed up late because his flight was delayed. And who the CEO of the company was staring daggers at when I interrupted the class an hour after it started.

The course leader hated me from minute one. Hated my questions. Hated my comments. I was a total pain. After the week of training, we were given an assignment: "mock" pitch the CEO of American Express on a specific project and secure a presentation to the board.

That night, while everyone else went and got drunk at the hotel bar, I was scanning the Internet for articles, reading Amex's annual reports, digging into the business processes of the divisions and internalizing their vocabulary. The next day, armed with video clips of the chairman revealing operational problems our software solved, and CEO quotes from internal documents explaining challenges our software solved, and analyst reports trumpeting issues our software solved, I made a seven-minute presentation that landed like a single bullet assassination.

The audience paused when I finished, then erupted in applause. The course leader, with the reluctance of someone cooperating with U.N. inspectors, handed me the $100 prize for best presentation. He uses it in his training even today.

Now, THAT is sales. Potent. Focused. Thorough. Rob intimately got into the world of his prospect, discovered what was important to that person and what technological challenge the company faced, and effectively showed how his product addressed those challenges. Pushy? High-pressure? Manipulative? None of the above. True sales, in the professional B2B arena, is infinitely more about matching your skills with the clients needs and challenges than about having to be pushy and aggressive.

Some time back, I contacted a bunch of experienced FLCWs around the country and asked them what "sales" meant to them, as illustrated by a specific story or simply their regular business practices. Arguably, some of the following aren't truly sales but actually marketing. However, the point is, here are successful FLCWs talking about what the term means to them and none of their responses fall into the typical negative stereotypes about sales. Some reflect more global business practices, while others are a single incident with a moral to the story. Check it out.

Sales As Staying in Touch

Lisa Sparks
www.integritywriting.com
Ft. Myers, Florida

I send out an e-newsletter each month (see Chapter Six for more detail on Lisa's e-mail marketing campaign), and what a difference it's made. It generates at least a client per month. Sales, to me, is more about keeping in touch—even with people who don't seem like strong prospects.

When first starting out, I had a meeting with a prospect who was bent on keeping the conversation social rather than business-oriented. I wrote the guy off as a less-than-serious prospect. Yet, through the advice of a friend (our own Peter Bowerman) I kept the guy on my e-mail list. A few months later he referred someone to me, putting $1,500 in my pocket. Then Mr. Less-than-Serious sent his own project my way for yet another $1,500. All because I kept in touch. I've found that the people you least expect to come through will reward your persistence over and over again. And I'm now in discussion with this client for more consistent work.

Relationship building isn't about heavy sales pressure. It's just about staying in the game and presenting a strong and credible image to your potential clients.

Sales as Being Aware, Creative and True to Your Nature

Heather M. Allard
Providence, Rhode Island

All my jobs as a freelance copywriter, starting with my first, came as a result of some type of "selling." And selling for me simply means having your eyes and ears OPEN at all times. It means doing homework. Getting creative. Being prepared. Valuing what you have to sell. Seeing infinite sales possibilities.

I live in a city where contacts are king and people do business with people they know. I knew I'd have to get creative and make use of every past experience I had. I used the local Yellow Pages, my college alumni directory, my high school's Web site and my local *Book of Lists* to get a feel for business owners in my area. I contacted several people—the mayor, a local philan-thropist, a Web designer my husband knew, the director of an artist's organization, and the head of the animal rescue league where we adopted our dog.

I made sure I contacted these people in a way that would "speak" to them. I e-mailed the Web site designer, I personally visited the animal rescue league, and wrote letters to the others. I crafted my approach with specific projects or suggestions in mind. And I always had my "port-faux-lio" (which I'd created from thin air before I had any real jobs) handy to show them some of my writing samples. From those initial five contacts, I got four jobs. Each one turned into several more, as well as some very useful networking.

The great thing about commercial writing is that you can gear your business, niche and marketing plan to your personality and to the speed you're comfortable with. If you're more of a creative introvert, there's plenty of business out there in non-profits, online newsletters, and graphic design firms. You can conduct your marketing from the comfort of your own shell…er, home, via e-mail, letters and phone calls.

If you're more of an extrovert, there's plenty of business with big corporations, politicians and entertainers. You can shop your high-profile self around at conventions, entrepreneur organizations and among the general public. There's business EVERYWHERE, and for every type of personality.

Almost every job I've ever had—from peddling hotdogs at the beach during the summer to being an account coordinator for a billion dollar cosmetics company—has involved selling, and being a FLCW is by far the easiest form of sales there is. We're not bashing people over the head with a briefcase full of B.S. We're filling a need that exists, selling a service that will only enhance others' businesses.

Sales as a "Disqualifying" Numbers Game

Tom Myer
www.myerman.com
Austin, Texas

Two general comments about the sales process:

1. Sales is a numbers game, and one with some pretty strategic pieces:
   - **Consistency** (doing it every day)
   - **Quality** (reaching the right people)
   - **Disinterest** (being passionate about what you do, but not caring about the outcomes so much that you're crushed by rejection)

2. To increase your effectiveness, it's in your best interest to disqualify as many suspects/prospects as you can. I used to let folks string me along (or I would pursue) regardless of what I knew about their needs, deadlines, budgets, and other key factors. I'd go days chasing back and forth, asking questions, preparing a proposal and then get a dramatic response (bring out the smelling salts, etc.) when they saw my price tag.

Now I qualify my prospects in the first meeting (or by phone, preferably) because I don't have time to waste by chasing tire-kickers or those who don't have the right budget, deadline or project for me. Those who find my prices too high go somewhere else. Fine. I have plenty of customers who love me for my "process," pay my rate and come back for more. I'm left with all "perfect clients" and the messy ones go away (ideally). This is not just beneficial in terms of time saved, but also yields enhanced peace of mind and an increased number of billable hours.

Sales as Regular Impressions
Jim Meadows
www.jimfreelance.com
Kansas City, Missouri

Sales means PERSISTENCE. Once I've done the fun work of cold calling and amassed a database of interested prospects, I put that list to work. I consistently and persistently keep in touch with those contacts. About two or three times a year, more if my time permits, I simply run a full mail merge of everyone on the list onto a one page "in-your-face" reminder of who I am and what I do, often receiving return e-mails and calls within hours or days from those who need my services. *Out of sight, out of mind* is so very true. I've frequently had clients say, "I'm glad you sent this reminder. I've got this project on the burner and I need your help."

At a recent networking meeting for freelancers and business people, the discussion topic was marketing. To my delight, the host speaker said, *And just to show you one real live example of how effective this technique is,* [holding up my recent mailing], *here's what Jim Meadows sent me last month!* He then passed it around the room for everyone to examine.

For my main prospect and client database, I use *Microsoft® Access.* Beyond the obvious fields such as name, company, phone, etc., I created numerous fields that will be helpful in metrics, tracking, searching, follow-up and marketing, such as: "Date of last meeting," "Date of last phone call," "Amount of last invoice," "Agency or End-user?" and "Notes/Special interests."

Then, using *Microsoft Word,* I simply create a mail merge letter that taps into the *Access* database. Because of the numerous fields I created in the database, it's pretty easy to do a "shotgun" mailing to everyone. Or, by performing various queries on the mail merge, I can target specific groups within the main database to receive the mailing. Normally I do a hard copy mail, but some prospects and clients specifically prefer fax or e-mail, and I try to accommodate them when feasible.

Sales as E-Networking & Building on Jobs

Andrea Harris
www.minerva-inc.com
Stow, Massachusetts (Boston area)

I get project leads delivered right to my e-mail box, thanks to an e-mail discussion list aimed at women who work in technology-related fields. A couple of months after joining the list, I saw a note authored by someone I had worked with seven years earlier in a large company. Now successfully on her own, she was answering a question about consulting that another participant had asked the group. I wrote to her to reconnect, and ended up getting hired for several thousand dollars worth of work. A referral from her led to second steady client.

Another lead from the discussion list was more obvious: a participant submitted a request for freelance writers. I ended up writing the media kit for a major technology news provider, and they have already asked me to do some additional projects. I make it a point to participate in the discussion list at least every couple of weeks to get my name and e-mail signature noticed. It's a free and painless way to connect with hundreds of business people in my area.

I've also piggybacked off work I've done for a client. After getting some of my clients' materials accepted for publication in a local business paper, I approached the editor about submitting my own article. She readily accepted, and now my article and contact information will be seen by tens of thousands of potential clients. Had I not approached her first with my clients' high-profile work, she may never have noticed me.

Sales As Raising Your Value in the Marketplace
Michele Lashley
www.karacomcreative.com
Raleigh, North Carolina

When I started my writing business (after 15 years in marketing communications and advertising), one of the first things I did was contact a local university about the possibility of teaching an advertising course. It wasn't a marketing ploy, because I certainly didn't expect to generate any business from such an endeavor. Instead, I thought it might be fun to share some of my real life experiences with up-and-coming marketing communications folks. Two wonderful surprises have come from this journey into academia. First, I absolutely love working with the students in my classes. They're excited, eager to learn and full of wonderful ideas and energy.

Secondly, because I'm constantly preparing lectures, keeping up on current advertising news and following integrated marketing trends, I've developed a knowledge base of information I can use in pitches to potential clients and in the day-to-day interaction with current clients. All in all, it increases my value to them because I'm able to provide more than just copywriting services. Now, I'm able to help them look at their overall marketing picture and work with them in developing a plan that will help them accomplish their goals.

Sales as Persistence and Suggestion
Michelle Zavala
www.studioz.ws
Colorado Springs, Colorado

I met with a new company about eight months ago and kept in touch regularly. It was going through transitions but I knew it had the potential to be a significant account if I was patient enough. The company is a subcontractor for a government agency but its management team wanted to move into the commercial market. I knew they were going to need lots of new collateral for their new audience. My persistence finally paid off because when they decided to move, they MOVED! We started out with an introductory ad, then their Web site content.

While I was sitting there, I created about 6 to 8 new projects for myself off the top of my head and they bit—HARD! Sure, they have some general advertising to do, but during our meeting, I mentioned a number of other ways to get their message out: direct mail, e-mail blasts, trade show displays, Web site updates, internal PR, an educational campaign to the target market, etc. Now they're really excited about moving forward and so am I!

Sales as Seizing Opportunities and Shifting Perspective

Casey Hibbard
www.compelling-cases.com
Santa Fe, New Mexico

Growing up as the introverted child of two sales pros, I was convinced the "sales gene" had skipped a generation. I wanted nothing to do with it. I would pursue the nobler profession of writing. Yet after five years as a FLCW, I'm proud to boast that I too am a sales pro. Though it took jumping some mental hurdles, I've found the things that work for me. More than anything, it was a shift in perspective: I realized that there are people out there who need what I have to offer. I try to recognize and seize opportunities when they arise by using a variety of strategies:

- While doing a Web site rewrite for a professional speaker, I noticed her list of clients included some of my top targets. I politely asked her for a couple of contact names—and ended up landing a software company that has given me thousands of dollars of work over the past two years.

  In that same vein, I make a point to learn where current client contacts have worked previously, and then ask if they still have contacts there. And I always stay in touch with client contacts when they move on to another company, and naturally grow my business in the process.

- Building on the power of face-to-face marketing, I attend events where I might meet decision-makers in my target group. Often, sharing casual conversation with someone sitting beside me at lunch has been the start of a solid client relationship. Similarly, I contribute articles to publications I know my prospects read.

- I do my homework by reading every newspaper, magazine or trade publication that covers my target audience. If I learn a company is growing, has just released a new product or has received funding, I know chances are good they will need help. When I call and mention the article, they're flattered that I took the time to learn about their company. In another case, I read in the paper that a local advertising agency had just won a prestigious award. A simple handwritten note of congratulations prompted the owner to call me with work.

- In one of my bolder acts, I contacted a company that had posted an ad seeking a full-time writer. I sent an e-mail to the contact, letting her know it might be more affordable to outsource. She agreed and hired me instead.

Sales As Being a Team Member
Paul Glickstein
Atlanta, Georgia

I have a client—a marketing/design firm—that I've now worked with for more than a decade. For the first few years, the firm's principals considered me to be a contract service provider and not much more. But that perception changed immediately and irrevocably one Christmas Eve.

The firm had shut down for the holidays and the principals were traveling to distant states to spend time with relatives. One of their clients here called a meeting on the morning of December 24. Without hesitation, I volunteered to attend the meeting on their behalf, take notes and prepare a summary prior to their return. You'd have thought I'd hung the moon. My transformation from service provider to team member was immediate, and it's remained that way ever since.

The "sales message" here: It's certainly worth pushing the boundaries of roles and expectations with clients. Copy is only part of what we offer; service and support are no less critical. And the payoff can be tremendous.

Sales as Honesty
Chris DiNatale
www.dinataledesign.com
Marietta, Georgia

PB: The graphic designer I've been working with for more than ten years (my book cover designer) told me this great story. Design is close enough to writing to make the tale applicable.

Chris had just gotten in the door of a huge fast-food company and wanted to make a great first impression on her initial design job for them. Unfortunately, she was using a new printer (recommended by a print broker) who was two hours away, making it impossible for her to do her standard "press check"—reviewing a sample at the printer to make sure the job was executed flawlessly. When she received the shipment of printed materials, she took one look and gasped. The printer had reversed her instructions: The parts of the printed pieces that were supposed to be glossy were now matte, and vice versa.

It was now Thursday, the client needed the finished product by Monday and the printer couldn't get it redone in time. Chris called a local Atlanta printer with whom she had a good, long-term relationship. While he agreed to print the job for just over cost, she'd still have to eat a huge chunk of change. But, in her mind, that was the cost of doing business if she wanted to work with this firm again.

Even with the second printer, the deadline was going to be tight, so Chris decided to call her client to let her know the deal. She explained the whole mess, what she'd set up as the contingency plan, and the possibility of a slightly delayed final delivery. When she was done, the client said, *Before you go through all that, why don't you bring in what you have and let us take a look at it? Maybe we can use it.*

In she went with flawed product in hand. Her client and client's boss flipped over it, the boss calling it "gorgeous." Bottom line, they used the piece as is. Here's the clincher. Her client's reaction? *Knowing that you'd unhesitatingly go to all this trouble for such a little mistake gives me a really good feeling about working with you. I know you'll do whatever it takes to get it done and done right.* And then she promptly set up a time to get Chris back in for some additional projects—all because she was thorough and honest, and laid it on the line. Honesty sells.

Sales as Being a Valuable Resource to Clients

Nancy Knauf
Cincinnati, Ohio

PB: Nancy is a dear friend of mine from Atlanta (now living in Cincinnati) currently working for an ad agency in strategic planning. She made a killer suggestion to me recently for raising your value in your clients' eyes. The Web site of the American Marketing Association (**www.marketingpower.com**), in addition to being a wonderfully rich resource by itself, allows you to receive daily and customizable news feeds via e-mail on any number of 150 subjects and industries. Let's say you write for a mortgage firm, a non-profit, and companies in the aviation and chemical industries. Just gear your daily profile toward those arenas and articles on those subjects show up in your inbox.

Nancy gave me an example of one client, a bank, who was looking for ideas for marketing themselves to college students. She added banking to her profile and one morning got a very cool article about some innovative things that a bank in New Zealand was doing that was nicely analogous to her client's situation. She forwarded it to her client with a quick, *Thought you might find this interesting.* As she put it, *It's nice to be able to show up in front of your client for a better reason than just to call and ask, 'Got any work for me?'* It's things like this that transform you—in their eyes—from just another vendor to a true strategic partner.

She also points to another overarching benefit: *Using the AMA site (and others) feeds your own mind with current ideas and information, so when a client has a problem, your brain will know where to look for solutions— ideally from many different angles.*

Visit the site and then look on the right side for a link to sign up and create your own profile. Also, as of early April 2004, Google added "Personalized Web Search" and "Web Alerts" to allow searchers to specify exactly what they're looking for and then get focused results based on those particular interests. That includes search results tailored to one's interests as well as e-mailing information on any given topic.

Sales as Distinguishing Yourself

PB: As I see it, "sales" is actions we're taking, things we're *doing*, not words we're saying, not some precise perfect turn of phrase. And forging alliances with graphic designers and other middleman clients by distinguishing yourself in their eyes as being good, reliable and easy to work with is definitely "sales" in my book. And these alliances put you in the position to land in some pretty high-profile circles. If they like you, you piggyback on their marketing efforts and are in place when they want to bring you in on a project they're doing for one of their marquis clients or when they simply steer you to one of their clients who's in the market for a writer. It happened that way for me with BellSouth, Mercedes-Benz, UPS, Cingular Wireless, MCI, DuPont and many others.

Useful Sales Tools

Given my 15 years of sales before starting my writing career, I thought I'd share a few basic sales techniques of particular relevance to writers. Use them or not, as you see fit.

Choice of Two Positives

I'll touch on this again in the expanded cold-calling script in Chapter Five. The idea is to ask questions with only positive outcomes as choices. Let's say you've determined there's some interest on the part of a prospect and you want to set up a meeting. Instead of asking, *Can I stop by next week to show you my book?* (which can easily elicit a *No*), say, *I'm going to be out and about next week and would love to stop by and introduce myself. Which day works better for you, Tuesday or Wednesday?* (Then, if they pick a day: *Is morning or afternoon better?*)

Or let's say you've determined that they need to get several newsletter articles written. Instead of asking, *So, you want me to get started on these?*

(which could invite a delay, while they ponder it), ask, *Should I begin the ones on (X subject) first or are the (Y subject) ones more pressing?* In essence, you're helping them bypass the human tendency to procrastinate and to instead get things done.

Series of "Yes"-es

This is a tried and true concept with a sound premise: Get a prospect to say *Yes* to a series of progressively more important questions, culminating in saying *Yes* to hiring you (again, using the choice of two positives above) or, at the very least, seeing the strong value of doing so.

For example, you've researched the company and have a rough idea of the parameters of a particular project. In your meeting, you ask questions, get answers and then confirm those answers by getting another *Yes*. You get the prospect to confirm what the company does, what its market is, what its market challenges are, what a writer can do for its bottom line, the project parameters, the project timetable, what the piece has to accomplish, what skills will be needed to do that (skills you possess, of course), etc.

And this is far more than some linguistic smoke and mirrors. The whole idea is to slowly build the case for hiring you by underscoring that you grasp their business and have the skills to do the job. You'd have to do all that anyway to get the job. This is, arguably, just a more expeditious way of getting there.

●　　●　　●

Okay, class is done. Now that we've reduced these not-so-ferocious critters from **"SALES"** and **"MARKETING"** to sales and marketing, it's time to talk about developing the mindset of the marketer....

Chapter 2

I saw a great series of billboards in Atlanta recently. It was for *Apartments.com*, an online clearinghouse for apartments that allows you to search for exactly what you want in any state. They could have devoted their billboard space to talking about *themselves* (like most companies do) and all the great things *they* offer: unmatched customer service, big selection, easy online access, etc. (I can picture big checked boxes, right?). They *could* have. But they didn't.

The first billboard had just one short sentence (their tag line, incidentally) across the middle: *"You want what you want."* Then, simply their logo and the *Apartments.com* name. Nothing more. A thing of simplicity and beauty. This company could have popped up yesterday for all we know. But, who cares? In one five-word sentence, they nailed THE hot button for their audience: personal taste and choice in an apartment. Heck, they used "you" twice in a five-word sentence. They know what people want to hear.

More to the point, people like to be acknowledged. Included. Talked *to*, not talked *at*. They want to know that they matter, that they've been considered. That what matters to them matters to the entity addressing them (in an ad, direct mail piece, marketing brochure, etc.). Remember that—it's key to cultivating the marketing mindset.

It's All About Me

In the process of letting me know they understood what's important to me, they disappeared from the process. Meaning, it wasn't about them at all. It was about me and what I wanted, and they were simply there as the vehicle to deliver that.

27

This example is a good way to introduce the three fundamental principles of sales and marketing I'll be sharing in this chapter—principles that apply both to marketing yourself as well as helping you write stronger marketing copy:

1. **The Audience**—they clearly understand the audience they're talking to and what's important to that audience.

2. **The Features/Benefits Equation**—they know how to keep the interests of the audience ahead of their own.

3. **The Unique Selling Proposition (USP)**—The fact that the company's search engine delivers exactly what the audience wants sets them apart. Or, at the very least, they're doing a better job than the competition of letting the world know what they're offering.

It's All About Communication

I had lunch with a budding FLCW in Atlanta a few months back. David, who was leveraging roughly 15 years of mortgage experience to boost his writing career, made a very keen observation based on his experience (and mine): "Most companies lose customers because of a lack of communication." How true. There will *always* be a need for people who can help companies communicate more effectively, both within their company and with customers. David added another truism—again, coinciding with my own experience—that most companies just aren't very savvy in the marketing arena and that it really wouldn't take much to make a positive difference for them.

It's Not That Scary...

This won't be some exhaustive study of sales and marketing because, frankly, there's no need to turn you into experts in order to admirably serve your clients and promote your own business. I hope by the time I'm done, you'll be viewing this arena not as some esoteric science, but rather as a predictable and intuitive reflection of human nature, and hence something that's already familiar to you. And what's familiar simply can't be scary.

As we discussed earlier, I get a lot of e-mails from people for whom "sales" and "marketing" are foreign and frightening concepts. Many of these folks have precious little experience in a business setting, hailing perhaps from academia, the media, whatever. For many, this perceived lack of a marketing background looms as a huge obstacle. But whether or not you're wrestling with this one, read on. It never hurts to be reminded of the basics.

"Why Do We Write Anything?"

In my seminars, when I get to the topic of marketing, I start out with the question above. And I get all the usual answers: *To inform. Educate. Inspire. Motivate. Encourage. Entertain. Move. Touch.*

All true. And yet, there's a far more basic reason why we write anything. Care to guess? How about this: *To have it be read.* I know, you're rolling your eyes, but frankly, none of the others are even possible until you accomplish the first. And that's what this chapter is about—boosting the odds that your intended reader will actually read what you've written, whether it's something designed to promote your own business or that of a client. It all starts there.

"Who's the Audience?"

As discussed in the *TWFW,* this is THE absolute first question you need to ask at the start of every project. When you buy a product that you heard about in a TV commercial, direct mail piece, e-mail or brochure, it's because something spoke to *you.* Someone knew what to say to make *you* sit up and take notice—which is exactly what will happen when a message is well-crafted. You're no different from anyone else out there.

Want some surprisingly good news? As simple and logical as this formula is, it's amazing—and tragic—how much marketing material out there is poorly written and doesn't consider the intended audience. If you can get it right, you'll set yourself apart.

It's Logical

Think about it. Don't you talk to your mother differently than your friends? Your co-workers differently than your boss? Somebody who has something you want differently than someone who wants something you have? Consciously or unconsciously, you're always thinking about audience.

Arguably, any project—even technical documentation, corporate training modules or grandiose documentaries—requires you to ask the same *Who's the audience?* questions in order to sell the audience on your approach or point of view. And that first question leads, as we discussed in *TWFW,* to a bunch of related ones:

 What's important to people in this group?

What motivates them?

How do they think?

How do they talk?

What words and language will get through to them?

What's going to turn their heads and get them to pay attention?

Once they pay attention, what will it take to get them to take action?

"Take action" can mean: buy the product, visit the store, take a test drive, make the call, order the bigger brochure, return the reply card, etc.

A Good Example...

A few years back, I did a brochure for a software company that specialized in doctor-patient communication solutions. They'd created a product that, by combining the telephone and computer, would call patients automatically and remind them of upcoming appointments, thereby freeing the front-office staff from those tasks. Another of their automated products allowed patients to use a PIN to retrieve lab results after-hours, again taking tasks off the plates of admin staff that would normally be fielding those calls.

By asking a few simple questions, I discovered that while the ultimate decision-maker would be the doctor, the primary user (and first audience) was...who? *Office managers.* If these people liked the product, they'd present it to the doctor with a recommendation to buy. If they didn't like it, the doctor would never see it.

Okay, so tell me about these people, I said. *What are their demographics? Their job description? What are they expected to accomplish?* Turns out they're mostly women, age 35 to 45, and they have many crucial responsibilities: reduce no-shows, increase revenues, improve patient relations, generally reduce the workload of the front-office and boost overall efficiency of that department.

I had a chance to see the previous brochure the company had created—it looked like a million others that followed the we-do model: *We do this, we do that, we do the other, we do it all, we do it better, we do it faster, we do it more reliably—buy from us.* A frighteningly high percentage of brochures seem to follow that model. Maybe a nod to the customer here and there, but mostly focused on the company and its product. All features. No one's talking *benefits* (and *that* discussion's next).

Well, that's easy enough to improve on. Once I'd gathered my information and discovered what the world of office managers was like and what they deal with on a daily basis, I knew how to talk to them and get their attention. I submitted my copy to my client, the design firm, and a few days later my contact called me and told me what every copywriter dreams of hearing: *The client loved it. They didn't change a single word.* Whoa!

Open the brochure and the first page of copy reads:

> *You have a simple job, right? Sure. Let's see…just increase practice revenues, decrease no-shows, reduce front-office workload and boost overall administrative efficiency. Oh, and build stronger relationships with patients. For starters.*
>
> *Well, imagine products that have been proven to do all that, while enjoying a 98 percent "thumbs-up" from patients and a remarkably high client referral rate. All from a company with a legendary industry reputation for customer service. Simply put, a company and product line with a mission to make your life easier and make you look good. Might be worth a look…*

I simply gave it all back to them. How hard is that? And by talking to the primary audience in language it could understand—by talking *benefits*—what did the company accomplish? It got the attention of the folks with buying power and won them over. Now I could continue with features, knowing the audience was listening. But even then, I tried to make it interesting by not just *talking* about the product features but telling stories that demonstrated how it worked. For example:

> *After a cholesterol screening last week, Mr. Johnson left with a **LabCalls** reminder card, complete with "results available" date. At 10:15 p.m. on that date, he called the dedicated **LabCalls** line, and using a PIN, accessed his results, delivered in the voice of his favorite front-office manager. To double-check the numeric values, he pressed 2 to repeat and then 3 to leave a message for his doctor. **LabCalls** automatically generated a report entry confirming his successful retrieval of the results.*

A Bad Example

I recently came across a great example of a company with zero grasp of audience. In Atlanta, we have an annual directory or "sourcebook" (the *OZ Creative Index*; **www.ozoneline.tv**), put out by the local magazine for the creative industry. In the back are business card-sized ads taken out by writers, graphic designers, illustrators, photographers, marketing companies, etc. One featured simply a photograph of an object and a Web address. Period. Not one other word. Nada. Just picture and Web address. I wasn't sure if this was arrogance or just plain cluelessness on the part of this company's managers.

Did they honestly believe people were going to be so intrigued that they'd just drop everything and go visit the Web site? Without so much as the simplest message to get the attention of their target audience? Amazing. Who knows—maybe they're drowning in work, though I'd never heard of them.

The Features/Benefits Equation

I recently had a meeting with a client from a successful marketing company that needed some newsletter work. This company had just had a banner year and the year ahead of it was looking bright as well. The client gave me one of his brand new marketing brochures, of which he was obviously quite proud. While it was certainly slick-looking, you had to wade through half the copy before it stopped talking about how great, experienced, knowledgeable and successful the company was and got around to talking about things that truly matter to clients: bottom line, image, market share, etc. Beaucoup features, few benefits. You see it all the time.

The Features/Benefits equation is an absolute cornerstone of sales and marketing. Yet, as you'll see in the broad array of examples and analogies in the coming pages, it's a concept we're already intimately familiar with.

Basic Definitions

Features *are all about a product or service and the company selling it.* Benefits *are about the customers—what's important to them and how a product or service addresses those issues. Always begin with benefits, follow with features.*

A few years back, BellSouth, the big Southeastern telecommunications provider, seemed to have an epiphany. Till then, its marketing campaigns focused largely on *technology*. Ads (like those of many other high-tech companies) featured images of computers, keyboards, data streams, switching stations, routers, etc. Of course, thanks to the graphic geniuses in BellSouth's employ, the images were all stylized and artsy, conferring a sexy patina over it all. Technology was cool. Everything was all about the latest fancy calling feature, network innovation, gadget, bell, whistle, etc. (translation: *features*).

It was as if, because the industry was so enamored with technology and its continual advancement, it was just assumed the public was as well. Then one day, someone woke up and said, *Hey, you know what? People don't give a rat's heinie about technology.* Exactly. After all, what's so interesting about technology anyway, beyond the gee-whiz factor? Not much. (The only exception is highly technical marketing materials directed largely toward "techies." These folks want all the gory technical details.)

Benefits Are King

So, what *do* people care about? Simple. They care about *how* that technology can enhance the quality of their lives—how it can free them from the confines of an office, give them more time for leisure, or help keep them in touch with their families (translation: *benefits*). And on some level, you know that.

People don't care about the speed of a DSL line. They care that that speed allows them to efficiently research their next vacation, find a date for the weekend, or get a great chocolate chip cookie recipe. *And* do it all so fast that they've got time to actually go on that date and make those cookies. They get to live their life, *not* learn all about technology.

People don't care that a cell phone is *this* small, has a cool blue display or a battery that lasts *that* long (all *features*). What they care about is that that cell phone gives them ultimate freedom and independence, while letting them stay connected at all times. It's not about technology. It's about connection, about making distance irrelevant. Those are *benefits*.

And oh, by the way, in case you're thinking, *Hey, you're wrong. I care very much that my cell phone has that way-cool blue display*, I disagree. You don't care about that display as an end in itself, but only as a vehicle for something much more important to you: It makes you feel like One Cool Dude(ette), and *that* is a Big Benefit.

Features Deliver Benefits

As a consumer, sure, you may like the 24-hour customer service a company offers, the Caller ID on your phone, or the aerodynamic design of a particular car, but you buy the product for what those features deliver to you in the way of *benefits*: the convenience of customer service 'round the clock; that sense of certainty about who's calling you and the ability to avoid unwanted callers; and yes, those feelings of pride and accomplishment at being able to afford a hot car. The features are simply the vehicle for delivering the benefits.

Soon after BellSouth had its realization, it launched a new ad campaign built around the tagline: ">>>connect>>>create something™." It was perfect—all about benefits. The new TV ads were rich in touchy-feely images, graphically showcasing the *benefits* of technology: business success, family closeness, romantic connection, etc. And nary a feature in sight. They got what was important to people—their lives, *not* bits and bytes.

IBM Gets It

Starting in 2003, IBM's new chairman and CEO, Samuel J. Palmisano, began taking the massive computer company in a new and very sensible direction: He moved away from simply being a supplier of hardware and software and entered the realm of business consulting. The acquisition of PriceWaterhouseCoopers Consulting and Rational Software were the most recent tools he employed to pull this off.

It's a classic features vs. benefits scenario. Before, IBM's approach had largely been about *them*: their company and their products. Features. Now the company was entering an arena that was about its customers and what was really important to them: reaching their goals of profitability, market share and competitive advantage. Benefits.

In another sense, the IBM story echoes the teaming concept I've discussed *ad nauseum*. When you team with a graphic designer (like IBM teamed with consulting and software entities), you're not offering writing services and design services. You're offering a complete solution to a business need. Customers don't want products and services (that's about you). They want complete solutions (that's about them).

Stop Talking About Yourself

There's a big difference between what your client wants to tell a prospect in a marketing piece and what that prospect wants (and needs) to know. Your clients probably often try to tell their prospective customers everything about the company and its products: years in business, commitment to excellent customer service, the superior quality of products (with all the technical specs), the highly experienced staff. In short, features. Prospects want to know how a company's product will solve a problem (or fill a need) they have and make a difference in their quality of life. That's benefits.

Just as importantly, it's unrealistic to think that someone will make a buying decision based on reading something. The goal is to get the prospect to take the next step—make the call, return the card, visit the showroom—and in effect, say, *Okay, I'm interested. Tell me more.* And you just don't need to tell all to get them to do that.

The Features/Benefits dynamic is everywhere. It's a cornerstone of human nature, not just something that plays out in business settings. You live it every day.

What Prospects Want to Hear

I came across an interesting article in the September 7, 2003, edition of The New York Times: *It's Not What You Say; It's How It Sounds* (by Claudia

H. Deutsch), about legendary image-meister Kevin Daley, founder of Communispond, a company that teaches communications skills. Here's a brief snippet, where he compares the approaches of two candidates:

> *Two copywriters applying for jobs at an advertising agency are asked what they would bring to the party. "Well, I'm very creative," one answered after a while. The winning applicant made no such claim but told of a successful and highly creative campaign he developed at another job. "A good presenter knows how to use a vignette to make a point without bragging," Mr. Daley said.*

The first copywriter, by describing himself as "creative," is just sharing a *feature* about himself to the employer. The second, by discussing a success story, quantifies the *benefit* to the agency of hiring him.

A "Love-ly" Example

What's one of the most common complaints you hear from both women and men about the opposite sex on the first few dates? *They spent the whole time talking about themselves!* That's *features*. How can that other party feel special, important or even relevant to the first when he or she can't even enter the conversation? It's the equivalent of a company going on about itself and its products.

It's only when one party shows interest in the other—through appropriate body language, asking questions, and *listening* to the answers—that the other person feels acknowledged, important and included. And when that happens, that other person has seen the *benefits* to him or her of hanging out with this person, not just the *features* of this person. This is the equivalent of a company talking about what's important to a prospect.

Robust Resumes

Given what we've established about features and benefits, let's map that onto something a lot of people can relate to of late: the creation of an effective resume.

What do most resumes consist of? Lists, right? Lists of accomplishments. Lists of experiences. Lists of jobs. Lists of degrees, awards and accolades. It's all about the job hunter. So, what does a resume highlight? All together now...*features*. If you're already competing with zillions of others, don't compound your primary challenge of getting noticed in the crowd by creating a resume like everyone else's.

Okay, given that lists of stuff about the job hunter are *features*, what would *benefits* be? Don't read ahead. Think about it for a moment.

To get that prospective employer's attention, you need to focus *not* on what jobs you've had or what you majored in, but *how* you plan to put your talents, skills, experience and expertise to work for the benefit of the hiring organization. Lists are about YOU, making them *features*. Describing the difference you can make for a firm, what you can bring to the table and the impact you could have is *benefits*. That's all about THEM, and it's all an employer really cares about.

Most resumes don't need a total rewrite, just a repositioning of the same information into a new framework that speaks first to an employer's needs *(benefits)* and secondarily to how the candidate's *features* meet those needs. Researching a company and its products can begin to reveal its needs and provide an opening for crafting an effective resume that powerfully speaks to those needs. Sound like something you could do for a company you want to freelance for as well?

Potent Press Releases

In the course of promoting my book, I've gotten a healthy amount of practice writing press releases. Given how inundated my target audience (media people) is with releases, it's always an uphill battle to get noticed.

Here's the plain truth about journalists: They couldn't care less that you've written a book (unless you're Stephen King, Tom Clancy, John Grisham, et al.). The rest of us? *Fuggedaboudit.* Send them a press release announcing you've written a book and you'll be lucky if they wipe their nose with it before tossing it. A release about a book and its author is… *features*.

That reporter wants benefits: *I SO don't care about your book. Tell me why that book is important to my readers/viewers, why they should care, why it addresses some trend or topical subject.* Not the book, but the *angle* represented by the book. Those are the *benefits*. Jane Journalist's job is to write stories that resonate with her readers (and earn kudos) so her good reputation and solid standing in the industry are affirmed. Cynically—albeit realistically—speaking, a journalist, fundamentally, is asking, *What's in it for me? How will writing a story about your subject make me look good?*

Lessons in Drill Bits

I like the old adage about the ½-inch drill bit. When you go into a hardware store looking for a ½-inch drill bit, you're not *really* buying a ½-inch drill bit. Think about it.

You're buying a ½-inch hole. A ½-inch drill bit is *features*. It's about the product. A ½-inch hole is *benefits*. It's about the buyer. It's always about the buyer.

USP – The Unique Selling Proposition

Marketing copywriting guru Marcia Yudkin, in her January 21, 2004, edition of *The Marketing Minute* (*www.yudkin.com/marketing.htm* to subscribe), underscores a wildly common error many companies make on their Web sites (and often in their marketing materials as well):

> *While rating Web sites for the Webby Awards this month, I shook my head at a mistake that's epidemic at sites for banks, consulting firms, tours and real estate companies. They explain their service offerings clearly but fail to make a case why someone shopping for a bank or consultant, etc., should choose THEM.*
>
> *They must be thinking that if the company describes what they do and how they do it, shoppers can easily draw conclusions about what they do better than competitors. Nope! Shoppers can't extrapolate like that, and they won't. Too often the qualities that make one service provider superior to others like them sit buried in one or two testimonials or are completely unstated.*
>
> *In a five-year study of 901 new products performed by the Eureka! Ranch, those whose sales messages explicitly stated the product's point of difference were 52 percent more likely to survive than those that didn't. Don't expect readers of your Web site to guess how you outshine the competition. Tell 'em!*

Every business entity is unique in some way. Once you determine the audience for a company's product or service, zero in on the *Unique Selling Proposition* (USP)—THE thing that sets that company apart in a marketplace full of competitors, and the reason to buy from them. Companies need to put their best foot forward, showcase their strengths and build on the thing they do better than anyone else.

Marketing guru and author Jay Abraham (**www.abraham.com**), in his book *Getting Everything You Can Out Of All You've Got: 21 Ways You Can Out-Think, Out-Perform, and Out-Earn the Competition*, talks about creating a

USP. He offers these useful guidelines, which you can employ as a copy-writer to drive the questions you ask a client in order to pinpoint that USP:

1. Ideally, the USP should address a clear need or void in the marketplace. When few (or none) are doing a particular thing, those who can will stand out.

2. Make sure you can deliver on the promise of your USP. If you're claiming, by way of a USP, that a company offers the "best in-stock selection and faster delivery" than anyone else, it had better be true or that USP will end up doing more harm than good.

   Most business owners don't have a USP, only a 'me too,' rudderless, nondescript, unappealing business that feeds solely upon the sheer momentum of the marketplace. Would you want to patronize a firm that's just 'there,' with no unique benefit, no incredible prices or selection, no especially comforting counsel, service or guarantee? Or would you prefer a firm that offers you the broadest selection in the country? Or one with every item marked up less than half the margin other competitors charge? Or one that sells the 'Rolls Royce' of the industry's products?

Once you've determined the company's USP, put it to work as the focus of brochures, Web copy and ad/direct mail campaigns. Identifying a company's USP also provides more clarity as to what its mission is, what piece of the marketplace it's claiming and how to protect it.

The Discovery Questionnaire

A truly boffo way to bring all these ideas together when sitting with a client is a "Discovery Questionnaire," an idea suggested to me by Seattle FLCW Sonya Carmichael Jones, which I featured in the September 2002 issue of the E-PUB. This piece, which can either be sent to a client prior to a meeting or filled out at the meeting, clarifies and quantifies the company's mission and project parameters. It'll enhance your credibility with the client and reduce your own anxiety about the process. I tweaked Sonya's basic survey, added and deleted a few questions and came up with the following. Tailor it to suit your specific situation:

1. Who's the audience for this piece? Is it the same as your target customer?

2. What are their hot buttons? When it comes to considering a product like yours, what issues are important to this audience?

3. *What makes your business, product, or service unique?*

4. *What do you do better than the competition?*

5. *What are your company's short- and long-term goals?*

6. *Who is your major competitor and where do you rank in the industry?*

7. *What's the purpose of this (brochure, direct mail piece, ad, etc.)? How will it be used?*

8. *How do you currently market your business, product, or services?*

9. *What are the main points you want to convey in this piece?*

10. *Do you have a company tagline or slogan? If not, have you considered creating one?*

11. *If money were not a factor, what would be your ideal marketing campaign?*

Are You Branded?

Developing a marketing mindset doesn't just apply to writing creative copy for your clients. It can—and should—also mean figuring out how to package the unique product that is YOU. No one has your specific distinctive gifts. No one walking the earth has your particular combination of talents and abilities. How do you showcase that?

The whole idea of "branding" is hot today. And no, a one-person shop doesn't *need* to be branded to succeed. While the need to do so is more obviously critical for a larger company, any business can benefit from exploring some fundamentals.

Some time back, at the local meeting of the Atlanta freelancers group I belong to, speaker Linda Travis (**www.brandrenovator.com**) shared her services branding expertise. Linda has isolated five components of branding that anyone, in any size business, can practice to varying degrees in order to more effectively stand out in the marketplace.

1. **Be Unique**—Identify your authentic point of difference in the marketplace (and we'll discuss how in a moment) and work to highlight that in your marketing materials. Maybe you have a skill in transforming complex subjects into layman's terms. Perhaps you can step inside your clients' world, quickly grasp their business and create effective marketing strategies. Maybe your strong point is helping clients find *their* unique voices in the marketplace.

2. **Focus Your Message**—If you want to be remembered, stand for something specific. As part of Linda's presentation, she had bars of Lava and Dove soap resting on the lectern. As has been famously opined, *a brand is a promise.* Those two soaps are textbook brands—each with its own culturally-entrenched promise. Dove evokes soft, gentle moisturizing while Lava conjures up the power to clean really dirty hands—you wouldn't buy one if you knew you needed the other. Similarly, if you want to earn the lion's share of your income as copywriter, then don't present yourself as a writer, designer, photographer and illustrator, even if you can do it all.

3. **Address the Buyer's Values**—What do your buyers value? Do they value what you do? How are you addressing that value? Ask what your buyers see and value in you and then make your marketing materials reflect this.

4. **Tell Other People**—Ponder the question, *What do I do?* You could just say, *I'm a freelance commercial writer* or you could figure out what's unique about you and translate that into a niche and a story you can tell—in short, a focused message.

5. **Convey Consistency**—People experience your brand with every contact you make. Make sure your "package" (literally and figuratively) conveys the message you want to send. Do that by maintaining consistency in your marketing brochures, Web site, e-mails, letterhead, etc.

A client will usually hire you initially because you roughly match the general criteria they have for a copywriter: a certain level of relevant experience, a decent portfolio, confidence and enthusiasm, interpersonal skills, etc. By definition, those are the only things they *can* consider because they don't know you personally and how you work.

But if they *keep* hiring you, you can bet it's because there are certain things about you that have real specific value to them, whether *you* realize it or not. It's worthwhile to ask your clients what that value is, because those revelations can be the building blocks of your brand identity. If there's something about what you do or *how* you do it that has clients hiring you over and over again, you need to know it. After all, it's logical to assume that other clients in similar situations and with similar needs would value those qualities as well.

In a sense, it's like a consumer focus group designed to find out why people buy a product, like it and continue to buy it. If the same things keep coming up, you can build those messages into marketing campaigns directed to the "not-yet-convinced" and turn one-time "snack" clients into long-term meal tickets.

•   •   •

Okay, now that we're a bit more comfortable in our marketing skin, it's time to talk about a most wondrous tool for business growth: the Web site. Let's go clickin'…

Chapter 3

I've got an online portfolio. Give me your e-mail address and I'll send you the link. Two short sentences that not only represent a dramatic simplification of your marketing efforts, but enhance your legitimacy in the eyes of your clients and prospects.

Okay, I want you to do something. Right now. Go get *TWFW* off your shelf, turn to page 95 and hold that place. Then, turn to page 102, grab those seven pages and rip them right out. Okay, perhaps a little drastic and unnecessary. But the point is, if I were writing the book today, I'd insert *this* chapter in place of *those* pages. I've become a Web site convert, almost obnoxious in my religious fervor.

As you recall, in *TWFW*, I described a systematic process for assembling packages of samples to send your prospects. Of course, that system will *still* work to build your business, and there are times when you'll absolutely want to send a client or prospect an actual sample as a way of continuing to stay visible. But for both the initial and ongoing prospecting and business-building parts of your enterprise, few tools are as efficient and expeditious as a Web site. When whoever it was coined the now-terminally overexposed expression *Work smarter, not harder*, they were talking about a Web site.

Remember the "before/after" prospecting scenario I painted in the first book? How, in the absence of a system, it could take you 30 to 45 minutes to put together a marketing package once you got a hot prospect interested in you? And how, with a system in place, you could reduce that to 5 to 10 minutes? Well class, today's "before/after" comparison starts at 5 to 10 minutes without a Web site, and approximately 60 seconds with one.

43

You're talking to your prospect and you get to the part where he or she asks if you can send samples. You say, *Tell you what—give me your e-mail address and I'll send you the link to my site* (which lets you capture their e-mail address and results in a greater likelihood of their actually visiting your site than if you simply give them the URL over the phone and hope they go visit). This approach will get a good reception for a few reasons. Not only will the existence of a Web site help the prospect view you as a more professional, established and legitimate businessperson, but in the process, you obviously dramatically simplify the task of getting samples into their hands.

The Whole Point

Let's cut to the chase here. That's really the point of a Web site—to showcase your samples. It's the main reason why someone will visit your site, *not* to learn about your terms, read your resume or see the list of projects you do. Yes, they want to know about those things too, but only after they see the caliber of your writing—the point being, don't bother putting up a site if you don't have samples posted. That said, how you craft the copy for other pages (especially the home page) will give prospects a taste of what you could do for them, copywriting-wise. So make it good.

Keep It Simple

Make it easy for prospects to get in and get out. Keep the navigation simple and don't overload it with too many sections. Dispense with fancy graphics and special effects. It's all the rage these days with many companies, and it would definitely make more sense for graphic/Web design firms as a showcase for their creative talents, but we writers don't need to gunk things up. If you insist on opening your site with some nifty-keeno graphics or a Flash presentation, at the very least have a prominently displayed *Skip Intro* option. Nothing will send prospects packing more quickly than being forced to sit through *your* creative vision on *their* time.

In addition to your home page and online portfolio, you'll probably want to include the following pages:

- Terms (How you work)
- Client list
- Services list
- Testimonials (see section ahead)
- Contact information

My Web site (**www.writeinc.biz**) is one way to do this. Not necessarily the last word in sites and certainly not overly flashy, but I think it gets the job done.

(Don't) Show Them the Money

A lot of people ask if their sites should include a rate sheet for different projects. Not necessary and not a good idea. I'd even go so far as to say that if you do include one, in the eyes of experienced writing buyers anyway, you might just appear a bit...green. Meaning, they know that there's no such thing as a "typical" project. Even within a given category, like marketing brochures, for instance, every project is different. It's for that reason a client doesn't expect to see a rate sheet.

If you do try to come up with a fair rate sheet, you'll likely end up with one of two outcomes—one ineffective, the other risky. In the first scenario, even if you were able to provide a realistic fee range for marketing brochures that would span the gamut from small-and-basic to large-and-complex, you'd end up with a range so wide as to render it virtually meaningless.

And if you try to narrow those ranges in order to provide a more meaningful number, you risk clients taking those numbers to the bank. What if their project is very simple and would actually cost less than your low-end figure? You might just lose the deal because you're perceived to be too expensive. What if their project is much more complex and would exceed the upper end of your range? The client might be disappointed when your actual estimate comes in way higher. Bottom line, there's virtually no upside to providing a rate sheet, and plenty of potential downsides. Better to use the site to showcase your competence, professionalism and reliability and hash out the financial details later.

Highlight Your Areas of Specialty

I had an interesting chat with my friend and fellow FLCW Steve Marshall recently about an intriguing idea: multiple Web sites focusing on different copywriting specialties. He'd looked at his portfolio, realized that he had a boatload of healthcare-related work and the idea occurred to him to create a site specifically geared to that specialty, in addition to his more general copywriting site.

The rationale is obvious: Any copywriting prospect will be more receptive to a vendor who's a specialist in that industry, and given the relative ease and low expense of creating another site (and business cards to go with it), why not do it? It's all about perception and Steve's keenly aware of how he can easily and inexpensively ratchet up his perceived value in a prospect's eyes. He's simply putting his best forward when approaching certain clients. A low-tech analogy to this is the creation of multiple versions of a resume for different types of work. Just makes sense.

The $75 Web Site

Low-cost avenues for personal Web site creation abound on the Internet. California FLCW Larry Rosenwinkel wrote an article for my October 2003 E-PUB on his success in creating a $75 Web site (using **www.godaddy.com** and including domain name registration, hosting, site creation software licensing, etc.). For $75, you won't get a fancy site with major bells and whistles, or one that's optimally designed for search engine maximization (my philosophy is that you shouldn't count on search engines to drive prospects to your site anyway—your personal ongoing promotion campaign should be doing that.) Here are a few more resources that can dramatically simplify the process of creating your own site while keeping costs at mind-boggling lows.

www.quickbizsites.com

www.homestead.com

www.citymax.com

Sales by Testimonial

There's nothing like a few compelling third-party references on your site to boost your credibility. At a past meeting of my local freelancers group, the speaker was Paul Johnson, head of the sales and marketing consulting firm Panache and Systems LLC (**www.panache-yes.com**). Paul's topic was "Let Your Customers Sell You Through Testimonial Letters." Great presentation, important topic and all summarized in Paul's excellent 20-page pamphlet entitled, *Let Your Customers Sell You: 120 Tips For Getting And Using Testimonial Letters To Win More Business.* This booklet takes the idea *far* beyond just getting a few nice blurbs—it's a treasure chest of excellent and provocative ideas for maximizing this strategy. Take a look at some good sample testimonial letters at **www.testimonialletters.com** (you can also order the booklet online).

Third-party selling has always been one of the most effective marketing techniques. Prospects would always rather hear from someone who has no stake in promoting your business that you're all you claim to be and more.

Some key points in Paul's talk:

YOU WRITE THE LETTER. People are busy. Why not ask your clients, over the phone, to give you three or four quantifiable benefits of doing business with you. Then *you* write it up and run it past them for review—saving them valuable time. "Quantifiable" means things like, *Joe's ad delivered a 25 percent increase in widget sales* or *Mary's direct mail piece really got the phones ringing.*

LAY THE GROUNDWORK. In the early stages of a writing project with a client, let him know you'll be asking for a testimonial letter when you're done. That not only gives the client a heads-up, but also lets him know you're planning on doing a job worthy of a testimonial.

GET VERBAL REFERRALS FOR WORK. In addition to requesting a written testimonial letter, ask your client directly for referrals to new business. And when asking, be specific: *Do you know anyone who'll need help putting together a marketing brochure, sales sheet or Web content in the next few months?*

Here's a brief sampling of some of tips included in the booklet:

Tip #1: Use a testimonial letter to prove that you can do what you say you're going to do. Help prospective customers understand how they can get results similar to what you've already produced for another customer.

Tip #29: Ask for a letter from executive contacts at the very highest level of your customer's organization. These people have responsibility for the direction of the company and can describe how your offering supports the larger strategic mission of the organization.

Tip #67 and #68: (When writing the letter for the client) Use the opening line, "Thank you for your recent efforts at providing solutions we needed for..." Or, "I'm proud to be able to tell people that we chose your solution..."

Tip #106: Build customer quotes into your fax cover pages.

●   ●   ●

Okay, now that we've got some marketing savvy under our belts, it's not a bad time to address a bunch of the nagging questions, concerns, myths and preconceptions I hear all the time...

TOP 10 LIST FOR CREATING TWFW'S WEB SITE
by Bay Area FLCW Kathy Steligo (www.thewordcompany.com)

Your Web site serves a practical and professional purpose: to sell your services or entice prospective clients to contact you for more information. Here are 10 steps to drive customers your way.

Reserve your domain name. You can register a Web address for roughly $16 a year (and often less), whether your site is up or not. Check the availability of your proposed URL, then register at a site like **www.000domains.com**, **www.buydomains.com** or others.

Plan before you build. Design each page on paper first. Create a consistent look with thoughtful navigation. Use appealing color combinations and readable fonts. Analyze other writers' sites to see what works and what doesn't.

Find a Web host. Search for "Web hosting" or visit HostIndex.com to compare costs and services. Your e-mail provider may be another option. Look for adequate space, fast-loading pages and accessible technical support.

Convert your paper design into Web pages. Use your browser, MS WORD, or Web authoring software like CoffeeCup HTML Editor. You can hire (or barter with) someone to build it for you, but you'll want to have the ability to update and make changes yourself; it won't take long to learn enough HTML to get you up and running.

Persuade with creative content. Your Web site is a subtle commercial for your work. Emphasizing customer benefits is better than blatant horn-tooting. Post convincing credentials, a client list and samples of your best work.

Keep it simple. Artsy and appealing are nice, but resist the temptation to add blinking lights and too many graphics, which detract from your writing and often reduce browsers to snail speed.

Proof and perfect. Your Web site attests to the quality visitors can expect in your work. If typos or grammatical errors abound, they'll assume that's what they'll get if they hire you. Proof your site before it goes live and have someone you trust do the same. Test it with different browsers. Check every navigational link.

Put your best foot forward. Your Web site represents your ability. If your forté is humorous writing, show it. If you're a technical whiz, reflect that in your text. Forget cute or bizarre...unless, of course, that's your specialty.

Make friends with search engines. Learn how to create META tags (embedded snippets of data that provide information to search engines).

Promote endlessly. Your Web site is only as good as your promotion. To drive traffic to your online portfolio, include your URL in all promotional materials, articles you write for print and online publications and your e-mail signature line.

Your Colleagues' Sites

I asked commercial writers across the world to share their Web sites for inclusion in the book. A nice list follows. You'll see a wide array of creative visions—things you'll like and things you won't. It's all about getting ideas.

Tom Myer—Austin, Texas: **www.myerman.com**

Kennerly Clay—Philadelphia: **www.eclecticcontent.com**

Jake Poinier—Phoenix: **www.mythreedots.com**

Steve Marshall—Marietta, Georgia: **www.samarshall.com**

Rick Waugh—Vancouver, Canada: **www.writemix.ca**

Simon Young—Auckland, New Zealand: **www.simonyoung.co.nz**

Amy Sorkin—Los Angeles: **www.amyswords.com**

Moira Shephard—Venice, California: **www.star-ink.com**

Maria Rivera—Austin, Texas: **www.redwritingshop.com**

Mark Lewin—Oxfordshire, England: **www.wordmeister.co.uk**

Peter Bowerman—Atlanta: **www.writeinc.biz**

Bob Bly—Dumont, New Jersey: **www.bly.com**

Michelle Zavala—Colorado Springs: **www.studioz.ws**

Bruce Lilly—Bloomington, Indiana: **www.BruceLilly.com**

Barbara Elmore—Waco, Texas: **www.wordscene.com**

Jill Shtulman—Chicago: **www.jsacreative.com**

Lisa Sparks—Ft. Myers, Florida: **www.integritywriting.com**

Jim Meadows—Kansas City, Missouri: **www.jimfreelance.com**

Kristina Anderson—Seattle: **www.easyreadcopywriting.com**

Andrea Harris—Boston: **www.minerva-inc.com**

Mary Guinane—Sioux City, Iowa: **www.twacopywriting.com**

Jill Taylor—Canton, Georgia: **www.taylorwrites.com**

John Barrett—Salt Lake City: **www.quillpro.com**

Patrick Leonard (a.k.a Lp Camozzi)—Montreal, Canada: **www.camozzi.ca**

Kathy Steligo—San Carlos, California: **www.thewordcompany.com**

Kevin Klemme—Bloomington, Indiana: **www.writingace.com**

Mike Klassen—Mill Creek, Washington: **www.mikeklassen.com**

Larry Rosenwinkel—Frazier Park, California: **www.winkwriting.com**

Marty Lamers—Atlanta: **www.articulayers.com**

Brad Dunn—Los Angeles: **www.vantagecorner.com**

Dave Riches—Prospect, Australia: **www.riches.com.au**

Chapter 4

Throw something out to the world, as I did with my first book, and things come back—the old action-reaction thing. Thankfully, what's come back has been overwhelmingly positive. But from the first reader e-mail, the first review, it starts: the inevitable wish that I could add another comment, paragraph or section to address a point raised, a misconception held, an opinion espoused. Hence, this chapter—my chance to say, *Let me clarify that…*

Of course, there's an ulterior motive here. Given that many of the points I'll illuminate are topics I get e-mailed about most consistently, maybe it'll reduce my e-mail volume, and that always makes me happy. But, this is more than just FAQs. There's a LOT of important information here. Let's go turn on a few lights.

1) How Good a Writer Do I Have to Be?

It hit me one day as I checked out one of my reader's writing Web sites. She was terribly excited to be starting her writing business and wanted me to take a peek. As I reviewed her samples, my heart sank. As much as I wanted to give her a rousing, heartfelt *Attagirl!,* they simply weren't good enough to get her hired by most corporate entities. After a handful of similar experiences, I figured I needed to address it. So here goes...

No one is going to hire you as a writer for $60 to $100 an hour if you're lousy (not more than once anyway). You need to have good writing skills. Not mind-blowingly pheno-menal, but good. Look at most brochures, newsletters and promotional materials you come across. If you feel comfort-able that you could write copy of that caliber or better,

51

you'll do fine. If not, rethink it. Granted there's a bunch of lousy writing out there (much of it attached to household name companies), but the goal here is not to add to it.

I suspect the first book gave a certain number of folks who weren't really writers the idea that the business world was ready to welcome them with open arms and checkbooks. Clearly, they'd surrounded themselves with friends who were kind rather than honest. Unfortunately, we're now entering an arena where the stakes are just a teensy bit higher.

Before you leap into the freelance life, solicit input from those who have zero attachment to protecting your feelings. Asking your mother or best friends about your writing ability isn't wise. You already know what they're going to say; that's why you asked them. What's worse—hearing that you're not the writer you thought you were *before* you invest a lot of time and energy into launching a business? Or banging your head against the wall for months on end, not realizing you'd be better off in another line of work?

Ideally, you should get an opinion from a corporate or creative writing buyer in a position to hire someone like you. They'll probably be flattered you asked. An equally good candidate would be from a fellow—but more established—commercial writer (besides me, please). Not sure where to look? Call an ad agency or graphic design firm. As you may recall, when I started out I contacted close to a dozen local writers. Virtually everyone was exceptionally helpful and encouraging. What did that tell me? That there was plenty of business and nobody felt threatened by a new face in the marketplace.

2) Do You Think I Should Take a Writing Course?

I have no idea. But if your "second-opinion" folks suggest that you do, ask them about writing courses. In the broad category of refining your writing skills, I've had a zillion people ask me what I know about the copywriting course offered through AWAI (American Writers and Artists Institute; **http://awaionline.com**)—the one promoted through the "Can You Write a Letter Like This One?" direct mail letter. Here's my two cents: Over the years, I've heard from plenty of grads and all have been overwhelmingly positive about it. If you want to develop some fundamental copywriting skills, you can't go wrong with it. Besides, Bob Bly's attached to it, so it has to be good. Visit this link for more info AND a special bonus for readers of *TWFW*: **www.thewriterslife.com/wellfedwriter.**

3) What's the Scoop on Business Names, Business Plans and Business Cards?

I get plenty of e-mail asking about *just* the right name for a business. Or how business cards should look. Or if a business plan is necessary. Yes, we need to handle these things, but if you're just shuffling papers to prolong the inevitable, I'll say it: *Stop stalling and start calling.* Heck, I did all the same things to put off picking up the phone and otherwise getting in front of my market—the only thing that really matters. But since these things do weigh heavily, let's (briefly) deal with them...

BUSINESS NAMES

Two schools of thought: One says it's better to have a catchy name for your business then to just call yourself, *Joe Smith Writes*. It lends a sense of being bigger than just one person *and* shows you're a creative copywriter. Of course, if Joe Smith markets himself better than the writer with the business named after the Swahili words for "river of writing," then Joe's going to have infinitely more work than Mr. Brilliantly Creative.

The other school says YOU, the writer, should be the brand. And this becomes especially important when you're building a Web site. The fact is, people might remember your name more easily than a company name, making your name a logical URL. Bob Bly does this (**www.bly.com**) and if you look back at the list of FLCW URLs in Chapter Three, you'll see a few others who follow this formula. AND unless your name is John Smith or Mary Brown, it'll probably be easier to reserve a domain name with your name than something with "write" in it (i.e., they're probably all taken).

Reader Gustavo Polit from Mexico sent me an interesting link for small business owners (**www.businessownersideacafe.com**). This lively, substantive site offers tons of resources for startups, including a place where you can post your request for a name and see what happens (click on "Starting Your Biz," then "Name"). Also **www.namingnewsletter.com**, **www.namestormers.com** and Marcia Yudkin's great tool, "Business Name and Tag Line Generator" at **www.yudkin.com/generate.htm** are other good thought-starter sites.

BUSINESS PLANS

A few years back, I was on a panel with several other freelancers doing a university-sponsored workshop on writing. One of my fellow panelists went on and on about the importance of creating a comprehensive business plan. I was sitting next to a colleague who had just finished her first full—and successful—year in the business and she and I exchanged puzzled looks.

To clarify, if by "business plan," we're talking about a list of marketing activities such as identifying prospects, cold-calling, direct mail campaigns, etc., great. Go for it. If we're talking about some exhaustive proposal with income/expense spreadsheets, profit/loss statements, and the like—it's not necessary (though if it makes you happy to do it, knock yourself out).

My business plan was identical to that of my equally skeptical panel colleague: *Make zillions of phone calls and keep following up with these people until I have more business than I can handle. When it gets slow, just repeat until it's not slow anymore.* It was a good plan. After all, it worked in less than four months.

A funny sidebar: One of my readers was planning his transition from journalism to commercial writing. His financial advisor told him to write a business plan so he could review it. He agonized over this little exercise for weeks until the fog lifted one morning: My book was his business plan! Not an altogether illogical conclusion, given that it's worked nicely for more than a few of us.

BUSINESS CARDS

Make sure your business card tells people what you do. Pretend you've never seen it before. Run it past others. Does it communicate? If a person found your card later but had forgotten the conversation you had with him, would it still be clear what you do? Don't make anyone guess. Make sure that "writing" or "writer" makes it onto the card somewhere. Seems basic, but you'd be amazed at how clever people try to be—to their own detriment.

When creating a business card, marketing brochure or a Web site for your business, get clear about what it is you're offering and, just as importantly, *not* offering. Keep your offering uncluttered. If I see one of the above that says, *I write, I do photography, graphic design, proofreading, marketing strategy, and voice-over*, my first thought is, *jack-of-all-trades, master of none*. A prospect reading such an unfocused message would likely think the same.

Here's the key question: What do you want to do? In which activity would you like to make the lion's share of your income? If it's writing, then present yourself as a writer, period. If you have other talents, great. Wait until you're in front of the client and then, *if* it's appropriate and relevant to what's being discussed, plant those seeds as an afterthought: *By the way, I also do a little photography and voice-over work.* If you're good at what you're suggesting, and the client has that stated need and likes the idea of a single-source solution, then go for it. Just make it clear what your "main line" offering is.

The only exception is if you truly are proficient at another skill (like graphic design)—good enough to compete on the open market with other practitioners. The ability to provide true one-stop turnkey solutions will make you very marketable.

And if you are planning on putting multiple shingles out to the world, then at least make up different cards (and as discussed, perhaps even have multiple Web sites) and hand them out only to the specific targets for those services.

4) What Should I Call Myself?

I've swapped e-mails with many folks in the last two years over the topic of *what to call ourselves*. One gentleman wrote: *When I tell people I'm a 'commercial writer,' they say, 'Oh, so you write commercials.'* Another woman adds, *If I say I'm a copywriter, they ask if I can 'copyright' their book.*

For starters, most of the people you'll want to be doing business with will understand what you do by either name, though in creative circles, you'll hear "copywriter" infinitely more often.

THE (self-proclaimed) Official Beater of Dead Horses on this issue has to be fellow FLCW (and adjunct writing professor) from Buffalo, Paul Chimera. But, all kidding aside, this is a relevant conversation. To make sure our market "gets" what it is we do, we need to identify ourselves with a name that communicates our functions without being confusing or too limiting. Here are some of Paul's musings (from a past E-PUB article):

> *Given the above-mentioned pitfalls of both "commercial writer" and "copywriter," and since many people simply don't know the term "copy" as we use it in our industry, I come back to these trusty alternatives:*

> **Independent business writer**   **Self-employed writer**
> **Self-employed business writer**   **Business writer**
> **Corporate writer**   **Marketing writer**

> *"Corporate writer" covers it—but more directly suggests the nature of your writing: corporate stuff—for companies and businesses.*

> *"Marketing writer" is perhaps better. Most people would infer that a marketing writer does things like ads and brochures.*

> *I prefer "Business writer" because it encompasses and implies BOTH marketing/corporate stuff, and journalism (if you do a little of both).*

Hey, call yourself whatever makes you happy—Most Excellent Word Dude, The Grand Exalted Scribbler to the Gods, The Princely Pen, or whatever floats your boat and doesn't confuse or turn off your clients.

5) How Do I Create a Decent Portfolio?

If your portfolio consists of a few articles from the church newsletter, several poems, and the brochure you created for your own business, corporate clients just won't throw work your way. You don't have to have the proverbial "overstuffed-with-Fortune-100-gems" book, but do get your presentation up to snuff. All the following ideas can be done while you're employed elsewhere. Smaller companies will be more open to less impressive samples and can provide juicy opportunities for boosting the quality of your "book." And you may already have some writing samples. Consider the following:

PAST LIVES. What if your samples are from a past life, say, 15 to 20 years ago? Use 'em. You might spiff them up by copying them onto glossy paper, or if you've got a graphic designer friend, maybe you drop the copy in a new, fresher layout. But, as a rule, good writing is good writing, whenever it was done.

PAST/PRESENT JOBS. If you have some writing projects from a full-time, work-for-hire position (past or present), absolutely you should use them. Just be sure you're not violating any confidentiality agreements. If they *are* politically sensitive in some way, simply purge the delicate information, replace with generic verbiage, repackage it and add it to your portfolio.

EXCERPTS. If the fruits of past efforts were thick manuals, user guides, reports or other voluminous projects too big or boring to make a good sample, pull out some engaging chunks and reformat them for easier reading. Even if that's precisely the kind of work you want to land again, it never hurts to highlight your best work to help prospects more quickly get a feel for your abilities.

JOURNALISM. If you came out of journalism and have a pile of news clips, yes, you can certainly use them. And while you will no doubt earn credibility points in the eyes of your prospects for your professionalism, writing ability and eye for the deadline, by virtue of your former line of work, you'll still want to beef up your book with some more corporate samples like brochures, ads, newsletters (similar to articles), etc.

RE-PURPOSE. Try to leverage *any* past writing efforts, regardless of the circumstances, if you can honestly say *you* wrote it. That means doing whatever you need to do to—forgive this loathsome, corporate-speak word—"re-purpose" the samples you do have. Whatever you ultimately have to do to add one to your portfolio will, I assure you, be less of a hassle than having to land another sample from scratch.

CREATE A PORTFOLIO. Remember my suggestion in *TWFW* about teaming with a graphic designer to simply create some ads or brochures for fictitious companies to demonstrate your creative abilities? Well, by definition, this is what grads from the finest arts schools in the country do. They don't get the chance to work on real jobs until they *get* a real job, so they build the book they'll cart around to interviews by simply picking existing companies and making up stuff. Yes, ideally, you'd land some *pro bono* work with real companies to build your portfolio, but just know that tapping nothing more than your imagination and writing skills is a perfectly acceptable strategy.

PRO BONO. A proven way to build up your portfolio when starting out. It's a great strategy for boosting visibility, getting and keeping your name out in the community, building up goodwill, gathering the right kind of corporate-type samples (brochures, newsletters, press releases, ads, etc.) and, in many cases, positioning yourself nicely to land paying work from those same entities (which often have healthy budgets) down the road. Below are a couple links for the kinds of organizations that would likely be receptive to a "win-win" *pro bono* pitch. Try to find the local or regional branches of these often-nationwide organizations and approach them as you would any prospective client.

http://www.southarts.org/SAF_links.shtml

http://www.njnonprofits.org/linksNCNA.html

Remember, I didn't start out working for Fortune 500 companies. I worked up to it on the strength of projects done for smaller companies. The bigger the company, the higher the expected quality of work and the more desirable that work is to freelancers. The smaller the end-user, the less discriminating they'll be because of limited experience and resources and the more likely they are to give a less experienced writer a shot. By all means, shoot high— especially if you can leverage some past industry experience or contacts. And if you don't get hired, ask what it would take. Mighty useful information. And sometimes, as it happened so many times for me, you'll land work with the big boys by riding in the door on a middleman's coattails.

6) "What Should My Portfolio Physically Look Like?"

Lorrie Lykins, a FLCW from Tampa Bay, shares this amusing tidbit about how *not* to present yourself and your work:

> It's not usually a good idea to show up unannounced at a
> potential client's place of business expecting everyone to

drop their phones and run over to ooh and ahh over your material. It's worse if you're clutching your son's long rejected Beastie Boys three-ring notebook (true story… really happened) into which you've glue-sticked your PTA newsletters and pictures of your dog dressed in the PTA fundraising event T-shirt with snappy captions you wrote as samples of your professional ability.

Amen to that. In my seminars, I love pulling out my first portfolio: an embarrassingly unimpressive three-ring binder (I cringe at the very memory), which, in terms of color, texture and variety of content, is the equivalent of unsweetened oatmeal. It had six black-and-white pieces in it, none of them with a nice layout, every one requiring oodles of accompanying chatter to pump it up into the outlying fringes of respectability. And I built my business on this near-disaster. It's a transcendent moment of relief for many of my seminar attendees.

If you want to make a good first impression, *don't* follow in my footsteps. I didn't know any better—you do. Invest in a professional portfolio, available at good *art supply* stores, *not* office supply stores. Just look in your Yellow Pages for Art Supplies, or ask another writer or a graphic designer where to buy one. Pearl (**www.pearlpaint.com**) and Dick Blick (**www.dickblick.com**) both have stores in many states, as well as online ordering.

A typical portfolio is a large (roughly 20 to 24 inches square, at least, and often bigger) black case, zippered on three sides, with 15 to 20 plastic sleeves lined with black paper (allowing you to use both sides) and secured in a multi-ring binder. A decent one will run you $100 to $150 and up. Just do it. It's the cost of doing business

Several colleagues (especially designers) take the portfolio one step further and mount their samples—angled stylishly—on loose pieces of stiff black cardboard (called mounting or matte board). They may use two copies of a brochure, opened and closed to showcase different sides of the piece. Perhaps they display several components of a larger campaign: pocket folder, brochure, insert sheets, etc. The separate boards are then stacked in a special large rectangular black suitcase. Very classy. Very optional.

7) Exactly How Hard is the Process of Breaking Into Freelancing?

Time for the adult conversation: It'll be harder for some, easier for others, and that's life. If you have no writing experience, you'll have a more difficult time than someone who does. If you're deathly afraid of marketing yourself—simply letting the world know you're out there—you'll have a tougher go in this business than someone who has little fear of the process.

If you live in the middle of nowhere, you'll have a rougher ride than someone in or near a major metro area. If you have marketing experience from a previous job, you'll have a smoother path than someone who doesn't. If you've never worked for yourself, then making to leap to self-employment is going to be more of a challenge for you than for someone who has flown solo for a while.

At this precise moment, you are where you are. You have a certain background, education, level of experience, portfolio, life situation, geographic setting, comfort level with marketing, etc. That's reality. You can choose to make these current facts of life reasons why you *can't* make it work, or you can accept this snapshot and do whatever you can to compensate for any liabilities (i.e., take a writing course, beef up your portfolio with some *pro bono* work, work on your fear of cold calling by doing it, etc.).

Being hungry helps. If you get discouraged easily and give up fast, it'll probably happen here as well, because this is hardly an overnight affair. If you're not particularly disciplined or have minimal pressure on you to make it happen within a certain time frame, it's more likely that you'll give up once it gets tough (which it will). Simply put, this is not a breeze of a business. It takes a lot of effort, the lion's share of which comes on the front end, to be sure. You do need to be motivated. You need to want more for your life. It *really* helps to have "had it up to here" with your current circumstances.

FLCW Wendy Knerr (profiled in Appendix B) talks about how being professional trumps lack of experience. If you don't have the portfolio, then you need to work extra hard, but one thing *anyone* can do is be ultra-professional. It's the great equalizer. That means showing up for appointments on time, calling exactly when you say you will and being prepared when you do. Five minutes late for a call or meeting doesn't cut it. It doesn't matter if everyone's always late, including your client. They have that luxury; you don't.

Colorado Springs FLCW Michelle Zavala echoes this:

> *I'm always fascinated that some of the simplest things make a client sit up and take notice. One potential client was shocked when I said 'I'll call you next Tuesday at 10'... and I did. He was 'wowed' with my ability to honor my word and follow through. And that contributed to him moving from 'potential' to 'regular' client.*

8) Is it True I Need Ad Agency Experience To Succeed In This Business?

I've heard this one plenty over the years. When I first started out, a lot of people asked me which agency I'd worked for, the assumption being that anyone who's going to freelance as a copywriter started out in an agency. When they heard I'd *never* worked for an agency, the typical reply was, *Oh—well, you're going to have a really hard time making it.* Thanks for sharing, I thought, and proceeded to go about my business, becoming financially self-sufficient in less than four months.

I even saw this fable rear its ugly head in an Amazon review of *TWFW*. It was written by a woman who worked for an ad agency, and she said, among other things:

> *While reading books is good, most people cannot be good commercial writers unless they first work in an agency with seasoned professionals. It's all about apprenticeship & mentoring.*

With all due respect, and pre-supposing that someone is a decent writer, she's just flat-out wrong. I am living proof that one does not need agency experience or even minor-league connections to agency people (I had neither) to be successful. And the hundreds of letters I received from other successful commercial freelancers, also without agency experience, further prove the point.

If she's viewing "copywriting" as primarily writing ads (not unlikely as it's a main activity of an ad agency), then I'd agree that mentoring and connections definitely count. But the true ad copywriting she refers to comprises an absolutely infinitesimal percentage of possible writing projects out there. You can be a very successful commercial writer making tons of money and never write an ad. How about newsletters, marketing brochures, sales sheets, Web content, annual reports, case studies, executive summaries, company profiles, etc.? None of these demand rigorous training in ad copywriting.

And FYI, I've seen quite a bit of mediocre copy coming out of ad agencies big and small. Here's how the industry often works: An agency Account Executive trained in sales lands a juicy account by parading the big-gun copy samples in front of the client—only to turn the day-to-day writing tasks over to the junior scribes (whose work may be adequate, but certainly doesn't reflect the brilliance the client was expecting—and paying for).

Might that client likely be receptive to a professional, hard-working freelance copywriter who represents herself honestly? Over my ten years in the business, I've found myself in many situations where I inherited a project from an agency—and often a BIG one—that was just not getting the job done to the client's satisfaction.

A few years back, I got a call from one of my graphic design contacts. He'd gotten a call that morning from a huge, national high-tech company that was rolling out a new service in two weeks. Their big-bucks international ad agency with offices in a zillion cities around the globe had taken five weeks to come up with one pretty lame concept. In addition to the shock of waiting that long for mediocrity, the idea of coming up with one concept for such a high-profile campaign was no doubt mind-boggling to the client.

In any case, the company took one look and sent their high-priced *artistes* back to the drawing board. A week later, they returned with one more concept, only a minor variation on the first and just as lame as Round One. I was listening to all this from my designer thinking, *I wish my readers could hear this, especially the ones who think they can't play in this game.*

The firm, staring at a swiftly approaching media deadline, dropped back and punted. They called my guy on Thursday morning and asked, *Um, do you think you might be able to come up with design and copy concepts for, oh, six different campaigns by, say, Wednesday of next week? And the first three by Monday?* We jumped on it, met all our deadlines, gave them 2 to 3 ideas for each one and they loved all our work. Touchdown!

Please don't get the idea I'm trashing the advertising industry as a whole. I'm not. Some of the coolest, most powerful and most effective marketing stuff ever created comes out of good agencies every day. I just want to take these entities down from the pedestal to which you've probably elevated them. Respect them; just don't be intimidated.

Readers of the E-PUB (my free monthly e-zine) will recall, in the July 2003 issue, my borderline obsequious fawning over veteran adman Luke Sullivan's killer book, *Hey Whipple, Squeeze This*. Out of respect for the craft, I won't claim that this book will turn you into crack ad copywriters. However, it will absolutely make you a better and more creative writer and help you avoid common creative mistakes.

And while the book is about writing ads, I was struck by how much of it was absolutely applicable to a broad range of marketing communications, from both the process and client angles. And Sullivan echoes one of my mantras: A lot of lousy stuff gets produced out there with big companies' names on it.

So, all you aspiring commercial writers out there without the agency credit on your resume, quit worrying. And speaking of not having a certain background...

9) I don't have your sales background. Am I doomed to failure?

Geez, me and my big mouth. I mention my sales & marketing background and suddenly a bunch of people decide their lack-of-same means they can't make it in the business. To paraphrase one of my mantras, *If you think you need that to succeed in this business, you're right. And if you think you don't, you're also right.*

Yes, I had 15 years of sales experience before starting my writing business. Yes, that helped me in the start-up phase. Yes, if you have a similar background, it will also help. But, most people in the business *don't* have sales experience, though I'm guessing you do have some other experience in a particular industry you could leverage.

Remember, I had no *writing* background and no paid professional *writing* experience. I'd never *written* anything for money. And I was entering a professional *writing* field. Think I could have used my lack of *any* writing experience as an excuse to not pursue this opportunity? Without a doubt. But I didn't, because I wanted it badly enough.

Veteran writer Lynn Wasnak (**www.lynnwasnak.com**) touches on the idea of positioning oneself in an article on **writersmarket.com:**

> Freelancers are not interchangeable widgets. What you as a freelancer offer for sale is simply yourself. The teeming contents of your brain—skills, abilities, personality, experience—form a unique combination that no one else can duplicate. It's no secret the pros make money writing by finding outlets where their special qualities meet needs for which others are willing to pay.

The bottom line? Figure out what you've got going for you, then use it.

10) Coming From Journalism, Commercial Writing Feels Like a "Sell Out." True?

I hear this fairly often from folks in the media, including freelance journalists. Many have been told that engaging in copywriting is akin to crossing over to…(cue the dirge…) *The Dark Side*. And at the heart of their dilemma is their training in objectivity.

Journalists get endless contacts from PR types who are trying to land media exposure for their products, services or clients. As a result, the average journalist is well versed in tuning out the pitch in order to stay focused on the newsworthy. Just imagine the conflict that develops when a career change to commercial writing means actually *writing* a pitch!

I got a note from a journalist who was making such a transition. It read:

*Journalism, ideally, is all about objectivity and presenting
all the facts of the case—good or bad. Corporate writing is
sales and marketing, and it definitely isn't objective. I have
to admit that this makes me a little squeamish.*

I have to smile when I read comments like this. As if, for those engaged in this field, it's a constant battle to keep from selling one's soul to the devil. I wish it was all so interesting and dramatic and that one was truly always flirting with eternal damnation. Alas, not so.

Certainly, it's easy to see how, after striving for a certain standard of objectivity for so long, after cultivating the habit of always presenting "the other side of the story," someone might view a marketing brochure as being decidedly one-sided. If you really want to move into commercial writing, however, you'll have to work on changing your worldview. Yes, this is an entirely different kind of writing, with an entirely different set of standards—not *bad*, just *different*. A company's marketing materials simply highlight its selling points—the things that make its products superior to the competition and hence, worth buying.

Some of the more squeamish out there might decide that that qualifies as "stretching the truth." I call it putting your best foot forward. It's what people and companies do when they want to attract the attention of the marketplace. It's not supposed to be objective journalism, and the target audience does not receive it as such. Today's media-savvy consumers know when they're receiving a pitch for a product or service and they employ the appropriate intellectual filters as they read marketing materials. I'd assert that most people do the same when reading or watching the news—which is always biased in some way, no matter how hard journalists strive for objectivity.

If "hard sell" materials like product brochures and direct mail campaigns still seem absolutely foreign to you, consider building your commercial writing business on projects like customer newsletters, internal communications, ghost-written articles for trade magazines, etc. These focus more on simply presenting information to the target audience than on selling anything. I promise, you'll sleep just fine at night.

The writer also raised another dilemma of erstwhile magazine writers:

*How do you go about contacting people you've interviewed
for articles in the past and asking them for work? Before,
I was the one with something they wanted—a mention,
maybe a feature mention, in a top-ranking trade magazine.
Now, I'm turning around and asking them to hire me to
work for them. It's a complete switch of positions, and it's
not easy to just do it.*

Check out the interview with California FLCW Chris Taylor, a former journalist, in Chapter Nine (*Full-Time Dream, Part-Time Reality*), where she navigates some of these issues. And also ponder this…

I have a friend who does executive article ghostwriting for top company executives. He works both ways: working the pubs and finding out what they're looking for and then finding the exec who needs to get his/her name out there, OR contacting the execs, offering his services to write an article and then finding the pub to run it.

He's very cognizant of the fine line between a good informative piece and PR for a company but here's his edge: He guarantees the executive placement of the piece. How? He's up on the current editorial "wish-lists" of many publications and knows precisely how to write it so that the pubs see the value to their readers. He offers the pubs a professionally written piece (i.e., no "newbie" inexperience leading to major rewrites, etc.) of real value to the readers, and at NO cost to them. He gets paid by the exec and instead of the $500 he might make for writing the piece directly for the pub, he gets paid $1500 to $3000 each. Smart cookie.

11) Coming From Academia, Commercial Writing Feels Like a "Sell Out." True?

In academia, especially creative writing/MFA programs, the focus is on "serious" or "literary" writing. Fine. But to look down one's nose at fields of writing that do pay well while providing precious few alternatives doesn't sit right with me. Fact is, many MFA grads truly believe they're going to be the next Jonathan Franzen or Patricia Cornwell, not grasping the lottery odds of that scenario.

I attended an academic conference a few years back for both professors and students of writing on the graduate and undergraduate levels. My book had been adopted as text in several universities at that point and I was there to stir up some more interest. With marked-up conference program in hand, I set off to visit several germane breakout sessions with titles like, "Five Years Out: What We Wish We'd Known When We Earned Our MFA" and "Alternative Job Options for MFAs"—where they actually asked, *What are the ethics involved in continuing to develop MFA programs* (and they're literally mushrooming) *when there are no good jobs on the back end?* Good question.

I approached the moderators at the beginning of the sessions, told them who I was and why I was there and asked for the chance to make a few comments about my field (and book) when the Q&A arrived at the end. They were all very receptive to my story and in one session, I handed out no less than 50 cards.

But I soon came face-to-face with *The Attitude*. I'd just gotten up and given one of my impromptu pitches—and people were listening. An older, grizzled academic in the back—full beard, rumpled jeans, untucked shirt—raised his hand. And judging from all the head-swiveling and murmuring going on within the audience and the panel, clearly, he was *Someone*.

He said, "Just keep in mind, that if you get involved in the commercial arena, you can become complicit in the exploitation of certain peoples…" (presumably banana republic sweatshop workers for big sport shoe manufacturers that hire copywriters…). I could almost hear the mental red pens coming out and crossing off that option. Afterwards, virtually no one came up to me for a card.

Fact is, the picture he painted represented a laughably small percentage of copywriting situations. Given the chance to reply, I'd have said: *With all due respect, don't you think you should give these students credit for being intelligent enough to decide for themselves where to focus their efforts, instead of standing on high and closing off doors for them while offering little in return?*

I ran this story past a gentleman I met at the conference. Full professor of English, two-time novelist, broad work background including software development, technical writing, marketing copywriting—in short, a true Renaissance man and firm believer in people having a wide range of writing experience and not becoming too insulated in academia. His response:

> *Academia is not a good place for young writers early in their careers. They need to see the world, and the corporate world and commercial marketplace offer important, eye-opening experiences. I find it terribly ironic that most of these young folks get treated like adjunct slaves by the very writing programs which, while certainly eager to take their money, seldom offer a decent job or adequate pay.*

He went on to tell how his son landed a job as a proposal writer in his second year out of school, earning $60K at one of the world's largest environmental engineering firms. He commented:

> *MFA teachers won't see that kind of money until mid-career, if ever. My son's getting a new window into another powerful world, an incredible education in a fascinating, high-stakes game—writing proposals for hundreds of millions of dollars. But our Exalted One* (the name he bestowed on my outspoken critic) *would not approve.*

12) Are Online Job Board Sites a Good Way to Land Assignments?

People flock to job sites like **elance.com**, **FreelanceWorkExchange.com**, **monster.com** and others because they require a relatively low effort (i.e., it doesn't entail cold calling, driving to client meetings or other more threatening modes of direct client communication). Here's an e-mail I got a few years back, followed by my response, both of which appeared in the July 2002 E-PUB.

> *While I've been trying to generate more business through [online job board sites] eLance and Freelance Work Exchange, I'm not having much success. I've gotten two low-paying jobs on eLance but no more, and one from Guru.com, but the client is VERY late with his payment. All in all, I'm struggling. Any suggestions?*

My response:

> *Online freelance writing sites, for the most part, are a waste of time—IF you're interested in maximizing your writing income. And for just the reasons you mention. Low pay and problems chasing your money down. I never mention them in my book because, in my humble opinion, they're a lousy way to make a living.*
>
> *It's a buyer's market—too many writers and too few jobs. So, when it comes to a bidding situation, there will always be those willing to bid next to nothing, just to build their book. And that's their right. I just don't want to play that game. That's why I outline the strategy I do and it doesn't include online writing sites. They're not worth your time.*

Then, the following month, I ran these two pieces of feedback:

> *I couldn't agree with you more! I played around with Guru and some of the others for a few months here and there, but NOTHING, and I mean NOTHING, ever materialized that was even close to meeting my criteria for how I want to spend my time and get paid for it.*
>
> *Thanks for finally telling people those writer sites are crap.*

13) While $75 an Hour or More Sounds Great, It's So Much More Than I'm Used to Making as a Writer. How Do I Deal With That?

Many people come to the commercial writing arena from that "starving writer" point of view—they're not used to having their writing skills valued by the marketplace, ergo, they don't value them (and hence, don't price them) very highly either. Then they find this field, with low-end hourly rates of roughly $50. They're thrilled and excited about making that kind of money, but it's not so easy to make the mental jump.

But it really *is* true that when you start believing you're worth it and begin exuding that, people will buy it. Look at this e-mail from Maryland FLCW Holly Minor:

> Thanks to your book, I may be one of the few non-starving writers out there! I charge as much as $80 an hour now (I'd been meekly asking for $35 to $50 an hour before) and am working most of the time. Every job seems to lead to another. Asking more seems to make people value my work more, too. Because of my rates, they just assume I'm great.
>
> And though I proudly carry my extensive portfolio to all client meetings, I have not shown it in more than a year, unless I push the issue. People just seem comforted knowing it's there (it could be empty for all they know.) Hah! I'm having a ball.

I recently ran into a friend who'd gone freelance after years of working for marketing firms. Her hourly rate? Almost apologetically, she told me: $125 to $150 an hour. And she's getting it. She voiced concern that it was too high, but the fact is, when in front of a client, she asks for it and acts as if she's worth every dime. Feel free to have your doubts. Just keep them to yourself.

14) I'm Not Particularly Self-Disciplined— Can I Still Make it in This Business?

People unwilling to leave the corporate nest (never mind that the corporate nest is leaving *them* in some pretty serious numbers) will ask this, followed by, *Maybe I need to stick where things are more secure.* My answer? Right now, you're on the other side and all you see in the plus column is this vague but quite desirable goal of working for yourself. On the minus side is how you could fail, go broke, lose your salary, benefits, house, car, wife, dog, etc.

Understand this: Once you get a taste of the freelance life—freedom, flexibility, not having to be somewhere, scrubbed and pressed, every day—I promise you'll do *anything* to keep it going. Discipline becomes a non-issue, because all of a sudden, the fear of poverty has been replaced by fear of The Alternative…

15) What Should I Charge For (Project X)?

The e-mail read: *I've been asked to quote a price to write a marketing brochure of six pages. What should I charge?* It was typical of the extraordinarily vague e-mails I often get on this subject. Without more information, there's no way I could begin to quote a number. There are so many questions that need to be answered first:

How many meetings?

Any background reading? How much?

Any research necessary? How much?

Any interviews of SMEs (subject matter experts)? How many?

How much copy on each page? (In other words, do they have a proposed graphic layout yet, so you know how much space you have to "write to"?)

By the way, the preceding is NOT an invitation to have you e-mail me with ALL this information in the hopes of getting a more accurate answer. As much as I wish I could, I just don't have the time anymore to answer inquiries like this.

Other than the suggestions below, estimating is an art I can't really teach you. But do it enough and you'll develop a sixth sense about it. Bottom line, there's no set amount for a marketing brochure, newsletter, ad, Web site, etc. With the project details just one Q&A session away, you're in an infinitely better position to estimate it than I could ever be.

As far as the actual mechanics of coming up with a reasonably accurate estimate, *it's all about time.* Break the project down into its component parts and estimate what each piece would entail, time-wise. And that means meetings, travel, research, background reading, interviews, concepting (brainstorming), copywriting and editing (though you won't have all these parts on all projects). Add up the hours, multiply it by your hourly rate and offer a project fee range (with a 10 to 15 percent spread).

As for what that hourly rate should be, do your homework, find out what the local market will bear for your type of writing and your level of experience (contact other writers or ad agencies/design firms for the local rate scoop).

16) Can I Still Achieve "Financial Self-Sufficiency In Six Months or Less," as Your First Book's Subtitle Claims?

For starters, as I'll share later in a bit more detail, unbeknownst to me at the time, I started my business in the midst of one of the worst creative recessions in Atlanta and was still paying all my bills through my writing within four months of kicking things off. All depends on what "financial self-sufficiency" means to you. If you need to make $5000 a month within three to four months, I'd say that's mighty ambitious. If your needs are far less, the odds improve. How hard are you willing to hit it out of the gate? That said, I'll allow that during the major growth period of my business, things in the marketplace were cooking. As I write this, they're recovering again from slower times, and by the time you read it, we may very well be in the clover once again. If you have NO writing experience, related background or portfolio, it will take longer than six months and probably more like a year. But know this: Your business growth will be a function, overwhelmingly, of your ability to market yourself, NOT the state of the economy (See Chapter 11: "It's Not the Economy, Stupid!").

And let's be clear: Any writing direction that pays $60 to $80 an hour, is flexible, home-based and can potentially earn you $75K or more annually in the space of a few short years, by definition, is going to require an investment of time to get established. Few professions meet those criteria. I truly had no paid writing experience, professional writing background or vast industry network. Yet, by using my sales and marketing background to prop up a pretty sorry starter portfolio, I was paying all the bills in less than four months. You may have the writing background but no marketing experience. We all come at this from different places.

Know that you'll build your business faster by building on your experience. Countless people have become successful by starting with the industry from which they came. A North Carolina attorney who hated practicing law but loved writing built a business approaching law firms to help them create their marketing materials. A gentleman here in Atlanta leveraged his technical writing background for the manufacturing sector by approaching that same industry, seeking their marketing collateral business. One guy had ties with the "repo" business. It's a surprisingly competitive field and these folks have to sell themselves constantly and what better way to do that (and boost their image) than to create brochures and Web sites? His pitch was extremely well received by most of the...um...practitioners he contacted.

And as for the flip side of the question, remember the subtitle of my first book? "Financial Self-Sufficiency as a Freelance Writer in Six Months or Less." Not six weeks or less. Or six days or less. And certainly not six hours or less. I literally had someone contact me after a particularly trying *first* morning of cold calling, whining about how haaaaaaaaaard it was. I was truly at a loss for words.

17) Writing For a Big Fortune 500 Company Feels Way Out of My League—How Do I Know I'm Good Enough?

One reader touched on this fear in an e-mail:

> *I've written for years—columns, articles, book reviews—so knew I could write. But, there wasn't a lot of money involved in that writing.*

Ah. So when you're not being paid that much, you don't worry as much about having it be so incredibly good. But when the pay is a lot higher, they'll expect more. And that cranks up the insecurity.

Clients do want a quality product and they're paying for the right to expect that. But that's beside the point. Give these people credit. If a client hires you, it's because he or she has talked to you, seen your work and decided you're capable of doing the job. With a few entertaining exceptions, as a rule, these people are not stupid and self-destructive. They don't willfully make their lives and jobs more difficult, nor do they care to risk the wrath of their superiors. And choosing a copywriter who's out of his or her depth would most certainly do one or more of those.

Consequently, these people are infinitely better judges of our abilities than we are, given our seemingly genetically hard-wired self-doubts. And I do mean we. You'd be amazed. Even after ten years in the business and a portfolio bursting with gems, I still experience pangs of self-doubt before every new job. I kid you not. I just don't indulge it. I simply notice it and move on.

Listen. Perhaps you're *not* a good enough writer to get in the door of the Fortune 500 (though writing skills *can* be improved), but understand that *other* Theory of Relativity. There are a zillion small- to medium-sized companies out there with either no written communications materials or stuff so gruesome it'd make your hair stand on end. Being able to take those companies to the next level of clarity and coherence—even if it's not on the par with, say, a brochure for BellSouth or Web content for DuPont—can often make a dramatic and glorious difference in their professional images and, as such, is an exceptionally valuable service. Not to mention an honorable calling.

That said, *just* being able to write nice sentences or to clean up poorly written ones probably won't earn you $75 to $100 an hour. To work up to the higher rates, you need to develop the ability to think strategically about a client's business—part and parcel of developing the marketing mindset we explored in Chapter Two.

While there's no substitute for actual experience, I hope this book will help shorten the learning curve a bit so you can begin moving toward higher income more quickly. Now, you won't always be called on for your strategizing skills. I'm not, and I still get my higher rates for straight copywriting. But, developing this talent is the surest way to healthier income. Don't worry if you don't feel you bring that to the table yet. Keep showing up at those tables, keep observing, asking questions, staying curious and turning out superior work and you'll become that valuable commodity.

18) How Do I Avoid Conflicts of Interests When Working For Different Clients?

I got this e-mail from Portland, Oregon FLCW Jeff Stephens (**www.creative-brand.com**) some time back:

> *"Conflicts of interest" are a big deal in the ad business: Agencies never do work for any two companies that might compete in any way. As a freelancer, I can see the same rules apply IF you are working as a freelancer through ad agencies. But as an independent contractor working directly with the end-client, do you feel like conflict of interest is a big issue? How about doing work, for example, for similar companies in non-competing markets? Seems to me as though working for multiple clients is the heart and soul of a FLCW's business, so you shouldn't be afraid to pursue other companies you can apply your experience to. Thoughts?*

It's not as big an issue as one might imagine. If I'm doing some writing for, say, two telecommunications companies, I just don't go out of my way to tell either one that's the case. I know I'll be discreet about protecting sensitive proprietary information. I might say I've done work for them in the past and will definitely do that if I'm not currently working for one company while I am working for a competitor. That lets them know I have some experience in their field, which they like to hear. And there's ZERO problem with working for similar companies in non-competing markets.

19) What Rights Do I Retain to the Writing I Do Commercially? And What If a Tagline or Slogan I Write Becomes Famous— Shouldn't I Earn More?

In magazine writing, it's all about retaining the rights to the work you create, so you can maximize income by selling reprints and rewrites to magazines in non-competing markets. Commercial writing doesn't work that way. You don't retain any rights and why would you need to? What are you going to do with brochure copy for a residential security system, for instance? Or newsletter copy for a financial services company? Basically, it's all work-for-hire, meaning you do your job, get paid, hopefully get a nice clip for your book and you move on. It's not something I spend ANY time thinking about.

As for higher pay for a tagline or slogan, I did mention the concept of "value billing" in *TWFW*—a situation where, when set up in advance, you could be entitled to higher compensation than just the time you put in, IF a slogan or tagline you've created ends up being very high-profile. I asked a few of my colleagues if they've had any experience with this. Below is what one had to say, with several others in vigorous agreement.

> *I recently quoted a tag line for a new company at $1000. When I discussed the cost with the agency people, I told them to think of the tag line as equivalent to a logo. They got it and apparently so did the client. Before pitching the cost, I also spoke with another writer who quotes up to $2000 for tag lines depending on the company. Bigger entities pay more, which makes sense (they not only have more money but will use the tag on a broader scale). If the client doesn't buy it, you've lost a few hours of billing. If they understand the value of what you're bringing to the table, you gain an economic reward that reflects your creative abilities.*

FYI, to clarify the comments about logo creation, the process of creating a company logo is universally understood to entail more effort and command a much higher fee than what would be the case with just creating any other graphic design element. And that higher fee reflects both the greater time involved *and* the greater value of that logo to the company's image and fortunes (think IBM, FedEx, Apple, etc). Hence the analogy with the tagline, the assumption being that a good tagline will entail much more effort and be worth that much more to the company, than just another line of copy.

As someone else pointed out, taglines for larger companies will also command higher prices because there are simply more levels of approvals and hence, a greater likelihood of many revisions. Now, not every client will buy the "tagline-as-logo" argument as justification for a higher fee, but to my thinking, it makes all the sense in the world.

20) Various Miscellaneous Questions To Which I Answer... Think Like a Businessperson First, Then Like a Writer

I recently had someone e-mail me and ask, very earnestly, *Given your advice about including business cards in client letters, should I also give out cards at networking functions, too?* Think logically. Use common sense. Of course you should. *Anything* you can do—legally, morally, ethically—to effectively get your name out there and have people remember you (positively) is a good thing.

Stop looking at this business as some arena that requires some specialized esoteric knowledge or some hidden keys. There IS no inner sanctum of knowledge here. It's not some secret society that requires secret hand-shakes and passwords. It's business, and certain things are common to all businesses.

I get people asking me which project category (brochures, newsletters, ads, Web content) is growing fastest and offers the most potential. That's thinking like a writer. A businessperson would look around and see that *any* business has a need for *all* those things (and Web content, especially, and not surprisingly, is proliferating) because *any* business needs to communicate and do so in a variety of different ways and will never *not* need to do so. Sure, a company might not choose to do all of them, but there's a place for every one of them within a comprehensive marketing communications campaign.

For instance, given how competitive business is these days, newsletters that help a company communicate more effectively with its customers or front-line people, if they translate to even an incremental uptick in competitive advantage, are a good idea. They could be external versions as customer retention tools or internal ones as vehicles for keeping people abreast of new products, changes, regulations, etc. And while many companies will have them, if one doesn't, and it seems like a fit, why not suggest it?

●　　●　　●

Okay, we've put this off long enough, but now it's time to face the music: cold-calling. But like most things, it's never as scary once we look a little more closely. And there's lots of good news along the way...

Chapter 5

An old expression reminds us, *When all you have is a hammer, everything looks like a nail.* When I started my business, my past sales experience (starting with door-to-door book sales) allowed me to forge a profoundly solid relationship with the Law of Averages. For years, I saw firsthand how absolutely ironclad it was: Make enough calls, you'll get the business.

With this in mind, and given my lack of a sprawling web of contacts, coupled with an aversion to meeting-based networking—which always seemed so mercenary—I decided to build my business by phone, something I did very successfully. Predictably, cold calling became the center-ring strategy for launching a writing business in *TWFW*; it became my hammer. And it's a powerful one—many readers have built solid businesses hitting the phones.

Welcome to Caveatsville...

But, is it the alpha and omega method of business building? Absolutely not. If you have a strong network of contacts, you should milk them for all they're worth. Do that and you might be able to avoid making many cold calls at all.

Sometime back, I mentored a budding FLCW in California. After close to three months in the business, he had yet to make his first cold call. He'd tapped fifteen years worth of contacts from software sales. Not that he knew all these people personally, but he called the ones he did know, got the names of five other people from them, then five names from each of the referrals, etc. As long as he could drop somebody's name, even if he didn't know *that* person, it wasn't a cold call.

Most everyone you know is in some sort of business. And it's a rare business that doesn't, at some point, have a need for copywriting. It's easy to compartmentalize our lives—put work here and friends there—and it can seem vaguely cheesy to hit up your friends for business. Yet if those friends like you and respect you professionally, why wouldn't they want to help you out? Wouldn't *you*?

Work the Network

Besides cold calling, you should absolutely pursue intelligent networking strategies—for example, attending meetings and association gatherings where prospective clients are likely to hang out. Remember, the rule is, *You'll be hired by one in ten people you talk to by phone and one in three who meet you.* Face-to-face networking establishes that crucial personal connection. And that means your next contact will be a "warm call"—one that's arguably as warm as or warmer than a good referral. We'll be exploring both these strategies in more detail later.

All that said, I assert that cold calling should still be a cornerstone approach to this business—because it works. Count on having to do some of it along the way. But regardless of how much of it you ultimately end up doing, there's enormous value in defanging the process. As long as you view it with fear and dread, you'll never consider it as equally viable and valuable as other methods, and such a mindset could absolutely hinder your progress. What if you're trying to penetrate a particular market or industry where you have few, if any, contacts? Cold calling (perhaps augmented by some targeted direct mail) would likely be the most expeditious way to make some solid inroads.

The ultimate goal here is to have a quiver containing a broad array of marketing arrows—cold calling, direct mail, e-mail prospecting, networking—all of which you feel equally comfortable employing, depending on the situation.

While fearless cold calling pros may view this chapter as elementary, most of you are likely to find some value here, regardless of your experience level. As for the novice, the nervous, and the terrified, this chapter is definitely for you. And I promise you'll feel *much* better about the process by the time we're done.

And incidentally, all five of the other members of my small commercial writer's group here in Atlanta—who've successfully been at this business an average of 15 to 20 years each—HATE to cold call and do almost none of it. They smile indulgently at me when I sing its praises, comfortable in their firmly held contention that they'd rather be strip-searched in a very public place than ever call a business stranger who doesn't come by referral. Most of them leveraged past experience to build their businesses.

Aluminum Siding, Anyone?

I was giving a seminar (I forget the city—not to sound like a rock star or anything) and we'd just gotten to the section on cold calling. Someone raised her hand and said, very earnestly, *I just hate the idea of cold calling, because I don't appreciate getting telemarketing calls and I think most people are pretty much the same.*

I gathered my thoughts, crossed my arms, looked at her and asked, *Is that who you think you are? Just an obnoxious telemarketer—no different from the people who cluelessly interrupt you during dinner to peddle aluminum siding, long distance service, carpet cleaning, and a zillion other things you have no interest in?*

This one point could be the difference between success and failure. Assuming you're a competent, reliable writer, if you pursue this business, you'll be a *professional* marketing a valuable and needed *professional* service to other *professionals*. Period. Regardless of whether the people you call have a need for your services (and 80 percent won't) or even have the time to talk to you, I promise they will *not* be viewing you as an irritating telemarketer. So, don't view *yourself* this way.

Think about it. Are you just a mouthpiece for someone else's business? Some interchangeable short-term worker? No. You have a skill that is vital to the success of any business. It pays upwards of $125 an hour. Those who hire people like us will tell you how hard it is to find capable ones. How *dare* you put yourself in the same category as a telemarketer?

And by the way, the big "DO NOT CALL" anti-telemarketing initiative of 2003 applies only to businesses calling consumers (B2C), not what we're doing—business-to-business (B2B) calling. Sorry, you're not getting off that easily.

Just in case you're still harboring feelings of kinship with the telemarketing rank-and-file, why not take this test and put the issue to rest, once and for all?

You Might Be An Annoying Telemarketer IF…

1. When someone clearly answers his phone: "Peter Bowerman," you reply "Can I speak to Peter Bowerman? (Or even better…)

2. When someone clearly answers his phone: "Peter Bowerman," you reply, "Can I speak to…um…Peter…uh…Borman?"

3. You call prospective clients during dinner or on weekends.

4. You're selling some consumer product like cellular service, home improvement, magazine subscriptions, cabinet refacing, home equity lines, etc.

5. You were selling something completely different last month, and next month you'll be exploring another "challenging and rewarding" career direction.

6. Your job involves reading a script (with all the enthusiasm of a county tax clerk) and trying to get people to part with their money—then and there.

7. You use law enforcement-affiliated organizations to give yourself credibility.

8. You call the same people over and over even if they hung up on you the first eight times.

9. You offer people things like steak knives or a set of collapsible luggage to get to them to do business with you.

10. Your only job is to get people interested enough to warrant turning them over to the next level of shysters… er, "sales professionals."

So, how'd you do? No matches? Well, maybe you're not an *Annoying Telemarketer* after all. Whew! That's a relief. (Can we move on now?)

Dissection Time

In typical human fashion, we make the marketing process dark, scary and gnarly. Our imaginations paint bleak outcomes and one-way roads to destitution. We conjure up images of the process being unproductive, embarrassing and agonizing. So, let's take this thing apart. We'll start by establishing a few truths.

We could liken the cold calling process to a battle. And who's the enemy? The prospects, right? WRONG. We are. We will *always* be our own worst enemy in *every* aspect of our lives. It's never circumstances or lack of time. It's never other people. Or the government or economy. It's *us*—along with our perceptions of the circumstances that affect us—that will interfere with our abilities to get what we want, every time. When we put external reasons in charge of the realization of our dreams, we put those dreams further out of reach. And that's a lousy way to live. *Only you are responsible for your success.* And only you can allow someone to stop you.

We Care, They Don't

So, what's at the root of our fear of phone prospecting? Our concern for what other people think. When we know we're alone, we'll sing *Feelings* in the shower at the top of our lungs in a helium-balloon squeak. But then we'll freak out about making an entirely legitimate inquiry as a businessperson offering a professional service to another businessperson.

Here's a news flash: *Other people spend an amazingly infinitesimal amount of time thinking about you.* You would be stunned at how little. Oh sure, your family and friends care about you. But when it comes to your business and the services you offer, it's really best to assume that people don't care at all—and that it's your job to make them care.

But the fact that people don't care can work in your favor. Let's imagine a worst-case scenario: You cold-call someone and proceed to absolutely implode on the phone. We're talking main-core meltdown here, culminating in an incoherent stream of babble. I promise you, the recipient of your call will spend no more than five seconds thinking about you after you hang up. Meanwhile, you're convinced a mass e-mail has gone out to everyone in the universe, sharing the details of this catastrophic exchange along with strict orders to never, *ever* hire this gibbering idiot.

Here's the truth: For all intents and purposes, you are a non-issue in the minds of your fellow human beings. And the day you finally get this will be your own personal Independence Day. After your "conversion," why not call back that client with whom you fell apart earlier on the phone? Chances are, they won't remember you anyway. Seriously.

Chutzpah Personified

Reminds me of a true story that made the rounds in my door-to-door bookselling days in college. This certain bookman knocks on a door at 8:30 a.m. A guy answers the door and proceeds to ream him out, going on and on about how all soliciting should be outlawed, salesmen should be shot, etc. He finishes his tirade and slams the door in our intrepid warrior's face.

The young bookman digests all this for a moment, makes a decision, runs around the house and knocks on the back door. The same guy answers that door, about to burst an aorta, when the kids earnestly exclaims, *I sure hope you're nicer than the guy who lives in the front of this house!* No doubt blown away by this audacious display of chutzpah, the guy bursts out laughing, invites the kid in and ends up buying a set of books.

Now, I never had the *cojones* to pull off a stunt like that, but just the fact that it really happened stuck in my mind as a sort of courage beacon. Someone took a chance and it paid off. File it away.

Grim Expectations

So, what makes cold calling so tough in the beginning? You're nervous. Perhaps you've never done it before. Or you've done it, but with limited success. Add to that our expectations of the process, which are:

It'll be hard

It'll be unproductive

I'll get my feelings hurt

I won't have any fun

I can't sell anything

They'll know I'm inexperienced

But I say there's another reason, one that's crucial you understand. On some fundamental level, *you don't really believe it will work.* I can sit here all day long and tell you that it works, and in the coming pages you'll read the same from a lot of other folks, but until you prove it to yourself, you won't believe it. And that's fine. But a funny thing happens when you do it long enough to discover—lo and behold—that cold calling *does* work. It ceases to be an unpleasant garden-variety exercise in futility and morphs into a proven vehicle to success. You may never love it—not required— but even that may change when you see the impact on your bank account. Would you approach the process differently if you *knew* you couldn't fail?

More importantly, cold calling will make you strong. It will be at the heart of your confidence and your sense of accomplishment. It's your battle— but one with yourself, your fears, your laziness and your fixed perceptions of your abilities. But, when you succeed, you will know that YOU have done it. Only you.

You'll Like This

Let me throw in a piece of very good news here: If your initial marketing push is big enough and thorough enough, *you only have to go through it once,*

When I started, I made probably 1000 calls in the first few months, but after that I never—repeat, never—put together a cold calling campaign even close to that magnitude again. Sure, from time to time, over the years, I'd do 25 calls here or 50 there when things slowed down, but the machine was cranked up enough that even those few calls were enough to get something going. Of course, after even a year in the business, the word-of-mouth referrals started coming in and that's what ultimately keeps you busy after awhile.

I got this great e-mail from FLCW Wendy Knerr (profiled in Appendix B), who built her business in Austin, Texas, making her first cold call on September 11, 2001.

> I started out by making about 600 cold calls over several months and that yielded enough work to keep me really busy all of last year. Now, I occasionally have to make cold calls, but I can rarely make even 50 calls before I land a project—either from someone I've just cold-called or from a previous client who's calling ME to offer work. Even better is the fact that the cold calling is so much easier now because I know it pays off.
>
> A big thing that changed for me since I started is that, even when I don't have work on my plate, because of past success, I know I'll find work again. Bottom line, I don't have the anxiety I had at the beginning.

Action or Results?

In my seminars, I'll ask, When you start cold calling, should you focus on action or results? Many participants immediately yell out, Results! Why? Well, we live in a results-based world. Or We're judged on results. Then I wait to see if some brave soul is willing to swim against the tide and say action. And usually someone does.

In my mind, action is the right answer. Think about it. What's true of action that isn't true of results, and which, consequently, makes it a much better horse to hitch your dreams to? If you answered, You can control action, but you can't control results, go to the head of the class.

What You Can't Control

You have no control over the results of any given phone call or e-mail. You have no control over how that man or woman on the other end of the line will react to your contact. You have no control over whether that individual will think your portfolio is good enough to consider hiring you.

Sure, you can improve your results by, say, getting more comfortable with your phone voice, choosing better prospects and beefing up your book.

But still, fundamentally, the one thing you have control over is the actions you take. You can't wake up in the morning and say, *I'm going to land three new writing projects today,* or even *I'm going to find three hot prospects today,* and have control over those results. But you can say, *I'm going to make 50 calls today* (action) and have total control over that. If your goal is the three writing jobs or hot prospects, and at 2:00 p.m. you've got nothing, think your calls might start taking on a bit of a desperate edge? If you're shooting just to make, say, 50 calls and you make them, you're done. Go chill out.

Focus on those actions, and the results—the hot prospects and the writing jobs—will come. Minus the anxiety. The Law of Averages is foolproof. I don't care how those calls turn out. Making 50 calls doesn't mean having 50 conversations (that's results again!). Just make the calls, regardless of the outcome (i.e., live contact, voice-mail, message left with a secretary, hang up, appointment, dinner date, whatever...). Frankly, you'll probably get mostly voice mail. Don't worry about it.

And speaking of voice-mail... when a receptionist answers the phone, and you determine whom you need to talk to (ideally, you had a name going in), why not ask for that person's e-mail address? Say, *In case I get her voice mail, can you give Ms. Smith's e-mail address so I can send her a link to my site and not have to bother her anymore?*

It won't always work, but given that those addresses are usually on the company's Web site, they're not exactly state secrets, either. Then if you do get voice mail, leave a brief message telling the prospect who you are and that you'll be sending him or her a link to your portfolio by e-mail and will follow-up in a week or so. It'll make the call that much more potentially productive, help your e-mail stand out from the mountain (I usually use a subject line like: *Copywriter following up on VM*) and let your site work for you while you're off doing something else.

TIP: Working Smarter

In *TWFW,* I suggested creating a variety of letters to send to prospects and new clients in the wake of different prospecting outcomes. If you've created a Web site, then essentially do the same thing by using the "stationary" feature on your e-mail program to create a variety of standard pre-written notes—with links to your Web site—to address different situations there as well (following up on voice mail, an actual conversation, a chat with an assistant, etc.).

Following up on these actions then becomes a simple matter of clicking on a particular stationary, which will populate an outgoing e-mail screen with the appropriate message (which perhaps, you then tailor to reference something you spoke about or a mutually agreed-upon next step), filling in their address, clicking "Send" and you're done. Here are several versions of stationary that I use for different situations—not the last word in eloquence and effectiveness, so create your own.

Hi Paul,

Nice talking with you today; thanks for your time. Keep me in mind if you need strong, persuasive copy written in an engaging, accessible style. My 15 years of sales/marketing experience prior to launching my copywriting career in 1994 means I understand audience and "writing to sell." Headlines, taglines, slogans and tasteful humor are specialties. Find my portfolio at: **www.writeinc.biz**.

I look forward to working with you down the line. Best of continued success.

Peter Bowerman
WriteInc.
987/654-3210 (h/o/m)
987/654-3211 (eFax)
peter@writeinc.biz
www.writeinc.biz

Hi Paul,

Peter Bowerman here, freelance copywriter, left a VM for you earlier today. As mentioned in my message, my online portfolio is at: **www.writeinc.biz**.

I don't know what your needs are for copywriting but look to me for strong, persuasive copy written in an engaging, accessible style. 15 years of sales/marketing experience prior to launching my copywriting career in 1994 means I understand audience and "writing to sell." Headlines, taglines, slogans and tasteful humor are specialties.

I'd love the chance to chat and perhaps stop by for a quick face-to-face. I look forward to hearing from you! Best of continued success.

Peter
(*Contact Info*)

Action, Not Results…Again

When I sold books door-to-door in college, our goal and key measure of accomplishment was 30 demos a day (the equivalent of phone calls made to prospects), a demo roughly defined as pulling the books out and beginning our pitch, whether we got in the door or did it *at* the door, and whether or not we got to finish it. Making sales the goal (i.e., results) would've introduced unnecessary and unwelcome anxiety into the process. More importantly, they *knew* if we made 30 honest demos a day or close to it, the sales would absolutely come. And they did. Same here.

You'll See It When You Believe It

There were days as bookmen where we'd put in our honest 13½ hours (8:00 a.m. to 9:30 p.m., Monday through Saturday; insanity, yes, but a true character-building strain of insanity) and come up with…bupkus. *Growth and Development Days*, we called them. Very, very rare. Our sales managers would congratulate us on having a G&D day, adding, *By the way, you do know that you'll sell the first three houses you visit tomorrow, don't you?*

And I'm telling you straight here, we always did, because, I'm convinced, we were, well…convinced. On my first call one morning following a G&D day, I remember approaching someone unlocking a car door in the driveway, about to head to work, and knowing, absolutely knowing, that despite the none-too-promising-looking circumstances, this person was going to buy a set of books (a $40 purchase, by the way). And I guess he knew it too, because he did. Approach cold calling with that same bone-deep belief in the Law of Averages and you can't help but win.

The Antidote for Attachment

Remember my discussion in the first book about the almost mystical nature of the Law of Averages? The point I made was that, once reasonably established, within a few days of making 50 to 100 cold calls, with eerie predictability, I'd get a few calls for jobs, yet *rarely* would they be from the people on my calling list a few days prior. It was almost always from somewhere else, as if the effort itself was the important thing. Stop getting attached to the outcomes of specific scenarios. It's about an energy and flow that gets released when you reach out. I got an e-mail from one of my mentoring clients in L.A., echoing this:

> *You really renewed my faith in the cold calling process, too. Our discussion about how you need to believe that the energy you put out will come back to you—but not necessarily from the places you reached out directly to—*

was exactly what I needed to hear. It's really helped keep me from getting attached to direct results from the places I call, and instead just increasing the numbers. I'm focusing more on the process of calling itself and not spending so much time worrying about who I'm calling or more importantly, how any call or round of calling turns out.

Not Busy Enough

In conversations with my mentoring clients as well as e-mails from budding FLCWs, I hear a lot of references to specific prospects, how they'd contacted this person or that company, how the conversation went, the types of projects this company did, whether it looked promising, etc. There's always an earnestness about these descriptions, as if a lot of psychic energy was riding on the outcomes.

Whenever I hear this, my reaction is, *You're not making enough calls.* Or contacts of any kind, for that matter. If you find yourself focusing, in detail, on a few specific prospects you've called, and seem to have a lot at stake mentally in having them pan out, you need more irons in the fire. Period. Sure, you've got a possible "live" one and you're nervous and excited. After all, it's the beginning of the proof that this thing really could work! Completely understandable. I've been there. But you need to have so many things going on, so many *Maybes* out there, that three things can't help but happen:

1. You can't even recall the specifics of any given situation or prospect without looking at your notes. And when that happens…

2. You don't care about any specific situation, because it's one of many. There goes the attachment. Bub-bye. And finally…

3. Some will inevitably come through.

Other Common Concerns

What if I don't have experience writing for the client's industry?

This is an immutable law of nature: A client's ideal candidate will always be someone who's written something exactly like the project at hand, preferably on multiple occasions. (This is especially—and justifiably—the case with technical topics).

Yet clients rarely get just what they want. They'll state their ideal, but will certainly entertain candidates who are close. Remember, they want to get it done, not spend weeks looking for the perfect writer.

So, the prospect asks, *Do you have any experience writing brochures for rabbit production farms?* In such cases, I'm tempted to ask, *Have you ever met anyone who did?* Regardless, your response (assuming you indeed have no such experience) should be something like:

> *Mr. Prospect, while I haven't had that specific experience, I have written brochures for many different industries and pride myself on being able to step into any new situation and quickly get up to speed. Writing is all about structuring the important information in a way that will have maximum impact. And I know how to do that.*
>
> *A good analogy is an advertising executive who can promote corn flakes one day and commercial airlines the next, without having much, if any, experience working in those fields. Unless it's a very technical subject that requires some specific training to understand the processes or vernacular, I feel confident I can deliver for you.*

It'll either work or it won't. If not, move on and let them keep stalking their elusive rabbit-production-farm-brochure copywriter. When they get tired of hunting, you might just get a call down the line. Contact made. Next?

What if I run out of people to call?

I heard this once from someone in the L.A. area. You're kidding, right? Even after close to a decade in the biz in Atlanta, I still regularly run across established commercial writers that I've never met. And with a whole different set of clients than me. There's plenty of work out there.

By the way, a great way to quickly build extensive prospect calling lists (especially for middlemen clients), broken down by city and category, is to use online directories like **www.switchboard.com** and **www.theultimates. com/yellow/**. Just enter categories like Advertising Agencies, Public Relations Firms, Graphic Designers, etc. Also use your city's *Book of Lists* (**www. amcity.com** for complete listing), chamber of commerce directories and any other local business directories (check your library).

Tom Myer, a FLCW in Austin, Texas, with a healthy amount of high-tech writing experience under his belt, simply got the Fortune 1000 list of companies (found at **www.fortune.com**), started at the bottom and worked his way up. Between that and another list, he made about 350 calls before landing about $35,000 worth of work in four months. Whoa.

I tried cold calling, and it didn't work for me.

To this I always ask, *How much of it have you done?* Not surprisingly, the answer is usually, *Not much.*

Let's establish a few things. Cold calling *does* work. It may not be working for *you*, but you simply cannot even come to that *flawed conclusion* until you've done a TON of it. We're talking 400 to 500 calls, at least. And given that it does work, if it's not working for you (i.e., no bites, no nibbles), then something else is going on. Like…

1. Your portfolio consists of a few poems, an article for the neighborhood newsletter, and your own brochure. If you're in a good-size market, that's not enough. There *will* be other more experienced writers ahead of you in line. There were plenty in Atlanta when I started out. But if those ahead of you are getting work, then someone's hiring writers.

2. You still see yourself as an annoying intrusive telemarketer. Retake the *"You Might Be An Annoying Telemarketer IF…"* quiz and continue to exorcise this demon.

3. Let's say it: There's something abrasive, obnoxious or otherwise off-putting about your personality. If you're willing to entertain this idea (i.e., you're more committed to your success than your ego), find a mentor—whether an experienced commercial writer or successful sales person—and have him or her critique your approach.

And there's something else. You take some action and nothing happens. You take a lot more action and maybe get a little movement, but still not much. But stick with it a little longer and suddenly, the floodgates open. It happens all the time. People who've been hitting the phones steadily for three or four months with minimal results just hang in there a bit longer, then send me an e-mail letting me know that (in one happy woman's words), "All heaven has broken loose."

Everyone I call already has freelancers they use.

I got the following brilliant—and wonderfully thorough—answer to the above from FLCW Spiros Psarris (**www.copycraftsman.com**) in Tacoma, Washington, used here with his permission. While sometimes it pays (especially for those in smaller markets) to educate customers who don't currently use writers as to why they should, this is pretty much right on target.

In marketing, there's a saying: "Find a parade and get in front of it." In other words, don't compete in markets where you have to convince prospects to try your product/service. Find a market where people already want it—then convince them to try a different brand (yours).

In this case, finding companies that will use freelancers is a big part of the battle. If these companies use freelancers already, great! You don't need to convince them that freelancers are an asset. Every company that already has a regular freelancer will need someone else later, **unless** all of the following are true:

1. The company never has a spike in their workload or a last-minute project beyond what the regular freelancer can handle.

2. The regular freelancer has no other clients, thus is never too busy with other work to accept every job this company needs to be done.

3. The regular freelancer never gets sick or goes on vacation, thus is always available on a moment's notice when the client needs him/her.

4. Every job the regular freelancer turns in is perfect, and never leaves the client dissatisfied or wondering if somebody else could do better.

5. There will never be a personality conflict between the regular freelancer and the client, even as people change jobs within the client company and different people use the freelancer.

6. The regular freelancer is expert in every possible area of writing, so that as the client needs brochures, radio scripts, speeches, direct mail, ghostwriting, PR, Web copy, event scripts, etc., the freelancer can do EVERYTHING with documented expertise, leaving the client no need to look elsewhere.

7. The regular freelancer is able to keep a fresh, "first-day-on-the-job" level of enthusiasm even after years of working on the same stuff—so the client never feels that new blood is required.

8. *The regular freelancer will never move, quit, die, retire, change careers, decide to devote more time to family or cut back on workload.*

   If a prospect already has regular freelancers, say, "That's great! I'm glad you've found someone that you're happy with. Maybe I can just stop by and drop off some information for when your freelancers are maxed out and you need somebody in a hurry."

   Or, "That's great! Are they also experts in [one of your specialties that you think this client might need]? If you ever need someone like that, I have [proof of expertise and results]. Maybe I could stop by and drop off some information, in case the situation ever arises."

PB: As I write this, in the past few weeks, I've met with three prospective clients, all of whom said things like, *I've used this writer for years, but, 1) I'm getting tired of his* prima donna *ways, 2) she's great but just not creative enough, or 3) she's headed out on maternity leave.* Nothing stays the same.

FYI, Regarding Big Ad Agencies

I read an interesting article recently in *OZ*, the local Atlanta creative industry magazine (**www.ozonline.tv**), about getting in the doors of ad agencies. Though it was directed to graphic designers, I suspect the same advice would apply to copywriters. And one recommendation was *not* to cold call or even cold e-mail the larger agencies. They're just too busy and won't reply if they don't know you. The best approach is a personal note (ideally steering them to your Web site), followed up with a call some time after that. Makes sense. But before you get excited, I have not found that same paradigm to apply with other MMs (middlemen) and EUs (end-users). They're still fair game.

One more thing about ad agencies. When reviewing the work of a copywriter, it's S.O.P. to have you drop your portfolio off (sometimes without even getting a chance to meet with them beforehand) and pick it up in a few days. Just the way it often works in that world.

The Expanded Cold Calling Script

My sincere thanks to Brian Egeston of Atlanta, one of my first seminar grads from waaaaay back, for volunteering the first version of this (Brian is a very talented writer and the author of four hilarious and often poignant novels; **www.brianwrites.com**). I tweaked and added some to it but the core is unchanged.

These guidelines are designed to give you some rough talking points when you prospect by phone. After the basic intro, I've included different prospect responses and possible replies to those responses. Remember—these are only guidelines. Vary them to suit your specific market, prospects, situation, circumstances, and temperament.

The Basic Cold-Calling Script:

Good morning, my name is Peter Bowerman and I'm a freelance writer, making contact with local banks, to determine whether you have any on-going or occasional needs for a good freelance writer to help create marketing collateral material: brochures, manuals, etc. Who might be the best person to talk with?

A small adjustment here: A few readers brought to my attention that if you don't have a contact name and a secretary or receptionist initially answers, you should dispense with the first part about who you are and ask any number of other brief questions such as:

(When calling larger corporations):

May I speak to the marketing communications department?

(When calling smaller companies):

May I speak to the marketing director?

(When calling agencies, graphic design firms, marketing companies):

May I speak to the creative director? (or assistant creative director—usually a better bet)

(If you're unsure who to ask for):

May I speak to the person in charge of hiring copywriters?

If they ask the nature of your call, then you can revert back to the original expanded version, but in most cases, you won't have to trot out the larger one until you're talking to the right person—or at least have left the administrative realm.

Additional Prospect Responses/Writer Replies

WE DON'T USE FREELANCE WRITERS

Might you have any clients, associates or industry colleagues that come to mind who could use a good freelance writer?

NOTE about the above from Jake Sibley, FLCW in San Diego:

If they respond with a referral (and it just happened for me), when you call the referral, if you get the "barbed-wire" receptionist who asks, "And what is this regarding," simply say, "I was referred by Anthony Jones over at Advanced Wireless." Once you get to the prospect, if he or she asks how you know Anthony, just say "Oh, he and I were discussing the possibility of my doing some work for Advanced Wireless." The truth is you just cold-called Advanced Wireless five minutes before and you don't really know Anthony from Adam, but so what?

I'M NOT THE RIGHT PERSON

I'm sorry to bother you. Might you be able to steer me to the individual who would handle folks like me?

HE'S NOT AVAILABLE RIGHT NOW

Not a problem. What might be a good time to check back with him? And who should I ask for? (AT THIS POINT, YOU MIGHT ASK FOR AN E-MAIL ADDRESS AND SEND THEM A RESUME/COVER LETTER LETTING THEM KNOW WHO YOU ARE AND THAT YOU'LL BE IN CONTACT.)

I'M THE RIGHT PERSON / THAT WOULD BE ME

Great! So, you do hire copywriters on a fairly regular basis? I'd love the opportunity to stop by, at your convenience, to drop off a resume and some samples and perhaps discuss how I might help you out. Would that be okay? (MORE AGGRESSIVE APPROACH) *Would sometime next week (or later this week) work for you?*

WHAT HAVE YOU WORKED ON? WHAT ARE YOUR SPECIALTIES?

I feel very confident handling a broad array of projects like: (LIST YOUR SPECIALTIES: I.E., MARKETING BROCHURES, NEWSLETTERS, ADS, DIRECT MAIL, WEB CONTENT, ETC.) *Currently, I'm working on a _____ for a _____ company. On what kinds of projects do you typically look for copy-writing help?*

DO YOU HAVE ANY SAMPLES OF YOUR WORK?

Certainly. I'd love to get them into your hands. I'm going to be out and about in (THE AREA OF TOWN WHERE THEIR OFFICE IS) *in the next few days. Would it be possible to drop them off and introduce myself?*

(OR, A BIT MORE "SALESY," USING THE "CHOICE OF TWO POSITIVES" APPROACH DISCUSSED EARLIER: *I'm going to be out and about in the next few days and would love to drop them off and introduce myself. What day works better for you, Tuesday or Wednesday?* (THEN, IF THEY PICK A DAY…): *Is morning or afternoon better? etc.*

DO YOU HAVE ANY SAMPLES OF YOUR WORK? (IF YOU HAVE A WEB SITE)

I sure do and I've actually got several loaded up to my Web site. If you give me your e-mail address, I'll send you the link. (BY DOING IT THIS WAY, YOU GIVE THEM EASY "CLICK–THRU" AND DON'T RELY ON THEM TO TYPE IN AN ADDRESS, WHICH THEY MAY OR MAY NOT DO. AND YOU NOW HAVE THEIR E-MAIL ADDRESS.)

NO, THE NEXT FEW DAYS AREN'T REALLY GOOD TO MEET

No problem. I could drop them in the mail. By the way, what types of work are you most interested in seeing?

SURE, THAT WOULD BE FINE.

Great! And in about a week or so, I'll follow up with you and if it makes sense at that point, perhaps I could swing by, show you some actual pieces and we can explore how I might be of most use to you.

WE'RE NOT INTERESTED.

No problem, I appreciate your honesty. Might I mail or e-mail you my resume and a business card (OR THE LINK TO YOUR SITE) *for your files?*

NO! AND DON'T CALL ME EVER AGAIN, YOU MORON!
(NEVER happens…)

I'm sorry to have bothered you. Have a nice day. Goodbye.

•   •   •

Now, that wasn't so painful, was it? Seriously, there are a number of ways to reach out to prospective clients and cold calling is just one of them— though it's certainly been a key one for me. But let's go take a look at some powerful and intriguing applications for direct mail, e-mail and even the humble fax machine.

Chapter 6

Got this from Philly FLCW Kennerly Clay:

As my database grew along with my confidence in my business, I started mailing out purple postcards (my logo color) each quarter to clients and prospects. I use them to announce Web site updates, new services (i.e., partnering with graphic/Web designers, print/fulfillment houses, etc.), or to simply flex my creative copy muscle.

Ideally, I call everyone in my database a few weeks before to confirm their contact info. I've been able to land a number of appointments this way, but from others who don't yet have a need for my services, I often hear, "I have your purple card right here in front of me." At least I know I'm first on the list if something comes up.

After my last mailing, I got a call from an IT consulting company that ended up hiring me to re-do their Web content, brochure and possibly more. Persistence paid off. The proof? My new client said he'd decided he'd call me the next time he received one of my cards.

Bottom line, direct mail is a solid strategy for staying in touch with your contact base of clients and prospects. And incidentally, given the tighter reins being put on the telemarketing industry (which doesn't affect our business-to-business phone prospecting efforts), direct mail will undoubtedly increase in prevalence as companies turn to other proven—and legal!—ways of reaching their target audience. Keep that in mind when pitching work with prospects.

Direct Mail Keys

With any direct mail campaign, the three catchwords are *consistency*, *clarity* and *frequency*. Show up regularly in front of your target audience, make sure your message is simple, clear and uncluttered and do it often.

As discussed in the first book, as you prospect and network for work, you build a list of contacts who've said that yes, they do have ongoing or occasional needs for copywriters. This growing list becomes your target list for postcard direct mailings. And over time, a list of 200 to 300 can be more than enough to yield steady work.

Most importantly, always consider the larger picture and the bigger goal. Remember the story of the dating service marketing campaign earlier in the book. The point is simply to move your prospects along the sales cycle until you reach the point where they either tell you they're not in the market for your services OR they hire you.

And there's no one right way to move someone along that cycle. Some send letters, postcards or e-mails first, follow up with a phone call and stay in touch with more letters, cards. etc. Others skip the first step, go straight to the phone and keep in touch with the other correspondence. Whatever you're most comfortable with. Just make those multiple impressions. While chances are good you'll do some cold calling along the way, it isn't necessarily the order that's key, it's the process.

Tips From a Pro

At a recent BMA meeting (Business Marketing Association—**www.marketing. org**; a good nationwide organization worth checking out), the speaker was Chris Coleman, a brilliant marketing industry veteran and Chief Marketing Officer of Atlanta-based Secureworks. Echoing the catchwords mentioned above—consistency, clarity and frequency—Chris made these points about direct mail:

TARGET. The more targeted your audience, the better. List quality is more important than quantity. (Chris' most targeted mailing had a ten percent response, mind-blowing, incidentally, given that good response rates are considered to be around two percent. Response rate for her least targeted mailing was .50 percent.)

FREQUENCY. Response drops over time, but the more "touches" you can make to your customer, the better response you'll get. Chris' goal in year one was eight touch points (direct mail, calls, releases, etc.). Year two: 12. Year three: 18. Probably more than FLCWs need to do but I can certainly see half that number spread across different approaches.

FREQUENCY TRUMPS NICE CREATIVE. Good creative in combination with a good list is ideal, but a fairly plain mailer sent often can do the job with a good list. It's all about continuing to show up on the radar.

For FLCWs, along with frequency, there's a lot to be said for a consistent look that allows clients and prospects to recognize your mailings—either because your cards consistently sport the same design and/or color or have a prominently identifiable logo. If you chose to go with one of the postcard houses below, this might mean sticking with one design and message—cheaper, for sure. And, if you make it easy, you're more likely to do it.

FOLLOW-UP. Following up will always boost response. The mailer with the ten percent response was repeated four times. Everyone on the list of 800 was called after each mailing. Leaving a voice-mail was considered acceptable.

Postcard Houses

In the first book, I detailed a process for creating your own direct mail postcards using *Microsoft Publisher*, some bright-colored card stock and your friendly quick copy shop down the street. You'd design the cards in *Publisher*, lay them four-up on an 8.5 x 11 inch sheet (or oversized versions at two-up on the same page), print out clean laser copies, copy them on the colored stock and cut them up with a paper cutter. And all for roughly $60 for 250 cards including paper, copying, and postage.

It's still a great strategy, and limited only by your imagination and creativity. Since then, many online postcard houses have popped up. They're more expensive given that the price doesn't include postage but the convenience and aesthetics factors are high. The company I keep hearing about is **www.modernpostcard.com** (a few others: **www.amazingmail.com**, **www.purepostcards.com**, and **www.postcardsplus.net**).

The drill: You choose from literally thousands of slick graphic and photographic images. You craft your card copy—typically, headline on the front and headline and body copy on the back—send it on and they print up 1000 cards with your message for roughly $200 ($125 for 500; prices at press time). You get a professional-looking card at about 20 cents a pop and leave the designing to someone else. If you're doing targeted mailings, 1000 cards can be plenty for 2 to 4 mailings. And every time your prospect and client base sees that card, it reinforces your image.

"Newsettes"

Another intriguing direct mail possibility is what's known as a "newsette"—a hybrid between a newsletter and a direct mail piece, with colorful graphics and two short 150- to 200-word articles on topics of interest to your audience, one on each side. Not only a possibility for your own personal marketing but something to suggest to clients, and a tool best suited for staying in touch with an existing database of clients already familiar with you. I did a bunch for a local mortgage company with a fun, friendly tone and good information on refinancing, 15-year mortgages, equity lines, etc. All designed to demystify the loan process, present different financing scenarios, and, of course, think of my client once they were ready to move on something.

A Novel Approach

I got a great e-mail some months back from a FLCW (who wished to remain anonymous) who's been so successful in marketing her writing business that she actually keeps a small stable of writers busy. She shared a most unique direct mail and cold-calling approach that's been steadily delivering the goods. She got the idea from Gill Cargill, a top sales training professional (www.cargillsells.com), and according to her, "an absolutely fabulous resource for anyone who needs to market his or her business."

First step: She bought a list of "suspects" (before they're prospects, she says, they're suspects) from a list broker—potential buyers for her different writing services, which include commercial, ghostwriting books and articles and others. You could create your own list from your prospecting and networking efforts, though the beauty of this approach is that it "warms up" cold prospects whom you've never spoken to.

Once she has her list, she makes just 25 contacts a week, five each day. She's put together four letters, and each week for four weeks, she sends one letter to each of these clients. Each letter focuses on a different writing service she offers and each is written in a different style—funny, serious, upbeat, etc. If you were doing it, you'd simply pick the styles with which you're most comfortable and proficient.

From Cold to Warm

She comments: "Over a four-week period, I showcase a broad range of writing talents. Even before I ever call them, they're getting to know me, so that by the time I do call, in most cases, it isn't a cold call any more. More often than not, they recognize me." Out of those 25 a week, she ends up booking three to five face-to-face appointments, which of course, is always the goal. Not that all the rest aren't interested; many of them remain on the "suspect" list for future contacts.

She figures you could do the same thing with direct mail postcards, using different writing approaches for different cards. In her case, letter copy lent itself better to the types of writing she wanted to do for her clients.

How does she up her odds that her letters get read? "Given that I'm not sending a huge volume of mail daily, I hand-write the delivery address and use stamps, as opposed to ink-jetted labels and metered postage, which, together, screams 'JUNK MAIL!' This personalized approach definitely gets better results."

As far as follow-up goes, she buys her lists in a format that's importable into *ACT* (THE name in full-featured contact management programs). She then loads her four letters into the program, picks her five contacts a day and generates the letters. The system's "tickler" function reminds her daily of what letter she needs to send to which person and who she needs to follow up with by phone on that day.

This approach affirms my own experience in getting far better results using a more personalized approach vs. the shotgun variety. I like it because it's innovative, not terribly labor-intensive and makes your eventual calls a lot easier and more fun. And most importantly, you can't argue with the results. Yet another way to come at this thing.

FREE Direct Mail From USPS!

Free direct mail. No catch. No kidding. The friendly folks at the United States Post Office have developed a very cool program called *NetPost*, an automated direct mail program which offers various types of postage-included mailables such as postcards, letters, booklets, flyers and newsletters. While they're obviously in business to make money, THE eyebrow-raising feature is a B&W, 4x6 postcard program that costs just 23 cents per card—i.e., ONLY the postage.

A full color postcard (also 4x6) is as little as 46 cents per card, postage-included. It's totally Web-based, meaning you can upload all your documents, images and mailing lists to the site, preview the final documents and pay online. Your project is then printed, addressed and mailed within one business day. Pretty slick. For all the details, visit **www.usps.com** and select "Send Cards & Letters."

According to fans of the program, once you've downloaded the USPS's list template, it's a breeze to cut and paste your list's name and address columns from an *Excel* spreadsheet into the template. You then pick your graphics and enter your text for the backside copy.

Because there's no minimum quantity, some use it to send "onesies" like welcome notes to new clients and post-project thank-you cards. Having saved their designs/text from earlier cards, it's simply a matter of entering a new name and address (the card is automatically personalized; i.e.,

"Dear Paul") and submitting it for next-day mailing. All online and all for simply the cost of the stamp. Such a deal.

USPS Direct Mail Seminars

If you're just getting your feet wet with direct mail promotion, check out the USPS' small business seminar "Advertising with Mail Made Easy," presented by an entertaining direct mail pro in major cities around the country. For only $59, you get a valuable five-hour seminar packed with tips about finding your target audience, buying lists, producing your own materials and tracking the results. According to a friend who went, the handouts alone are worth the price of admission. For the current schedule, go to http://www.usps.com/directmail/seminars/schedule.htm

Follow-up is YOUR Job

I'm amazed at how often I hear someone say, *I sent out a bunch of direct mail cards (or packages) and I haven't heard back from anyone.* For starters, never send a full-blown marketing package to *anyone* who isn't expecting it. It'll be a waste of time and money. But once you do a mailing, it's your job to follow up, not theirs. They're not thinking about copywriting. It's your job to have them think about it more.

In fact, you're doing them a favor by following up. How many times have I called clients and heard, *I'm glad you called. I've been meaning to get ahold of you but I've just been so busy.* When you hear that, what's just happened? You made their life easier *and* moved the project that much closer to paying work. And if they're not in the market, you'll find out quickly and painlessly and move on.

The ABCs of E-mail Marketing

Given my dearth of personal experience in e-mail marketing, I called on others to share their experiences. After the basics below, we'll talk to Florida FLCW Lisa Sparks, who's made e-mail marketing an integral component of her success. We'll also get some interesting insights from "across the pond."

The Five Basic Rules of E-mail Marketing

1. **Don't Spam.** Sure, the law of averages could work in your favor in one sense, but you could blow your reputation at the same time.

2. **Personalize.** The more you can send your e-mail to specific, named individuals, the better your hit rate will be.

3. **Keep It Simple.** Use fancy graphics for e-mails only if you're sending them to those expecting them (i.e., regular e-newsletters). If they're going to cold prospects, make them as simple and personal-looking (and un-spammy looking) as possible.

4. **Cross-Market.** Do a mix of marketing by mail, e-mail and phone. Be everywhere your prospects are. Any one mode of communication is much easier to ignore than several in succession.

5. **Keep It Brief.** Your audience gets too much e-mail. Make whatever you're sending worth their while. Keep your message brief, (ideally) link them to a Web site, and let them know you'll be following up by phone (and then DO it).

Sunny E-mail Success

Florida FLCW Lisa Sparks is one of my heroes in this biz. We'll visit her again in Chapter Eight (*Eating Well in Smaller Markets*). I met Lisa in 2002 when she contacted me before coming through Atlanta for a conference and we grabbed dinner. Here was this extraordinarily impressive then-27-year-old African-American woman, who, through a winning combination of moxie, persistence, enthusiasm, resourcefulness, ingenuity, strong faith and plain old hard work, was building a thriving writing business, *Integrity Writing* (**www.integritywriting.com**) in the small and predominantly white Ft. Myers, Florida market area (population: 50,000).

Crucial to her success has been her mastery of e-mail marketing, and she's turned that expertise into a published program entitled *Power Words: Increase Your Sales with a Click*. I've seen it and it's great—very comprehensive and easy-to-follow.

Yes, this is a plug as a returned favor for the great info she's sharing here. Her price of $47 is a bargain for all the legwork she's done. This is a specific, detailed chronicling of the actual successful steps she's taken to dramatically impact the growth of her business. For more information, contact Lisa directly at **lisa@integritywriting.com**.

Focused on What Works

For Lisa, e-mail marketing (and specifically, her monthly e-newsletter) isn't just another way to attract business. It has become THE focal point of her overall marketing strategy. Yes, she still goes to networking functions, undertakes periodic cold-calling campaigns and sends out postcard mailings, but all contacts generated from these efforts—if they don't yield immediate fruit and even if they do—feed into her subscriber base for her newsletter. Why? Because e-mail marketing has proven to be the most consistently profitable avenue to build her business. The approach may not be for everyone, but if you choose to make it part of your arsenal, Lisa's game plan is an excellent one.

How Big A Difference Has It Made?

Lisa's response: *Since I began in October of 2002, I've more than doubled my business. I get calls at least once a week from new clients who want to work with me. When I ask how they heard of me, it all traces back to a forwarded copy of my monthly e-mail newsletter,* **Copywriting Secrets**.

From Fax to E-mail

Initially, Lisa sent a fax newsletter to the people on her client and prospect lists. While it was a great way to keep in touch, it had some serious downsides. It provided precious little measurement ability—she couldn't see who was getting or reading it—and, thanks to long distance charges, it was getting expensive. Most importantly, during the three months she did it, she received no business from it. So, she decided to switch to an e-mail version. The results? *I received new business after the second issue. Sure, it was just a $200 project, but in the coming months I landed two $1500 projects back-to-back plus some consistent, monthly newsletter work—a copywriter's dream.*

What are the different applications for e-mail you might want to try? Well, what's your goal? To reach a new, untapped group of people with a strong pitch? To simply stay in touch with an existing group of contacts—either with periodic e-mails or perhaps a regular e-newsletter? Once you've established your objective, the first step is to generate a list of recipients. How?

Marketing to Existing Clients/Prospects

If the goal is keep in touch with an existing group of clients and prospects, you will have been collecting e-mail addresses over time through prospecting or networking (from both current clients as well as prospects who said they use freelancers, occasionally or regularly). Make sure you get permission from these people—*especially* with clients—before sending them regular correspondence. If you do, they'll come to respect your experience and industry expertise as you build the case for hiring you. Without it, you'll likely irritate them and reduce your chances of ever being hired.

Lisa suggests, *Just make it very easy-breezy: 'Mr. Prospect, I put together a great monthly e-newsletter with good business-building tips, success stories and a lot more. Can I add you to the distribution list? I think you'd enjoy it.'* Make it easy to say yes.

And remember, while you'd love for them to read every word of your handcrafted e-gem every month, clearly, the power of this approach is your *regular* monthly presence in front of your client and prospect base, saying: *I'm still here and ready to serve you.*

Make It Good, or Else

In fact, assume recipients are *not* reading the whole thing or even most of it. Then it becomes a question of grabbing their attention with invitingly bold and snappy headlines that speak to the things dear to any businessperson's heart: increased profits, enhanced reputation, competitive advantage, etc. But that said, make *all* the content good. As Lisa points out, *Some will read it and if it's lousy, self-serving or self-promotional, they'll unsubscribe.* Poof! You've just lost your monthly "access." Give people good information and it *will* pay dividends in new business.

Marketing to Cold Prospects

At some point, you'll want to move beyond your contact base and start approaching cold prospects by personalized e-mail. How? Over time, harvest cold e-mail addresses from company Web sites and build a targeted list of prospects (something our United Kingdom FLCW, whose story follows, did). More labor-intensive, but arguably worth the time.

And if you're going to make cold e-mail contacts, always personalize them. Yes, this takes more time, but, as mentioned, my experience in marketing both my business as well as my books has more than proven the value of the personal contact.

In countless cases, I got the appointment or job, or landed the TV, radio or newspaper interview because I picked up the phone and found someone to talk to, or at the very least, crafted a personal e-mail to a specific person. In addition to addressing the person by name, tailor your e-mail by making a specific reference to his or her company, something you saw on their Web site, an article you read about their firm, etc.

Inexpensive, Targeted Ads

Lisa suggests another clever strategy to attract cold prospects to your newsletter subscriber base (and lead to more work): *Every industry has an e-mail newsletter. Buy an ad in one with an already huge subscriber base and offer an incentive for subscribing to yours (i.e., a special report that helps solve the target audience's biggest problem). Ad rates for these kinds* *of pubs are often very reasonable—I've seen them as low as $10 to reach 12,000 people, all with similar interests. You should see a huge increase in subscribers. And best of all, the people who sign up have given you permission to send them information.*

Buying or Renting a List?

What about buying or renting a list of e-mail addresses? Thumbs-down, says Lisa, because: *There's a pretty high likelihood that you'll get a list compiled by a spammer who gathers addresses without permission and sells it as a reputable 'list.' And even doing a background check on the list owner may turn up nothing.*

Just as importantly, sending anything to even a reputably obtained list of people means you've obtained no permission—and that means you're officially spamming. Yes, you could send personalized notes to people on a list but obviously, that's time-intensive and defeats the purpose of getting the list in the first place. But spam is spam and penalties can be steep. Your ISP could block you from making legitimate, permission-based contacts or even drop you altogether. Think hard.

And is it even worth it? As Lisa notes, *It's hard enough to get the attention of people who **do** know you and **are** expecting your correspondence, much less those who aren't. Don't compound your problem by sending mass, unsolicited e-mails.*

Content is King

Okay, you've got your list—either people you've met through networking (Audience A) or cold prospects who don't know you (Audience B). Next step? Crafting the content of your e-mail message, which will obviously be different for Audience A (which has granted permission) than Audience B (which hasn't).

It's to Audience A that you might consider sending a newsletter—which will get you in front of your market on a regular basis. Here, your content can and should be a bit more familiar, and less "sales-y" because the key is relationship-building—ongoing reminders that you're out there. Maybe you provide tips, success stories of how your writing services have helped other companies like them, useful resources, etc.

Alternately, you could focus on just one of those components, sending out a much shorter piece, which can allow you to send one more frequently. But be careful. Just the perception of "too much e-mail" and they may opt out.

With Audience B, you need to grab their attention, so whatever you send should be more hard-hitting and promotional. You don't have a relationship established with this audience yet so you can't afford to be as low-key as you'd be with Audience A.

And as Lisa reminds, *Given people's notoriously short attention spans, whatever you write needs to be brief, concise and meaningful to that audience. It has to pass the test: 'What's in it for me?' and if the answer is, 'Nothing,' it's gone.*

Being Style-Conscious

Okay, how will you send that content? Fancy HTML-style graphics or simple text? I don't know about you, but unless I'm expecting it, any e-mail with slick graphics in the text window gets deleted immediately. Heck, it looks like every other spammed sales pitch. Remember the concept of camouflage?

If you're sending to cold prospects, a plain but personalized text message might work better. When I receive such a message with a subject line that's addressed to me specifically, I'm exponentially more likely to read it than one with fancier graphics. And personalizing means *Peter* or *Mr. Bowerman,* not *bowerman*. I swear I do not know what these idiots are thinking when *Hello bowerman!* is their idea of personalizing an e-mail. I'd have to have an I.Q. in mid-double digits to fall for it. It boggles the mind.

If you're sending to people who are expecting it, you can be more graphically creative. And as Lisa points out, if you want to take a graphically snazzier approach, there are tons of programs, both software- and Web-based to help you look good—easily and inexpensively. She says, *The Web-based, in my opinion, are the easiest use. I use* **Constant Contact**®, (**www.constantcontact.com***). It allows you to use a wide variety of pre-set graphic templates to lay out your message, while merging your list of names into the program." And if your list is in a program like Microsoft Excel, it's easy to import the names and addresses, and the merge function will yield personalized e-mails.*

Constant Contact charges by the number of -e-mails sent: 250 or less—most likely sufficient for an existing prospect list—costs a flat $10 per month (at press time) and prices rise from there.

Programs like *Constant Contact* and others typically provide tracking information on your campaigns—very important. They can tell you how often different links have been clicked in the body of the e-mail so you can learn what interests your audience and what causes them to take action. Use that information to follow up with prospects and ask them specific questions about upcoming projects. If they're willing to click for more information, they're the people you want to put on a preferred subscriber list. These people often become very dedicated and consistent clients.

Here's a listing of several e-mail marketing programs:

Constant Contact: **www.constantcontact.com**

Cooler Email™: **www.cooleremail.com**

Vertical Response®: **www.verticalresponse.com**

IMN™ (formerly iMakeNews): **www.imakenews.com**

Ezine Director℠: **www.ezinedirector.com**

Topica: **www.topica.com**

Visit this link (again, available at press time) for an article providing brief (and independent) reviews of a bunch of these programs: **www.wilsonWeb. com/wct5/listserver_intro.htm**

Success or Failure?

What are some of the key factors determining the success or failure of your e-marketing campaign? Content, of course. But before they'll even read that content, you need a subject line that draws them in. Lisa says, *If it's a recurring piece like a newsletter to an "opt-in" group, it's best to stick to the same subject line, as they come to expect it and won't confuse it with spam. Think about the ones you get regularly. I'd wager they always come with the same subject line.*

If it's to a cold group, again, it needs to be bold and attention getting, just like ad copy or direct mail, and needs to speak to what's important to that group. Experiment with different styles.

And of course, mix up your direct marketing approaches, doing some direct mail postcards, some e-mail marketing, cold calling, etc. They all complement each other and it's about reaching and interacting with clients and prospects as they do different things: read their mail, check their e-mail and answer their phone. Lisa says,

> *I send out promotional e-mails twice a month in between issues of my e-mail newsletter. I'm careful because my audience of writers, marketing managers and small business owners get inundated with e-mail. If my "in-between" messages aren't relevant, my list will begin to shrink. Twice a year, I'll send out a postcard mailing. They're effective for building a list, but can get expensive when you're a cheapskate like I am. That's why e-mail is so much fun for me. The profit margin is almost 100 percent*

Lisa also does speaking engagements and picks up clients that way as well. She attends local chamber of commerce events and always asks the people she meets if she can add them to her e-mail list, a sure business-builder. And usually once a quarter, she'll do some cold calling. But again, all these activities—calling, postcards, networking—feed into her e-mail marketing. She sums it up: *E-mail has become the mainstay of my marketing strategy and it's paid for itself many times over.*

Samples of Lisa's regular e-newsletter are archived at **www.integrity writing.com**; also check out the site of Boston-based Andrea Harris (**www.minerva-inc.com**) who puts out her monthly *Minerva Minute*.

English E-mail

Got this intriguing e-mail from U.K. FLCW Richard Jebb in October 2002, describing a simple e-mail prospecting campaign. By his own admission, the approach bordered on spam, but I found the process and post-mortem interesting, as were his observations about smaller-market businesses vs. those in London. Given the precipitous rise in most people's e-mail volume since then, it's hard to say how such a campaign would fare today. But food for thought, nonetheless.

> *I'm excited about an e-mail campaign I just completed and wanted to share it with you. While the e-mail I sent was a bit on the spammy side, it wasn't very "salesy." It was in the form of a question: "Have you or anyone in your company that you know of used a freelance copywriter in the past 12 months?"*
>
> *I then explained I was a freelance copywriter wanting to know how buoyant the market was and suggested they look at my Web site. I've had a pretty good response. I sent the e-mail to 770 marketing agencies (the U.K. way of saying ad agencies), a list of varying focus and accuracy that I created earlier this year. About 150 were returned undelivered, meaning about 620 got through. Out of that 620, over 80 have responded. Roughly equal yes/no responses tilted slightly to "no," but many have asked for more info. Only one response called it spam and even he still asked me to contact him if I have "any in-depth financial writing experience."*

> *I now have two meetings in London, one locally and have
> landed a project writing an in-store radio ad for Safeway.
> I don't plan to continue in this way, but the process helped
> qualify the list nicely. I now have a better idea of which
> companies are responsive to unsolicited approaches and
> are therefore, in my belief, worth researching and
> contacting personally, either by e-mail or phone.*

> *I'm also planning to target companies closer to home. I'm
> in Tonbridge, in Kent, about 40 minutes outside London.
> Agencies around here, whilst having London-based clients,
> are not as frantic and harassed as their London-based
> colleagues, so I think I'll face less competition and stand
> a better chance of getting noticed.*

Just the Fax, Ma'am

A few months back, I received an e-mail from friend and fellow commercial
freelancer, Steve Marshall, here in Atlanta. Steve had background in
technical writing, amongst other things, and he'd successfully made the
transition to commercial writing as the IT crash unfolded. He shared a brief
history of his path to the present, culminating in these words:

> *Now my average true rate—that is, income received, minus
> expenses, divided by actual hours worked—often reaches
> substantially higher than $90 per hour. Not always, by any
> means—I've made my share of pricing mistakes, and I
> don't expect I'll ever be completely error-free. The aim in
> this area, as in all others, is continuous improvement.*

> *Those hours don't yet average 20 a week, but they're
> approaching it. And here's the interesting thing: I haven't
> seriously approached the Atlanta market. I did a little bit—
> some cold calls, a mailing to manufacturing firms, a few
> ads, some networking. And I got some results. But until now
> I haven't "declared a footprint" here. Eventually I will.*

Needless to say, I was intrigued. So I plied him with eggplant and garlic sauce
from our favorite neighborhood Chinese joint, Uncle Wong's, and he spilled
the beans. He'd pulled off this pretty remarkable feat—building a very healthy
income stream while barely touching the local Atlanta market—through
some targeted fax marketing. It's a pretty cool story and he even graciously
agreed to share the sales letter he used. Here's how it unfolded.

Exceptionally Profitable

Apparently, he'd actually done several prior fax marketing campaigns to some non-Atlanta-based design firms and ad agencies, which yielded a decent chunk of business as well. But his biggest effort was a sales letter to marketing executives at 10,000 mid-size manufacturing companies across the country. He commented:

> There were no high-quality results immediately—the first few months brought in some lunch money. But then things began to move, and over the next year I got a few solid new customers from the campaign. Spreading the total cost of my fax project among them, they had cost me $200 to $300 each (depending on the value I assign my own time on the project). In 2003 they paid me an average of $4200.
>
> But the pudding comes next: I'm budgeting 2004 income of nearly $50,000 from them. And surely my $300 investment for one of them—a $30,000 customer—has to rank as one of my better ones.

What percentage of his current workload came as a direct result of these campaigns? According to him, more than half. The rest comes from some targeted direct mail he did to Atlanta-area manufacturers (mailed, incidentally, on September 11th, 2001) as well as some healthy word-of-mouth contacts. Which just naturally comes with the territory once you start building the business and doing good work. Another reason why you shouldn't ever have to mount a marketing push as big as your initial one.

I noticed that the actual fax letter, while richer graphically than just a page of text, didn't seem all that involved. He'd designed it himself, adding, *You need only the most rudimentary design skills when you're dealing with fax technology.* Stands to reason. People aren't expecting brilliant design in a fax.

The Nuts and Bolts

Now, I fully expect many of you will read the following technical details and say, *Forget it. Too much trouble.* But whether or not you choose to duplicate it, what I want you to take away from this is the innovative thinking—and elbow grease—that went into it. This was a thing of beauty.

The basic building blocks:

- 🐚 Data available in public libraries
- 🐚 Two Windows-based computers

🐝 Telephone service with free long distance—both land-line and cellular

🐝 Software including *WinFax, Microsoft Access, Word,* and *Excel.*

We'll get into the how-to of it all in a moment. For starters, who was he contacting? Given that most of his business came from outside Atlanta, I assumed he'd bought a list. Where did he get it? According to him, he used data available for free in the *ReferenceUSA* database in the public library. He commented, *It wasn't perfect, but the price was right, and it allowed me to send every fax to a name, not just a title.* Key distinction, because it takes the campaign out of the realm of a "broadcast fax," which would make it more like "fax spam," opening it up to other potential restrictions.

Putting the Pieces Together

Once he had his list, assembling all the technical pieces—the data, the fax technology, the phone lines, and in essence, integrating products from several vendors—was a formidable challenge. Along the way, he contracted out "data collection, *Microsoft Access* code creation, and some preliminary testing." Meaning?

In the realm of data collection, he said, *At the time I was gathering the data from **ReferenceUSA** at the library, you could only download 50 records at a time. Given that my initial list was 18,000 strong, the time involved would've been significant. Since my time is worth $90+/hour, I hired someone to handle this step—for a lot less.*

How about the *Access* code creation? His low-tech explanation: *I decided that Access, which is a true database program, would be the right vehicle with which to extract the necessary data (i.e., first and last names of marketing executives, along with salutation, plus their fax number). Integrating Access with Excel would accomplish this task. But I needed to hire a programmer to write a small program that would start with the raw data in one Excel spreadsheet, extract pieces I needed and dump them into a second spreadsheet. That Excel spreadsheet would then be integrated with Word (for the sales letter) and WinFax, my fax software program.*

Overworked Cell Phone

Okay, so he's collected the data and put it in a transmittable format. The last task was, of course, the actual transmission, which was where the preliminary testing came in. And he's a mighty clever guy. Given that he enjoyed unlimited night and weekend calling on his cell phone, he wanted to figure out a way to link a computer fax program to the cell phone. As he observed, *In theory, it's easy. But rather than spend hours on it, I hired someone, basically, to prove to me that it could be done.* Incidentally, he ended up hiring my own computer guru, Dave Morrow, who handily pulled it off.

How successful was the campaign? Well, he already shared his exceptionally positive ratio of cost per customer vs. sales per customer, which, as he puts it, *is the only measure of success I understand.* Beyond that, he doesn't know how many faxes reached the named addressee (or another equally qualified decision-maker). Apparently, roughly 13 percent of them failed on the first attempt, and he chose not to resend them.

He wisely made it clear on the cover sheet that requests for removal from his list would be honored, and about a third of one percent of recipients requested removal. Only a few of these expressed resentment; the rest were businesslike.

FYI...

Which brings up another issue: It seems that two such requests for removal made reference to state and FCC rules, which they claimed prohibit certain forms of fax advertising. He and his attorney are reviewing the rules, and he suggests that anyone planning a similar campaign investigate the matter as well. Incidentally, this is totally separate from the recent "Do Not Call" legislation, which concerns residential solicitation, and doesn't address faxing at all.

Both these respondents, in form letters, threatened to "contact the authorities" if he continued to send them faxes. *(See the Disclaimer and supplementary info on this subject following Steve's letter.)*

In case you're thinking, *Well, scratch that idea—don't need that kind of heat,* in my experience, out of any given group of people, a few will bluster and threaten, when in reality, they're more bark than bite. Was Steve intimidated? His response? *Barking intimidates me not at all, although I give biters a wide berth. Using the telephone to contact specific marketing executives, and offering them a standard marketing product—copywriting—certainly doesn't seem unethical to me.*

Make $ While You Sleep...

After culling down the initial 18,000 names in his raw database—eliminating records without contact names or other pertinent info—he ended up with roughly 10,000. Using *WinFax* software and transmitting on his cell phone, given that it was a three-page fax (cover letter + 2 Pages), it took nearly two weeks—automatically, while he slept—to get through all of the names.

As he saw it, one could send a fax simply to "Marketing Executive," but, he says, *It wouldn't be as effective—but send ten thousand, and you'll get something back. Kind of like your 'dog and his order book' story from the first book.* Thanks, Steve. Some stories have some serious shelf life.

Most impressive about this whole approach was that Steve did it without tapping the local Atlanta market much at all. I assumed he hadn't personally met many of the folks he was working for now. No question, he said, there were times when sitting down across a table from his client would've been ideal, and that's not possible. Though recently, he flew to Cleveland for a personal trip, and while there, met one of these new clients.

Steve says: *Obviously, this is a "self-selecting" system. Meaning that those who have responded clearly didn't have a problem dealing with me even though I was in Atlanta, Georgia. I'm sure plenty of recipients took one look at the fax and said, 'Why would I work with someone in Atlanta, when I've got local resources?' But also obviously, enough of them did to make this endeavor worthwhile.*

Benefits Roundup

Faxing isn't a high-tech medium, but for certain very small fish, like us, it offers some great advantages. For starters, Steve points out, there's the format of faxes. It accommodates copy of any length, allowing a writer to…write. And as he noted earlier, no one expects breakthrough design. In addition, by including your Web address, you give your prospect access to your full presentation.

Secondly, there's the data. Fax information for businesses—names, titles, and fax numbers—is available in quantity at low cost. By contrast, e-mail addresses are generally a much more expensive proposition.

And finally, there's the technology, which is advancing on several fronts. As he sees it, *The race toward free long-distance service is well underway, and will continue. Meanwhile, software vendors will improve their faxing programs.*

And incidentally, in a recent update from Steve he observed, *Since the first solid round of results rolled in (the $50K clients), there have been a few dozen other inquiries; maybe 12-15 of which became clients. A few were worthwhile, even if they were small and/or one-shots. I still get calls now and then, more than a year after someone received a fax. The work has produced samples that greatly improve my portfolio.*

If You're Interested...

Clearly, Steve has done all the technical "heavy lifting" to turn a good idea into a feasible and technically proven strategy. If you're interested in implementing a similar campaign for your business and would just as soon not re-invent the wheel, Steve is available for fee-based consultation. Contact him at **steve@samarshall.com** or through his Web site at **www.samarshall.com**. He's a good man—friendly, down-to-earth and thorough.

The Letter

Steve's letter is below. It's strong stuff. And it has to be to get someone's attention. Bold and brash, it has a confident tone without being glib. While it has a tough sales edge, it never strays very far from the benefits he knows the reader cares about: sales, profits, results, and beating the competition. Bold subheads draw the reader in and hit those hot buttons one after another.

Prospects reading this can't help but "get" that this guy's on their side and knows what's important to them. He talks in certain tones—about what he *will* do, the results he *will* get, where he *will* take this client and their business. You won't find any of the weak "may... might... maybe... can... possibly..." language here. This isn't the place.

In these days of lean manufacturing . . .

Put your ad agency on a diet.

Stop overpaying for second-rate copy.

Dear Mr. Last Name,

Who's calling your agency fat?

I am. My prescription: trim them down, with exercise and diet.

First, exercise. Sweat 'em—make them compete against my writing. (But get a signed release first, because strenuous competition is dangerous to incompetent copywriters.) Then, starve 'em—limit their consumption of your marketing dollars. When they try to sell you mediocre writing, just say NO.

It's tough love, and they'll complain. But it will be good for them, in the long run, to stop selling a service they can't deliver. More important, it will be good for you—if you hire me, your copy will work harder and produce better results.

Writing for the market is a skill, an art and a science.

Some ad agencies have plenty of talent—in other areas. Some deliver precise analysis and media strategy, others create stunning visuals. Which work great—until your prospect starts reading. Then weak copy takes over and squanders an opportunity, or even drives your customer away.

Every aspect of marketing is important—but language is what sells.

I write sales copy that works.

I'm better than ad agency copywriters at two things: analyzing business and writing for the market. And unlike agencies, I only want one award: a note from you, saying my piece outpulled your last one. I'll frame that.

Let's take some work from your competitors.

Strong language? Yes, that's what I'm selling—manufacturing isn't Mr. Rogers' neighborhood. You have every right to compete, and your competition has only one right: to qualify prospects for you.

I'm a veteran writer with more than twenty years of broad experience in business and industry. I write all varieties of marketing, technical, and corporate communications, to the highest standards. (And that's guaranteed: you simply won't find grammatical errors, flawed logic, or verbal mush in my copy.)

Price and quality both?

You bet. As a marketer, you know that most price-and-quality offers are fakes. Not this one. I charge more than agency copywriters are paid, but with my low overhead I bill less than agencies bill. You win with better writing at a better price.

To learn more about my capabilities and client history, please visit my Web site: www.samarshall.com.

And if you have a writing project coming up, please call me today.

Best regards,

Steve Marshall

DISCLAIMER: Okay, while I personally feel (and I'm guessing Steve would concur) that you're more likely to be struck by lightning on a sunny Thursday than ever get sued by anyone as a result of a fax marketing campaign, nonetheless, it's CMA time:

Due to the possible legal issues raised by business-to-business faxing, this material is being presented solely as a possible business-building strategy. I am not specifically recommending or endorsing its use, and as such, will not be held liable for any legal problems that arise as a result of its utilization in whole or part, as described here. Please conduct your own due diligence and investigate the specific statutes relating to the practice of business-to-business faxing for your state and any others in which you will be conducting business.

And as mentioned earlier, these possible legal issues are *not* related to the national *Do Not Call* initiative that took place in 2003 to crack down on telemarketers. Again, that program was related specifically and exclusively to telemarketing to consumers in their homes and did not apply to business-to-business calls. Please research the specific statutes related to business-to-business faxing for your state. In my state, the text of the Georgia No Call program description states (and I quote):

The **Governor's Office of Consumer Affairs (OCA)** is responsible for enforcing the Georgia No Call Law. The law does **not** apply to unsolicited faxes or unsolicited calls to a business. The full text of the law can be found at: **http://www2.state.ga.us/GaOCA/nocall.htm**.

And under the Q&A related to the National Do Not Call Registry, the response to the question: *Can I register my business phone number?* was:

The National Do Not Call Registry is only for personal phone numbers. Business to business calls are not covered by the National Do Not Call Registry.

•   •   •

Some intriguing ideas to ponder. Now, let's check out some intriguing markets—ones that might not have made it onto your radar…

Chapter 7

Meat and potatoes. It'll sustain us, but we'll always be wondering about those little ethnic dives on the other side of town and what tempting culinary treats they might offer. While many a well-fed writer has thrived on a diet of projects served up by corporate end-users (EUs) and middlemen (MMs), there's more to eat out there—even within supposedly familiar corporate corridors.

Just as importantly, concerns over an up-and-down economy are a good reason to broaden our tastes. Though, for the record, I don't think the state of the economy really has that much of an effect on one person's business-building efforts (See Chapter Eleven—*It's NOT the Economy, Stupid!*).

In any case, thanks to some legwork of my own and the generosity of several of your fellow FLCWs, who have graciously shared their experiences in other arenas, we'll peek into some new doors. The not-for-profit sector. Some rarely-tapped departments within corporations. Writing opportunities in colleges and universities. A wonderful list of possible writing clients that underscores how much potential work may be sitting right under your nose. And a few other juicy side dishes.

One caveat—this exploration is not meant to be exhaustive. My goal is to plant some seeds with basic overviews, steer you in the right direction, and let you check it out.

Not-For-Profits (NFPs)

The following piece appeared in the July 2003 E-PUB, thanks to Bloomington, Indiana FLCW Kevin Klemme (www.writingace.com), and is used here with his permission. Nothing theoretical here; just the delectable real-world details we love so much.

115

Writing For the Not-For-Profit (NFP) Sector
By Kevin Klemme

I spent six years as the primary writer for a consulting firm with a client base that was 90 percent NFP, and continue to serve that market on my own. Based on that experience, I'll list a few types of clients and discuss the needs, contact points and general revenue potential of each. The rates suggested reflect what I've seen in the Midwest.

School Districts

I've often approached school districts through the superintendent's office and usually end up reporting to the assistant superintendent during the project. Most districts of any size have a community relations office serving a marketing function, and it's not unusual to work with them on a project. It's usually the superintendent's office, however, that makes the final decision and approves the spending.

School districts most often need help with grant proposals and planning documents. (If you have the background to help with strategic planning, they sometimes need that, too). The consulting firm I was with charged up to $150 per hour for my time on very large (eight figures) grant proposals from large districts. Rates for freelancers working on more common projects would be $75 per hour for big, urban districts, or $60 for smaller ones.

Local Economic Development Organizations (LEDOs)

"LEDO" can refer specifically to an economic development corporation, or it can be a catchall term for any organization with "economic development" as part of its mission. In the latter sense, it can include Chambers of Commerce, Workforce Industry Boards or other locally created business or workforce development committees. LEDOs typically need writers to prepare white papers, grant proposals and planning documents. Usually, I've dealt with the president or vice-president of the organization. Larger LEDOs, such as the Chamber of Commerce in a large city, will have directors of arenas such as education, legislative issues and others. I've worked for them as well. Rates can go as high as $100 per hour or more for big organizations, but $50 to $75 per hour is more common.

Local Trade Associations

Councils, forums and associations formed around businesses in a specific industry or geographic area are promising prospects for freelancers. Entities that lobby state or local governments have an ongoing need for white papers and reports on studies they've funded. Often, the experts conducting the study write in jargon, which the trade association needs translated into plain English for public use. Associations also produce educational materials for the general public or for distribution to schools. I've always worked for the president or vice president of these organizations. Rates are about the same as for LEDOs.

Community Service Organizations

From regional United Way chapters to small committees trying to meet local human needs, all need grant proposals written. CSOs of any size tend to have tight budgets: Larger ones pay but smaller ones typically don't have much ready cash. If you're interested in the cause, it's often a toss-up whether to charge a small fee or do it *pro bono*. I've done paying work for United Way chapters or affiliates conducting community needs assessments. In cases like that, it helps if you know how to design a good survey, because the same person or company will usually be expected to write the survey instrument and the report on the results.

Three other points regarding NFPs:

1. Most prefer flat rates to hourlies, because they usually have firm project budgets.

2. Each NFP has its own jargon (especially the LEDOs). You'll need to know it or learn it, whether you have to write with it (for industry-specific jobs) or translate it (for public consumption).

3. Brush up on potential clients before calling. No one will hire a writer ignorant of local events or industry trends. Check your local paper for recent stories on school districts and CSOs. See if the national version of your local trade association publishes a journal. Many of the organizations listed above will also have Web sites with news sections.

Hidden Corporate Treasures

I ran this tasty piece (by Mary Anne Hahn, and used here with her permission) in the March 2003 E-PUB. Mary Anne comes from 15 years in corporate America and is the editor and publisher of *WriteSuccess*, a free biweekly e-zine of ideas, information and inspiration for writers (subscribe at **writesuccess-subscribe@yahoogroups.com**).

This opened my eyes to some avenues I'd never explored. I've always said one should tap other departments within corporations; this quantifies that suggestion. And if you're already in the door of a corporation and they like your work, ask them for referrals to other departments—perhaps some outlined here. If you're making your first call to a company, as you'll see, one call can't do it all!

Corporate Roads Less Traveled

By Mary Anne Hahn

When targeting any corporation for work, most freelancers contact the communications department. Makes sense. After all, the department responsible for the majority of a company's external and internal communications would have the greatest potential needs.

But 15 years in a large insurance company taught me that the need for strong writers exists throughout the organization, not just in communications. And while the management folks in these other departments may realize that need, they probably won't think to seek out a freelancer, unless you let them know you're out there and show them how you might help them address their specific communications challenges.

This advice applies as well to utilities, banks, hospitals, brokerage firms and a wide variety of other organizations, which frequently have similar departments with similar needs.

Customer Service Departments

Having spent a good deal of my career in the customer service sector, I know first hand what kind of writing needs exist there.

A lot of customer service functions happen through form letters or more personalized responses from a representative to a customer. Often these letters could use a professional writer's touch, or at the very least, these representatives could use business writing training. Some organizations might even hire a writer to assist them with correspondence backlogs or in creating new form letters.

Why not offer a newsletter targeted to customer service department staff? It might include *Employee of the Month*, customer service tips and articles, motivational quotes and stress-reducing techniques and exercises. Those who've worked in customer service departments understand how valuable such a newsletter can be for employee morale.

Human Resources Departments

HR departments generate a large volume of written materials. From developing company policies to job descriptions, from posting fliers announcing upcoming company events to handling employee benefits paperwork, HR professionals (for whom writing may not come easily) need to constantly communicate to the rest of the company in writing. Can you help them get their messages out clearly and professionally? If so, freelance opportunities await.

Marketing Departments

Next to communications, marketing departments probably produce the most written material. Product brochures, business proposals and direct mail sales letters all fall under the marketing umbrella. This written work is often outsourced, which frees up the marketing and sales staff to study trends, identify potential new business and make sales calls. If you have desktop publishing as well as writing experience, even better.

IT (Information Technology) Departments

The need for writers in this area is tremendous and the gateway is IT department heads. Not only are technical writers needed to document system specifications or create system user guides, but also non-technical writers can assist IT with the creation of Internet site content for a company's customers, or Intranet content for its employees. People who excel in writing HTML appreciate those who excel in writing clear, crisp content.

Training Departments

My current day job title is "Document Development Coordinator" for the training department: I support the trainers by creating and editing a wide variety of training manuals and procedure materials. When they're actively training a class, these people have little time to research and update the materials they use. Writing needs include putting together corporate glossaries of terms and acronyms unique to an industry and organization, editing training and procedure docs to ensure they're user-friendly and training the trainers themselves on how to write clearly and effectively.

Do your research. Make the phone calls to identify the people who head up these various departments. But the effort could be well worth it in terms of uncovering dozens of "hidden markets" and new clients for freelance writing work.

Back To School

A classic easy-to-overlook market. Big cities AND smaller markets are often home to colleges and universities. It's a mixed bag and not always high wages, but nonetheless, worth investigating.

A few years back, I got a call from someone in the marketing department at Emory University here in Atlanta (referred by a too-busy colleague). Could I help revamp her Web site copy? I was getting ready to leave town, so I had to steer her to yet another writing colleague (are you getting the power and potential of a writer's group?) I asked her if we could huddle up when I returned. Her reply? *Absolutely. I have a constant need for freelancers.*

Just Like a Corporation

Okay, consider that: Emory University has a marketing department. I hadn't thought about it, but of course they would. They're a business like any other. They need to market their product through brochures, newsletters, direct mail, Web sites, orientation materials, educational CDs, tons of internal communications, etc.

Next story. I was in Champaign, Illinois a few months after that first phone call, attending a luncheon for the local chapter of the international technical writing organization, Society for Technical Communication (**www.stc.org**). The Champaign/Urbana area is home to the University of Illinois, and seated across from me was a woman who worked in publications for one of the big academic departments. I asked if she ever outsourced writing projects to freelancers. *I use freelancers all the time*, she replied. Interesting.

Research Reveals...

I recently spent a few days contacting some universities around the country to see if they hired freelancers and if so, what they paid. Unearthed some good stuff. A representative from a midwestern university's technical department said he hires freelancers to write articles for the department's magazine—both general interest and technical stories adapted for the lay person. $50 an hour. A possible avenue for those with a technical background (or a technical major in college).

A manager of Editorial Projects in the Public Affairs office of a Southeastern school said she hires an assortment of freelancers to help with writing and designing publications and Web projects for the university. Projects ranged from articles for an alumni magazine to copy for ads and brochures, Web sites, etc. For articles, they generally pay about 50 cents a word. Not great, but as a way to build up a portfolio, it could work.

Formal Community Networks

One west coast institution, much to my delight, had a most interesting program: a network of writers that it farmed out to anyone in either the academic or local business communities who needed copywriting services. Projects might include internal communications, marketing, publications, Web content-design-creation, etc. Rates ranged from $25 to $130 per hour. Now, we're talking.

Interested writers would formally apply to become part of the network and provide a price list, either per project based on size, or based on an hourly rate. As my contact explained, *We want to provide competitive products to our clients. But we also seek to provide variety, which includes variety in pricing, experience in higher education, etc.*

Not surprisingly, they like to hire people with a proven track record (several rely heavily on referrals). One woman elaborated, *The people we use must consistently meet deadlines, produce good and clean copy, be careful about fact-checking, be receptive to revisions requested by their client and be great to work with as a team member.* Imagine that. Pretty much true for any commercial writing arena.

If you're going to contact universities, try poking around on their Web site first. Good target departments are: human resources, university relations, media relations, public relations, public affairs, communications (NOT the academic "communications" department), marketing and others. Drill down within those departments and find the directors, assistant directors, managers or similar titles.

All in all, academia is a reasonably promising market. Sure, most universities won't pay the highest rates, but they're usually competitive—and as a place to beef up the book, they can be great. For writers in smaller markets, where there are fewer large corporate entities and where cost of living is less, they can be an excellent direction.

The BIG Small-to-Medium Sized Business Segment

I had a prospect meeting recently with a successful graphic design firm looking to expand its copywriting resources. The designer I met with made an interesting comment about small-to-medium sized businesses: While he'd like to pursue them, the services he offered tended to be more than they really needed *or* could afford. I commented that they sounded like an ideal client profile for a two-person freelance writer/designer team.

Absolutely, he replied. While he might charge $15K to $20K (plus printing) for a brochure (given his market positioning and high overhead), the humble freelancers could likely deliver an appropriate product for roughly half the cost. I assert that his comments point to a large *and* largely ignored segment of the marketplace.

I've been discovering more and more companies in this sector—firms with 25 to 100 employees. They have a marketing budget, but with fewer employees (many of whom are already multi-tasking), they often lack the time or expertise to craft their own marketing materials. Even if they do have communications departments, it's usually one or two people—almost never enough to handle all the projects that need to get done. (See the case study in Appendix C, for an example of a ten-year old company with no printed marketing materials and a one-page Web site.)

THE UPSIDES

Smaller companies make up a substantial market segment and the work is oftentimes challenging and innovative (they can take creative risks that larger companies, with their big-'n-scary legal departments, cannot). At smaller firms, you're more likely to be viewed as an expert, your opinions valued, and your work regarded as an important team effort. And today's small-to-medium sized companies become the medium-to-large firms of tomorrow (often with your help!).

THE DOWNSIDES

While in a strictly relative sense small companies aren't as financially flush as a Fortune 100 firm, in my experience, they're usually just as solid and reliable as the big boys and typically pay even faster. Just do your due diligence, get your up-front deposits, etc. Smaller companies, by definition, have less work than a large firm would, though a medium-sized company can still keep a freelancer plenty busy with ongoing projects.

Often, smaller companies do their writing in-house, but usually only because they never knew there were other options. Meaning, you'll need to educate these folks about the field and the writing process, which also means they'll tend to follow your lead: If you say a one-third deposit is standard, they'll write you a check. Speaking of educating...

Don't Ask, DO Tell

Ask these folks if they have any writing jobs and they're likely to say *No*, either because they do it all in-house or because they haven't considered how communications materials could further enhance their marketing message and ongoing strategies—both within their organization and with their client/prospect base. Remember, in smaller firms, people may need to wear many hats and it's often a challenge keeping up with what they *know* they have to get done, without thinking up more projects to take on. And this is where a strategy-minded FLCW—with talented designer in tow—has the opportunity to become a marketing consultant, suggesting ways in which the client can improve profits, customer loyalty or in-house cohesion, simply by creating the appropriate marketing materials.

SUGGESTIVE SELLING

Brian Scott, founder and Webmaster of the great site **www.freelance writing.com**, wrote an in-depth article about tapping the smaller business segment for another fine site, **www.writefromhome.com**. While his suggestions also encompass *very* small businesses—a segment I usually see as more trouble than they're worth—the piece nonetheless had tons of great advice. One excerpt discussed Atlanta FLCW Paul Murray and his "suggestive selling" success in landing a veterinary clinic as a client:

> *Murray discovered that his local veterinary hospital lacked a regular newsletter because the owner didn't understand how his hospital could benefit from one. "It wasn't because the owner couldn't afford a copywriter or he had other print materials that substituted for a newsletter," says Murray, "it was because he was uneducated as to how a newsletter could positively contribute to his business."*
>
> *Murray's selling strategy was simple: He showed the owner how hiring him to write and produce a monthly newsletter would convert initial customers into repeat clients, bring in more referrals, sell more products such as flea control and sprays, and enhance the hospital's image.*
>
> *The bottom line, says Murray, is "the newsletter would boost the hospital's sales; that's what the owner really wanted to hear." Murray got the job.*

Check out the full article at:

www.writefromhome.com/marketingprarticles/128.htm

Then look around your own community. What other business scenarios could you build from this kind of thinking?

Your Partners in Profit

As a sidebar, your graphic design colleagues often cross paths with businesspeople who write their own copy (at least they're not trying to do their own design work, so maybe there's hope). As a designer discovers a client's homemade copy is lousy, he or she can then suggest going outside for copywriting services. This way, the designer can make the client look even better, and everyone wins. No designer relishes the thought of designing around garbage, and ending up with a sample he or she's reluctant to show!

And sure, much of the time, the folks who write copy in-house won't be interested in your services. But why not come up with a flyer offering a brief overview of what you do, a few *Why Hire a Professional Writer* benefits-driven selling points (an investment, not an expense; strategic copywriters offer fresh "outsider" perspectives on, and suggestions for your business; focus on the profit-generating activities you do best and hire out the rest; etc.), and perhaps a few juicy before-and-after examples of copy improved? Give a bunch of these fliers to the designers you work with regularly and then forget about it. Who knows? You might catch someone at just the right moment.

ALL THAT SAID...

IF you're in a major metro area with plenty of prospects and business is booming, then stick to the clients already accustomed to using copywriters, as opposed to trying to convince the others to begin outsourcing.

If, however, you find yourself in a smaller or tighter market, you might want to cast your net a little wider and be open to the idea of educating prospects at smaller-sized firms, many of which absolutely need to outsource to a good writer but just don't realize it yet. Regardless of the strength of the market, just keep in mind that most writers are ignoring this smaller-sized segment, which contains many industries that may never have occurred to you—read on!

Right Under Our Noses

At the university-sponsored writer's conference I mentioned earlier, all participants were provided with a list of possible writing clients, straight from Lucy V. Parker's great book, *How to Start a Home-Based Writing Business* (4th edition, published in 2003; the excerpt below is used here with her permission).

I loved it for the wonderful "thought-starter" it was. Yes, you'll see some of the usual suspects, but for the most part, it was chock-full of new prospect targets. Many had never occurred to me, yet there they were, right under my nose. Use it to fire up your own imagination and come up with even more ideas. Thanks, Lucy.

Sixty Potential Writing Clients

By Lucy V. Parker

1. Accountants, attorneys
2. Advertising agencies
3. Art galleries, public and private
4. Associations
5. Athletic teams, sports promoters
6. Book publishers
7. Churches, denominations, religious organizations
8. City guide publishers
9. Colleges, universities, private schools
10. Concert promoters
11. Conference planners
12. Consultants
13. Convention centers
14. Corporate human services departments
15. Corporate marketing departments
16. Corporate public relations/communications departments
17. Corporate purchasing departments
18. Design firms, architects
19. Direct-marketing firms, especially direct mail
20. Directory publishers
21. Engineering firms
22. Fitness centers
23. Fund-raising departments and consulting firms
24. Government departments—federal, state, county, township, city
25. Government-funded special agencies, such as water districts, school districts, and libraries
26. Greeting card and gift companies
27. Health clubs
28. Health insurance firms, health maintenance organizations (HMO)
29. Hospitals, medical centers
30. Hotels, resorts, casinos
31. Importers, exporters
32. Individuals, families
33. Labor organizations
34. Laboratories

35. Magazines/Newsletters—business and trade
36. Magazines/Newsletters—consumer, including single-sponsor publications
37. Magazines/Newsletters—employees, alumni, organizations
38. Marketing agencies
39. Medical professionals, including physicians, dentists, psychologists, chiropractors, nutritionists and others.
40. Museums, public and private
41. Newspapers—community and regional
42. Newspapers—business and trade
43. Performing arts centers, theaters, performing groups
44. Political parties and candidates
45. Private clubs—yachting, golf, etc.
46. Producers: industrial/educational/promotional films, video, broadcasts, CD-ROMs and DVDs
47. Public relations agencies
48. Research organizations
49. Restaurants
50. Resellers
51. Retail stores
52. Shopping centers, malls
53. Small businesses
54. Social service agencies
55. Software publishers
56. Theme parks, recreation centers
57. Transportation/shipping firms and agencies
58. Travel agencies
59. Web site developers
60. Wholesalers

In That Same Vein...

Atlanta FLCW Bobby Hickman (**www.blhickmaninc.com**) sent me these tidbits, which appeared in my March 2004 E-PUB (and are used here with his permission), regarding these four novel avenues he's pursued for business. It's all about being creative and keeping the radar up!

Four Business Roads Less Traveled
by Bobby Hickman

1. **Business Expos.** I get a lot of leads here—not so much from the visitors as from the other exhibitors. I get there early, set up my display and wander around to meet everyone else. People who take part in expos are usually start-ups, or small concerns trying to expand, and all are trying to get the word out on their products and services. I did a free expo at a local Staples and got newsletter work from a chiropractor along with a brochure job from a computer network provider. My Staples said most stores try to hold one expo per year. Contact your nearby Staples and ask to be notified if/when the next one happens.

2. **Business Seminars.** Attending Small Business Administration seminars can generate leads while improving your business skills. I attended two classes at the local college (Kennesaw State University in Georgia). Attendees are generally entrepreneurs preparing to go out on their own. I was hired by one guy to do a brochure and Web copy for his new contracting firm, and have promises of work this year from a new bakery and a coffee service when they launch.

3. **Pro Bono.** Leads To Profits. To build my portfolio, last year I volunteered to handle my local business association's newsletter. That led to several writing opportunities—all *pro bono*—and a seat on the board. But as my business grew, I had to curtail the free stuff. The board asked me how much I'd charge to keep doing the newsletter. I'm now being paid every month. (Also, the ex-president steered me to several other valuable contacts which could lead to future work.)

4. **Coaches/Mentors.** Business/career coaches and professional mentors—folks also trying to expand their businesses—are a good source of leads. I used a coach to help me develop a marketing strategy; she's sent me several new clients *and* become my client. I'm helping her with publicity and I'll be ghostwriting her book this year.

The moral is, you never know when or how your marketing will pay off. Even when it feels like you're not getting anywhere, you're probably accomplishing more than you realize. While my marketing coach and I are making progress targeting bigger jobs with insurance companies (my industry for 20 years), it's these little things I keep stumbling into that keep me going until the long-term plan starts to pay off later this year.

Easy to Overlook

Here's another right-in-front-of-us idea. A few weeks back, while waiting at the carwash, I picked up the Atlanta version of a home improvement magazine. Frankly, it was little more than a quarter-inch thick advertising vehicle for every home improvement-related company under the sun. Just a cursory glance revealed half a dozen ads with headlines and body copy that looked like an office manager had written them. Not to mention a bunch of companies without Web sites.

Given this cacophony of voices vying to be heard in the competitive din, it shouldn't be too hard to convince these folks of the importance of strong copy—as well as having a Web site to direct traffic to (given that most of their competition has one). And I have to believe there are plenty of other industry-specific ad circulars (er… "publications") like this. Be on the lookout.

And a Final Few More...

Melanie Rockett of Proof Positive (**www.proofpositive.com**) coaches writers and other freelancers to generate more clients and more jobs. In a two-part article on her site, she highlighted a couple of rarely considered avenues for finding work, excerpted below.

Upcoming Events Mean Increased Opportunities

Melanie discussed the 2010 Winter Olympics, to be held in her hometown of Vancouver. Even though it was seven years away, she painted the following picture:

> *The athletes' village must be designed and built. The event venues must be designed and constructed. Millions of dollars will be spent on planning an event that will have hundreds of thousands of visitors pouring into the city. Hundreds of new Olympic focused businesses will start up. This means tens of thousands of documents, illustrations and photographs. Hundreds of new Web sites. The work has already started.*

And, no doubt, so has the need for a flood of written materials.

No upcoming Olympic games? Tap into local, city and state events by contacting:

1. Chambers of Commerce

2. Convention bureaus

3. City, regional and state tourism boards

4. Local and national government Web sites and publications

5. Press announcement lists or Web sites

6. Event coordination companies that produce large events

There may be needs for plenty of event-driven brochures, pamphlets, press releases, Web sites and more. In addition, virtually all of these entities have business/marketing communications facets that are worth investigating.

News Articles Filled With Hints

An article about a company's newly hired PR or marketing director—a fresh face with fresh initiatives—might spell writing work if you make the contact. A story about a startup or expanding company might hint at a need for writing projects to support that growth. How about a story on a new hospital breaking ground? That could mean press releases, policies and procedures manuals and most importantly, a communications department with ongoing needs for brochures, ads, direct mail, Web sites, internal/external newsletters and magazines and much more.

Disasters Create Communication Needs

According to Melanie, hurricanes, fires, flood and explosions leave more than destruction in their wake—they can create plenty of writing projects of the honest, reputable and non-ambulance-chasing variety. She gives an example:

> Many years back, an oil processing plant I did occasional work for had a huge fire and explosion. As a freelance writer/producer/director I was asked to document the aftermath of the fire on video and in writing. Some of the information was used for insurance purposes. The company also used the information to develop special emergency methods, strategies and procedures in the form of videos and manuals. As a freelancer I got over a year of ongoing work out of this disaster. I believe I performed a valuable service in helping to prevent accidents like this from ever happening again.

Now, *that* should keep us filled up for a while. Toothpick, anyone?

●   ●   ●

But what about those of you who live in smaller markets? Are you out of luck? Hardly—just read on. (And all of you in big cities, I encourage you NOT to skip the next chapter—there's lots of great advice for *anyone*.)

Chapter 8

If I had to guess which question I've been asked most often since this whole wild ride began, it'd have to be various versions of: *I live in the middle of Nowheresville, Montana (population 18). Can I build a writing business work out here?*

Actually if you literally are in Nowheresville, Montana, no, you probably won't be able to make a go of it—if you're trying to draw only from local work. That said, there's a lot of middle ground between Nowheresville and New York or L.A. We're talking about a lot of medium-sized cities and regions holding onto *beaucoup* freelance work.

While I have no personal experience building a writing business in a small market or rural area, I *do* know people who have done just that—and who've been generous enough to share their experiences. And these folks just blow me away. They're sooo resourceful, creative and ingenious about digging up the work (they have to be!) Yes, there are advantages and disadvantages both to starting this business in a major metro and a smaller market. And while the advantages of the former and the disadvantages of the latter are obvious, the flip side of both may be less so.

The Differences

In a big market, you'll have far more competition than in a smaller burg, where you may be the only game in town. While chances are good most big-city prospects will know what a commercial freelancer does and how you operate, you may need to educate small-town prospects about the value of hiring you. Bigger markets command higher fees, but your cost of living will be dramatically lower in that small market. Big-market writers know it's all about marketing,

131

direct mail and showing up consistently. Their small-town counterparts have learned the value of networking and relationships.

Through conversations with folks working in smaller markets, I've gleaned the following golden tips and strategies. But know this: *The following ideas are applicable to ANY marketing campaign in ANY size market* (and the same goes for larger market strategies). It's just that they're especially crucial when building the business in a smaller market.

1. **Network.** Join the Chamber of Commerce and any other group that draws local businesspeople. Get involved, volunteer, be a presence, be generous. Seize opportunities to showcase your skills. People remember, and they talk.

2. **Build relationships.** While people everywhere are most likely to do business with those they know and like, this is especially true in a smaller market. View people as friends and neighbors first, possible sources of business second. Remember birthdays. Do small favors. Be that good neighbor. And yes, let people know what you do for a living.

3. **Educate.** Be sure the businesspeople around you know what's in it for them. Don't ask what they need—chances are, they might not perceive any needs. Instead, suggest projects. Show them before-and-after scenarios with other similar small businesses. Open their eyes. Let them picture it. Talk benefits (profits, enhanced reputation, life simplification), not features.

4. **Persist.** Small-town folk often take a while to accept new ideas and people—their mindsets are simply different from their urban counterparts. Stay in the game. Even if you're not getting work or even a response from a particular business, keep in contact (unless they tell you to get lost). Over time, many will come around. Project a positive, low-key attitude. Foster the impression (and mean it) that it doesn't matter to you whether or not they ever do business with you, that it's the relationship that matters.

5. **Stay aware.** Keep your radar up for opportunities, but not in an overbearing way. Keep abreast of business openings, expansions or ownership changes—then send off a note of congratulations or suggest ways your services can support sustained business growth.

6. **Barter.** Small businesses with lower budgets may be happy to trade for your services. Ideally you want paid work, but if a restaurant, travel agency or health club you'd likely patronize is willing to barter—and the terms work—go for it. *Note: Barter is typically based on the retail price of both products/services, not a discounted rate.*

7. **Branch out.** An obvious solution to the small-town dilemma is to prospect for work *anywhere* outside your area, even across the country. This can potentially offer the best of both worlds: You can live wherever you want, including places with much lower costs of living than a major metro (and where prevailing rates for writers would likely be far lower), yet given that you might be working with big city clients, you'd very likely be able to command big city rates.

As we discussed in Chapter Six, Steve Marshall's innovative and aggressive fax marketing campaign generated a ton of work for him, largely from two new clients in Ohio and North Carolina, who together, he figured, would account for roughly $50K in income the following year.

Then there's Tom Myer, whose massive cold-calling campaign I featured in the December 2002 issue of the E-PUB. Tom made close to 350 calls in a few weeks, calling companies in over 30 states and landing close to $35K worth of work—again, the bulk of it beyond his home base of Austin, Texas.

Michelle Zavala, a friend and colleague in Colorado Springs, has three main clients outside her home base—in Denver, Virginia and Atlanta (her anchor client). During a recent conversation, she was lamenting her lack of social life, given the 35 to 40 hours a week she was billing her Atlanta client (a mega computer firm), plus hours billed for the other two as well.

Incidentally, she picked up both her Atlanta and Denver clients through cold calling, and the Virginia client through a referral from another writer. Michelle notes, *Since she focuses on case studies* (Casey Hibbard; see Appendix A) *and I do creative/marketing copy, we frequently refer business to each other. Locally, I refer on tons of PR work and in turn, other referrals come to me.* Keep that in mind. Your fellow writers may be competitors but they're colleagues as well.

Remote prospecting could work for anyone. After all, why limit yourself to your own region, given the optimally wired world in which we live? Personally, I have always found enough work in my hometown of Atlanta to preclude the need for interstate marketing campaigns, but if it were something I wanted to do, I'd see no obstacles.

The remote scenario will always be a more likely scenario for two groups: specialists in a niche industry who are running out of prospects in their local market and those in smaller markets and rural areas where there simply isn't as much work, period.

Just know that the way you'd market yourself long-distance is the same as the way you'd market locally. Of course, it's imperative that you have a Web site—given that it's THE single most expeditious way to neutralize the distance factor. No question, digging for work cross-country will probably be more of a hassle, but given the Internet and cheap cell phone and pre-paid long distance plans, there's no reason it should be particularly daunting, or even more expensive.

From the Trenches

What follows next are accounts from four impressively intrepid women across North America (Ft. Myers, Florida; Sioux City, Iowa; Ontario, Canada; Loretto, Tennessee) who've built successful FLCW businesses in smaller markets. Again, I don't care what size your market area is, you will learn a lot from this crew.

Gulf Coast Gumption
Lisa Sparks—Ft. Myers, Florida; Integrity Writing
(www.integritywriting.com)

How did you get started in the business?
When I first started as a FLCW, I was working for one of the largest B2B newsletter publishers in the U.S.—*Progressive Business Publications* in Philly—and was covering four diverse industries: e-business, non-profit and a few others. I learned I could handle different clients and handle them well. After a move to Ft. Myers and a few unsuccessful attempts to land a job, I decided to do my own thing. Within three weeks, I had my first client.

Describe the challenges of working in southwest Florida.
Learning to market yourself, while crucial, is not that difficult. I attend free seminars in marketing education at Florida Gulf Coast University and trade ideas with other people—contractors or professors. I also get great advice from my clients…sometimes. When I first started out, they told me that the one big season here is "snowbird" season—December to April. After that, according to them, there's little work for ad agencies or contractors. But I still find work because I refuse to believe it.

It's attitude that separates you from the pack. Many of my competitors are more experienced or qualified, yet I keep plugging away. I have confidence when meeting with clients—and it shows. I come out, more often than not, with a signed letter of agreement and a deposit check. Confidence makes the difference.

What's your definition of "marketing"?

Marketing means being outgoing, organized and prepared. Have a plan on how you're going to present yourself to the world. Have a clean and neat work space and take the time to set up processes and systems, whether it's a client info packet and how it's put together, how you approach a meeting, how you phone-prospect or what your 15- to 30-second elevator speech is (the sound bite that passionately explains what you do and what sets you apart from the competition), etc. Get these things set and do them the same every time so they aren't so daunting anymore.

Network. That means thinking, *Even though these people might not bring me much business directly, by getting to know them, who knows who they might eventually refer me to?* Pound the pavement. And be patient—every action isn't necessarily going to lead to business, but it's all about momentum.

How do you overcome the challenges of working in a smaller market?

Be prepared to educate your clients about what copywriting is. Develop relationships with graphic designers so you can offer end-to-end solutions. Consider adding "project management" to your repertoire—nothing more than simply overseeing the project (a job that usually falls to the graphic designer). Break everything down into bite-size pieces and think like the client. Pretend you know nothing about copywriting and ask yourself, *How would I explain this process to someone who's never dealt with a copywriter before, someone who doesn't think they need one?* Focus not on selling your services but on solving their problems.

I always emphasize the time factor with clients. I find a lot of prospects that think they're great writers. I'll tell them, *Well, of course you don't necessarily need me from a writing standpoint* (often not true), *but given the demands of your core business, you just don't have enough time. As a smart businessperson, you need to focus on servicing your customers. I'll end up bringing in customers for you. How? Through my writing.* Just break it down into simple principles that every businessperson can understand.

Set up a small five-page Web site that clearly explains what you do, what you've done in the past, and what you can offer. Also, collect e-mail addresses through the site. A Web site costs little to maintain and will convey professionalism to clients. I get back my investment many times over.

What are the challenges you face as an African-American FLCW?

Most people I call on are not part of my racial group. It can present a challenge *and* an opportunity, because sometimes people want to give someone outside their own ethnic group a chance. People will often listen to me just because they want to hear what an African-American person will say! I think I'm the only AA-FLCW in Ft. Myers. That uniqueness often gets me in the door, but once there, the novelty quickly fades, and I have to almost *over*-deliver and be *more* professional than my white counterparts, in order to close the deal.

I always dress in a suit, even though it's burning hot outside, at least for the initial meeting. I have to spend more time gaining trust, but once I get it, I can forge a pretty solid business relationship. People need to see I'm not a welfare mother; I'm not going to take their money and run. But there are those who'll believe those stereotypes, regardless, in which case, it really doesn't matter how I present myself.

But most are practical businesspeople—the only color they see is green. Once you start talking about profitability and markets and how to get them there, it doesn't matter who you are. But to African-American writers, I'd say, be even more professional than you think is necessary to gain the client's trust and then keep those standards up, because old thinking can pop up anytime. It's not fair, but it's reality.

The monthly newsletter I started is an example of something that adds value and which few others are doing. It's all part of always trying to bring benefits to my clients—this is how you can be a better businessperson, etc.

Have you ever run across some real prejudice in a client?

Yes, in a strange, reverse kind of way. You go into a meeting to talk about business and all the prospect wants to talk about is civil rights and how they like black people and how they knew Martin Luther King and all that. They flip through your portfolio but they're not really looking and you want to say, *I'm here to perform a service for you, are you interested in that?* Sometimes I've walked into an office for a meeting, after having only spoken to the client by phone, and the people are shocked when they see me. And I'm thinking, gosh, must be the nice dress I'm wearing!

I always try to turn the conversation back to business and reinforce my professionalism at every opportunity. And I always follow up, though in many cases, the client never calls back (which happens to ALL of us, so get used to it).

There are times you'll hear a particular client has a huge copywriting budget, you meet with them and they try to get you to reduce your rates. It does make you wonder, but whether blatant or not, I'd advise AA-FLCWs to not blame it on race, even if it feels that way. It's a daily fight to choose humanity and not to choose hate.

I've been tested a lot on my rates but I don't give in. Some don't like it, but that's often just the attitude you need to avoid problem clients. When you have basic standards you won't compromise, people will either respect that or they won't. But you can always walk away from a situation and feel good about it.

That strategy is finally bearing fruit. Clients are coming from everywhere, mostly from my e-newsletter. Some have only met me at a few networking events, and all of a sudden they call out of the blue with a project for someone they know. And these people are more than willing to pay my rates.

What challenges do you face as a woman in the business?

I think it's easier to get a meeting out of a client if you're a woman. If it's a male client, they're sometimes just curious as to what you look like. It certainly doesn't mean you'll get work, but it can get you in the door. And a lot of my female clients will send work my way because they want to see me do well. They've actually come right out and said, *I'm glad you're doing this, and I want to give you business and I'm going to get my husband to do the same,* and so on.

How have you gone about landing most of your work?

In the beginning, it was definitely phone prospecting. I'd call people and introduce myself and deliver a short script that fairly closely followed the script in *TWFW*. I lead with the fact that I do newsletters, then mention other types of work, like brochures, business letters and press releases. Sometimes, I'll simply ask for the marketing manager and not deliver a formal script at all.

But frankly, it's more fun and interesting to meet people face-to-face. So I go to Chamber meetings and hand out cards—and I can land four or five meetings out of a function. And regardless of whether I get work from them right away, I have a name and e-mail address to add to my newsletter (with permission, of course). And through the Chamber, I've been able to write an article for their publication that goes out to 1500 businesses. The piece allowed me to promote my business and explain to this huge audience all the benefits of dealing with a copywriter.

So, presently, I get most of my business and referrals from relationships I've formed at networking functions. They work wonders. They *do* produce business. AND I still do plenty of phone prospecting.

My Web site, coupled with my e-newsletter, is creating tons of business for me. It gives me a professional, polished look that prompts visitors to believe in my business. It's a great way to look "big" even when it's just me.

What do you wish you'd known when you started out?

It doesn't take slick sales ability to be successful, mainly because it's insincere. You only have to resort to that if you don't believe in what you're selling. I believe in myself and my abilities, so I don't need gimmicks.

What advice would you give to someone in your position starting out?

Look at things from a client's perspective. Ask yourself, *If I were a client, how would I like to be approached by a copywriter?* Know your audience. Don't focus on *I have to make money to pay my rent.* Believe me, they can sense it and that will drive them away. Just be of service and the rest will fall into place.

A Heartland Harvest
Mary Guinane—Sioux City, Iowa; The Write Answer
(www.twacopywriting.com)

Because I live in a tri-state metro area with a population of only 100,000, I'm all about networking and relationships. Here, laying relationship groundwork is just as important as building a portfolio. A small market means that someone always knows someone.

Getting Started

Plan on higher start-up costs because your initial impression will have more ripple effects in a small community. Keep quality first rate, but quantity in moderation. For example, start out having your brochures printed professionally, then, after you've distributed them *en masse*, begin printing them as needed on your home printer. You may only end up paying for professional printing once, so do it when it counts.

If your marketing materials are done well, you'll attract clients who understand the value of quality. More than once, I've had someone refer to my brochure and say, *I want something like yours.* You can build your client list *and* get paid to build your portfolio by doing some of these simple projects for smaller businesses.

For my Web site, I purposely went to a well-known, award-winning designer with a reputation for quality. In addition to building me a good site, he's been happy to play the mentor role. I was able to ask him lots of questions about the bidding process, rates in our market and his expectations for a good copywriter. I've since done work for one client of his and been part of two other bids for large projects.

Building Momentum

Though they may not be billable hours, time spent at community events and networking functions weigh heavily in launching your business. In the beginning, view relationship building and networking as projects that need your time and attention.

I had a connection with the local Advertising Federation Club and helped them out with some freebie stuff. I was happily surprised when they paid for me to attend the District Conference and I'll be the Program Chair on the Ad Fed Board starting in several months. We only have about seven ad agencies in town, but they're all part of the club and I've been able to make good connections at each.

I also joined the Chamber and will be helping with a project the Ad Fed will be doing for them—a *Buy Local* promotion. Lots of small businesses are being affected by my work—a follow-up gold mine!

Next, I joined the Junior League—very strong here. It helps balance my solitary work place and provides more networking opportunities. In this town, if you're in the good graces of the right groups, good things happen. In Iowa, people are very loyal to the companies they deal with. In fact, the sales guys complain about how strong a factor that is when it's *not* in their favor.

Valuable Volunteering

Don't underestimate the power of one job done free, but done well, for a committee; it can be as effective as time spent on cold calls or mailings. Volunteering feels good, but never give away anything less than your best work. Other committee members will appreciate your hard work and who knows who they'll tell? They all have bosses and companies who just may need you, too.

Whatever you do, do it right. Your reputation will precede you by the time you're meeting with your third client in a small business community. Being professional at all times and producing solid work on deadline isn't just important, it's crucial.

Even if you don't get work from outside your market, build your knowledge base by expanding your information network. Use the Internet to learn what happens in other markets and find resources to help you think like your clients. Find message boards to exchange with copywriters in other markets—of course, *TWFW* message board is a prime example! (PB: See signup info in Appendix E). Use business and entrepreneur Web sites and newsletters to find out what the decision makers you're meeting with are discussing. The more you know about their problems, the easier it is to offer them solutions.

I've played the "new person" card as a copywriter, but made sure everyone I met knew that a high level of professionalism was my transferable skill. I may have changed industries, but simple things like thank-you letters and letting people know that you followed up on the lead they gave you are always appreciated. It's okay to be new, but never let that translate into naïve or unprofessional behavior. Consider tapping community leaders for their expertise, but don't expect them to do your legwork for you. Figure out how you can reimburse them for their time with your skills. Focus on building a relationship with that person, not coming out of the meeting with a paying job.

Becoming Established

Don't evaluate the success of your first years in business solely on income. Take time to evaluate each project for its potential for repeat or referral business. One small job for a well-connected client may have a higher long-term return than a one-time gig with a big price tag, but no other potential. Select new projects for the same reasons.

Think and act like a businessperson, not a freelancer, when you're with other business people. Those stuck in an office each day don't want to hear about you writing in your pajamas. They do enjoy an exchange on how your business is similar to theirs, so keep the conversation in their comfort zone. (You can always pity them later when you're doing the project you landed with them, in your PJs, of course.)

Be a source of solutions for clients, on committees and at networking functions. In a community where people cross paths often, you need to be part of the network. Find out the area of expertise of everyone you meet, then refer others to them. The more you know about what *other* people do well in your community, the more folks will think of *you* as a source of expertise and solutions.

Canada CAN-DO
Pam McInnes—Ariss, Ontario, Canada; A-ha! Writing Services
(www.ahawritingservices.com)

I registered *A-ha! Writing Services* on September 5, 2001 when I lived in Fergus, a small town of 7,000, located in Ontario (I'm presently in Ariss, even smaller). I'm currently fulfilling two yearly contracts, have a few repeat clients, and pick up new clients every now and again. I'm making decent money and still have time to work on my novel, children's book series, and business e-book.

Market Research

Even before choosing a name and registering the business, I conducted a phone survey directed at businesses in Fergus and the surrounding area (a 50km radius). I asked the businesspeople I talked to if—and how often—they used freelance writers, and if I could contact them once I had my business up and running. Most said, *Sure.*

My research never stops. After I have completed a project or a long-standing contract, I send out a Service Evaluation form to my clients. It asks if *A-ha!* communicated billing information and procedures effectively, if my work met their expectations and how they would rate the company on a scale of one to ten. It also has an area for client comments—with a clause stating I may use their comments in my promotional materials.

I also started using my monthly newsletter, *A-ha!'s Acumen* as a means of gauging my client's needs by turning it into a Q&A forum. The readers (small to medium-sized business owners or employees) ask questions about writing, customer service, technology and marketing and either myself or another expert will answer. This is a new venture, so its effectiveness has yet to be determined.

Networking/Volunteering

I joined the Centre Wellington Chamber of Commerce and was immediately ambushed by the staff. Their newsletter was in pretty rough shape and they desperately needed a professional to help them out. Given the strong potential for meeting local business owners, I decided to give them a hand. At the first meeting, they tried to promote me to newsletter editor, but I declined, citing unfamiliarity with the local businesses. I countered by offering to work as an associate editor. Agreed.

Six months later, the editor stepped down. Business was picking up and I told them I couldn't do any more volunteer work. They asked for a quote. I won a client for a year.

I also joined The Kiwanis. In addition to enjoying the meetings and volunteer events, I've gotten a few writing projects. Most members of service groups are serious business people with hearts of gold. If they can't use your services, they'll try to refer you to those who can.

I've participated in one trade show and would do it again in a second. It allowed me to invite prospects out to meet in neutral territory, while also networking with new prospects. I landed one project, which more than covered my show expenses.

Advertising and Marketing

Advertising didn't work for me. The general lack of understanding locally as to what a freelance writer does necessitated a more personal approach to getting my name out into larger nearby cities: Guelph, Kitchener-Waterloo, Cambridge, and even greater Toronto. I thought of standing on the highways wearing only an *A-ha! Writing Services* sign and a smile, but better judgment prevailed. I ended up doing something even more painful—I cold called. I still cold call.

My first cold calling campaign was three-part: an intro call explaining what I do and determining the prospect's current and future writing needs; a follow-up mailing with an info sheet and portfolio to interested businesses; and a final phone call to verify receipt of info, answer questions and invite that business to join my newsletter mailing list.

Summary

Trustworthiness and dependability are crucial in smaller towns. Once I've made a contact, I have to prove that I can provide what they need, when they need it. I contact them when I say I will. I communicate effectively by saying exactly what I mean. Once the client feels comfortable enough to hire me, it's imperative to maintain solid communication lines and to exceed all expectations.

Advice? Be flexible, use the technology available, and don't be afraid to branch out. In my case, it was important for me to realize that I couldn't make a living just from my small town. Perhaps it's the small-town experience, but I've found the Canadian market not as open to hiring freelancers as the U.S. market, and explaining about what I do is more difficult. Calling myself a *business writer* is best, though in my small town most businesses don't see the need to spend money on professionally written brochures, sales letters, newsletters and in many cases, even Web sites.

PB: Obviously, there's a difference between a town of 7,000 and a region of 100,000 or a city of even 50,000. No surprise that Pam quickly got that she needed to move beyond her small town and hunt in greener pastures.

Tennessee Tenacity
Karin Beuerlein—Loretto, Tennessee

I'm building my business in Loretto, Tennessee, in the middle of nowhere (Nashville is the closest city at one and a half hours away). It's going well. I have a major client that provides steady income now, one that came about through—you guessed it—cold-calling! I'd called the state's Department of Agriculture (in the course of phoning several government agencies) and the public relations rep had said the agency had no budget at all for writing projects. But he also said he thought the Farm Bureau was starting some kind of magazine, and asked if I would be interested in a project like that.

After considering *not* following up on the lead because it sounded too vague, I sent my info to the editor-in-chief, who forwarded it on to the managing editor, who in turn contacted me months later and was amazed that he'd found someone who could crank out two or three articles per issue right in his backyard (me!) Now I write for this publication regularly and am starting to take on some editorial duties as well. I'm also starting to get jobs by word of mouth even though I'm out here in the sticks. So the system can work for rural dwellers!

Get some great brochures and business cards printed up and fling them to the winds. The work will come from the darndest places.

I seem to remember reading in *TWFW* that sending out postcards or doing a fresh cold-calling session will work weird magic. I recently started a new round of cold calling, and on that very day two people I hadn't heard from in ages called me with work (it had nothing to do with the people I was actually calling). I didn't even do my usual naked writer's booty-shaking rain dance this time! It was amazing.

PB: Karin's living in Knoxville now and provided me this update/warning when I checked in not long ago.

After several years of experience, my advice is this: Never stop your marketing efforts to new businesses and regular contacts with your old clients. I made this mistake in 2002 as I was planning my wedding— I was impossibly busy and thought it would be okay to coast on the steady work I was receiving. My two biggest clients folded and I was stuck building everything from scratch again. Not a pretty situation to be in. But I'm still plugging away. After tasting the freelance life, it would be a grievous disappointment to return to the grind of working for someone else. I know that marketing myself will always eventually pay off.

●   ●   ●

Impressive bunch, eh? They've got to work extra hard to make it. Hopefully, you big-city folks appreciate all the advantages you have. Okay, now we head to another common scenario—the part-time business-builder. Right this way, folks…

Chapter 9

The Question:

> I've read your book and would love to carve out my own little island of freedom, flexibility and financial security as a writer. But presently, I'm in a full-time job, working nine-to-five, five days a week. What's the answer?

Having built the business full-time from Day One, I'll defer in a moment to those who built their businesses on a part-time basis. Conversations with these folks have generated some thoughts and strategies. Any way you cut it, it'll be tougher building your business this way than full-time—but if it's your only option, here are some ways to approach it.

1. **Get Real.** Given the embryonic state of cloning technology, you're simply going to have to face the reality that you can only be in one place at a time. If you're locked into a job during the same working hours as your prospects, it means you're not available to take business calls, and that's a problem. At the very least, make it clear to your market that you are doing it part-time and are best reached by e-mail or after-hours. Speaking of which…

2. **Get Honest.** Be honest with people about your current level of involvement in the business (even if it turns some clients off, and it will). If you act like you're full-time and then can't be reached or have to start sneaking around your real job, that's not going to serve anyone. Your full-time employer deserves a full-time effort. And your part-time clients also deserve the best.

145

3. **Get a Web Site.** This is absolutely the next best thing to being in two places at once. Make sure you have a decent number of good samples loaded up. It's hard enough building a business part-time without a weak portfolio working against you as well.

4. **Get Smart.** If you can't make calls during the day, what's left? The obvious second choice is e-mail prospecting. Build a list of target prospects through your city's *Book of Lists* (**www.amcity.com**), Chamber of Commerce listings or other business directories that provide e-mail addresses—obviously not possible with the Yellow Pages. If you want to target a particular industry, compile a list of companies, visit their sites and contact key decision-makers that way.

5. **Get Personal.** As discussed, the catchword with e-mail prospecting is *personalize*. Don't even think about spamming—it's just not worth it in terms of poor returns and the potential damage to your reputation. Send brief, personal notes to specific people, providing a link to your site (and samples), and again, be honest about your time limitations. You might even use the strategy I suggest in the cold-calling chapter: calling after hours, knowing you'll get voice mail, and then leaving a brief message stating who you are and that you'll be sending a follow-up e-mail with a Web link. And after hours, who knows who might answer the phone? It's often decision-makers—and overworked ones at that.

6. **Get Flexible.** Obviously, the ideal short-term solution is to craft some flexibility into your schedule, to perhaps have one or two days off a week or be able to come in earlier and/or leave later to free up part of a day. If you're not willing to make some fundamental changes, maybe the desire isn't there. As the old expression reminds, *To get something you've never had, you need to do something you've never done.*

7. **Get Out There.** Try to attend after-hours networking functions where prospects might be hanging out. Chat up these folks, give them your card and tell them what you're up to (AND explain your time limitations.) I'd wager that, presented the right way, you'll impress some people with your enterprise and ambition.

8. **Get Outta Town.** Plenty of FLCWs pursue clients outside their main geographic area. If you're an east- or west-coaster, pursuing clients on the opposite coast can give you a three-hour working window before or after your normal workday to conduct business. So, keep that option open, especially if you've decided to pursue an industry with limited local prospects.

My First Test Case

Jim Meadows from Kansas City, Missouri (**www.jimfreelance.com**) is both very talented as well as an extraordinary time manager. He contacted me in August 2000, right about the time *TWFW* came out. He was launching his freelance business and had a fairly impressive resume—23 years of varied business experience. At the time, Jim was employed full-time with AT&T and was also an evangelist, a college instructor and a published author in the ministerial field (*and* a husband and father). He planned to leverage that multi-faceted background to help him launch his writing business.

Jim's goal was to generate a $2000 to $3000 in monthly income within four months. Given his experience, I thought it was quite doable. He kicked off his cold calling campaign in early September 2000, and by January 2001 things were popping. In March 2001 (the six-month mark), he e-mailed me, letting me know he'd finally hit his income goal. He wrote:

> What you have predicted is coming to pass. I've met my initial goal and I can see it getting even better moving forward.
>
> This week I finished a press release for a medical center for $300. I'm working on a mailer for a seminar presenter for $750. Next week I am doing a marketing letter for a local trainer for $225. I just finished a quarterly newsletter for a professional association for $400. And, I just got a check today for $938 from an advertising agency for some ad copy. Best of all, one of my contacts in the marketing field called me today to subcontract a booklet-writing job for $2,500. There are ongoing projects in the pipeline and lots developing on the horizon. As you predicted, I am exceeding my original goal. And to think that I have accomplished all this with just a very **part-time** effort (emphasis added).

Huh? Very *part-time?!* Somehow, I'd missed that *he'd continued to work full-time at AT&T.* Wow. Turns out, he had a fairly flexible schedule with them, which allowed him to come into work late some days and leave earlier on others. He was spending his freed-up morning hours doing his cold calling and his night hours for writing.

Right about that time, I'd started a seminar swing and decided to put Jim on the agenda as a call-in testimonial. He'd tell his story over speakerphone to the attendees (minus the part-time detail), who'd then do a little Q&A.

Even as a full-timer, it would have been a darn good story. Once the questions tapered off, I asked him—*So Jim, what you do for living?* Puzzled faces all around, as Jim replied, *I work full-time at AT&T in management. I've been building this business on a strictly part-time basis.* I chuckled as jaws dropped all around. Suddenly, this opportunity went from doable to *amazingly* doable.

So how did this great story unfold? Well, here are selected e-mail snippets from the preceding six months, outlining his strategy, approach and results.

September 27, 2000 (one-month mark)

A quick update on my progress. In the last three weeks I have made about 300 cold calls. Out of those, I have a database of about 110 people interested enough to have me send them materials. Of those 110, I have already had or will have about seven face-to-face meetings. And out of those meetings so far, I have several clients who may have immediately pending projects. So far, I've had only one negative reaction to my $75 rate, with mostly no reactions or a response of, That's about the going rate. *My significant working experience has impressed prospective clients. I've gathered about 20 samples from my past lives and it seems to be enough.*

December 21, 2000 (three-and-a-half-month mark)

I've made about a thousand cold calls over the last couple months. From that I have a database of about 200 prospects. I've had a couple dozen personal meetings and snagged a handful of small jobs.

I have called every listing in the Kansas City Yellow Pages for advertising, public relations, marketing, events, writers' agents, and graphic designers. I have called every company, public and private, listed in our local Book of Lists. I have just started some of the smaller area lists such as Chamber of Commerce members, etc. I also did a fresh mailing to each of the clients and prospects on my 200-member client and prospect database, reminding them of my availability. I have also recently set up my own Web site to enhance my image and marketing efforts.

Incidentally, here's the 30-second pitch I use when I get voice mail:

Hello, [Name]. My name is Jim Meadows. I am a freelance writer in the Kansas City area, checking in with your office to see if you need any project help. I do have a 23-year career that has had me involved in all aspects of the writing and editing process, producing material for AT&T, Eastman Kodak, and other corporate and private clients. If I can help with a project, whether large or small, give me a call, XXX-XXX-XXXX. Feel free to visit my Web site at www.jimfreelance.com. Thanks for your time, [Name], and you have a great day!

VOICE MAIL PITCH

It seems to be effective, and I do get a lot of callbacks.

December 27, 2000 (one week later)

I spent some time today following up by phone with the first 50 contacts of my hot-prospect database. Most were gone for the holidays but I delivered a renewed sales pitch by voice mail. The ones I did talk to were quite glad to hear from me and most mentioned that they anticipated possible projects moving into the New Year. I won't complain if it all hits at once, as you predict it might!

January 18, 2001 (four-month mark)

Interestingly enough, much of what you said is coming to pass. Shortly after the first of the year, I started getting lots of activity: a direct mail project for an ad agency, a technical proofreading job and a marketing proposal for a seminar company. And the phone continues to ring. Of course, I'm not going to let up on the aggressive marketing and prospecting work so necessary to keep it all going.

And then in March 2001, at the six-month mark, Jim contacted me with the e-mail you read previously. In November 2001, I got this update. Note his reflections regarding his experience marketing his services on a national level:

Things are going very, very well. I've got about $10,000 in receivables, more work coming from existing clients, and new clients in the wings. Still all on a part-time basis.

The vast majority of prospects I contact in remote markets do not seem put off in the least that we're several hundred or thousand miles apart. Their attitude seems to be that we live in an electronic age and distance has lost a lot of its meaning for these situations.

*I've decided to continue to let AT&T give me my base salary
and benefits for a while. As I see the writing income get
progressively more lucrative, I believe I'll cut the apron strings.*

*My one thousand cold calls have resulted in a database of
about 200 very hot prospects and a steady stream of calls
requesting my services, plus referrals that just seem to
come out of the blue!*

Reflections

I caught up with Jim recently and asked him to share his thoughts, both on
doing this business part-time and general business-building advice. Some
we've heard before but repetition isn't a bad thing.

1. Do some *pro bono* work to build a portfolio.

2. Stick to your guns on fees. There are plenty of people out there who
   will pay you well. I stuck to my $75 hourly rate, and while I've lost
   some potential clients over it, once they walked, it just opened my
   calendar for the more serious ones.

3. In your research and marketing, try to find companies with key
   contacts on-site around the clock. There may very well be prospects
   that would appreciate a freelancer being available at odd hours.

4. Be absolutely certain that the phone number you give out as a
   writer has a good messaging capability. Several times while at
   AT&T, I remotely checked my voice-mail at my home office, and
   was able to catch up quickly with a client or prospect. Or perhaps
   just provide your cell phone number on your outgoing voice-mail,
   if that works for your circumstances (*PB Note: OR just forward your
   VM number to your cell, as I do*).

5. Create a Web site that can "duplicate" you while helping you avoid
   the extra work of copying samples, assembling packages, mailing
   costs, lengthy follow-up times, etc. Targeted (i.e., NON-spam)
   e-mail prospecting—definitely advisable if you're building the
   business after-hours—is more productive if you can offer
   instantaneous access to your work at the click of a mouse.

6. Capitalize on whatever flexibility you have to shift hours or free
   up some weekday time, and then milk it for all it's worth. Consider
   cutting back to part-time on your day job. If you're stuck in a
   full-time job with little wiggle room, plan on building your client
   base over several years rather than a few months.

7. Consider teaming up with a family member or associate, and have that person handle cold calling and meeting coordination during the day. It might even impress some prospects (*I'm his publicist* or *I'm her client coordinator.*)

8. Believe that the system really does work. Yes, I had more experience than many first-timers building a writing business, but, upon reflection, I followed the blueprint laid out in *TWFW* closely and that's what brought me success.

9. Cold calling and marketing are all-important. Get on the phone and run through the lists, no matter how unproductive it may feel at times. Some of my best clients have been from lists I initially looked at and thought, *I'm not going to pick up anyone here!* But I went ahead anyway—and it paid off, big time.

10. Leverage every resource, contact, and life experience you have. Realistically assess your past and identify the key qualities that will sell you to prospective clients. Sure, you won't catch every kind of fish with the same bait, but you will catch the ones who find you most attractive to them.

11. You can't harvest what you haven't planted. Constantly keep marketing. Every *No* gets you that much closer to a *Yes*. The law of averages is vividly real. You simply must make X number of contacts to achieve Y number of paying clients. Even when you start getting busy with work, spend at least a few hours each week doing the marketing—whether cold calling, mailings, door-to-door, whatever. Today's marketing is what plants the seeds for tomorrow's business.

12. Continually research and network. I am constantly scanning the daily newspaper, business journals, radio and television, etc. to capture leads (company start-ups, new marketing/creative directors, etc.). Take advantage of business luncheons and groups to spread your name around and grow your network.

13. Strive to make an excellent impression on every contact. Everything you do and say must communicate professional reliability. If anything about your presentation communicates lack of quality, why should someone hire you? If you're uncertain about any aspect of that presentation, bounce it off a trusted business professional. And hand-in-hand with that, maintain the highest ethical and professional standard in every aspect of your business—it will serve you well.

From Journalist To FLCW, Gradually

In May 2002, I got an e-mail from former high-tech magazine writer Chris Taylor (**www.keywordwriting.com**) of Wrightwood, California that shared the highlights of her new life as a FLCW. A few lines caught my eye:

> *In my first four months, I painlessly grossed $2500 a month from part-time freelancing. I've cut back to part-time at my magazine and am looking forward to making the jump to full-time freelancing next year. I'm undisciplined and don't like to work hard, but I know my stuff and write fast and well—a perfect combination for a relaxed freelance career.*

On the basis of that, I asked if she'd be willing to let me tell her story here. She agreed.

In 2000, the 15-year IT veteran was offered a job as an editor for a high-tech publication, despite having zero journalistic experience. (Lesson: Credentials don't always matter; in this case, the pub was in a jam and willing to take a chance.) While she thrived at it for several years, the long commute, combined with the stresses of single parenthood and the high-tech crash finally nudged her to begin exploring other home-based writing avenues. She came across *TWFW* and the light bulb went on.

Chris decided to merge into her new direction gradually, scaling back her full-time position one day a week at a time until she'd made the transition completely. Her juicy story of creating a life on her terms will resonate with several groups of FLCWs: at-home-moms (single or married) looking to launch their own writing biz, journalists switching to copywriting, and anyone else who finds themselves juggling several lives.

• • •

Interview: Chris Taylor

What gave you the confidence to pursue this?

I'd just spent the last year and a half interviewing marketing directors and product managers for the magazine, and so was well set up to network. Luckily I had a good reputation with them and their PR reps, both because I knew my field (high-end computer data storage), and I was easy to work with. My PR contacts have been invaluable for landing nearly all my writing jobs. Bottom line, I've done zero cold calling.

What types of projects did you discuss doing for them?

I had to be very careful when I talked to them about freelancing since I was still employed as an editor for the magazine. I had to avoid conflicts of interest by refusing to ghostwrite any articles that would be submitted to my own publication. I could not appear to be selling the decision-making power of my editorial position for freelancing money. However, if the article was slated for another publication, I cheerfully took it on. I also wanted to do white papers, which are quite similar to trade journal articles. From there I figured I could branch out to press kits and perhaps direct mail. But until I quit the magazine completely, I had to be careful with my prospecting.

How easy was it to land the work?

I'm very surprised at how quickly and easily it happened. When I started networking in late 2001, largely with my PR contacts, I was prepared for the long haul. But even with minimal marketing, the frequency of assignments and the money have been great. Once I went full-time with freelancing, I felt more comfortable contacting the hordes of people on my networking list.

What sort of projects did you end up doing and what were your rates?

I charge either by the project (like press kits or sales training manuals) or by the word (white papers and articles). For my first press kit I charged only $60 per hour, but the $1 per word projects that are my bread and butter net me $90 to $100 an hour because I'm a fast writer and know my subject. The $1 per word charge still works for me now that I'm full-time, and I base other projects at $100 an hour.

How has commercial freelancing compared to writing magazine articles?

Many high-tech trade journals have no freelance budget and don't pay at all, because vendors and analysts, eager for the exposure, fall over each other to contribute articles for free. So, I never believed I could make a living that way. However, I'm making a very good income ghostwriting magazine articles for corporate clients. These folks aren't looking to make money from article placement; they're trying to boost their exposure and credibility in order to land clients. If a client thinks an $80K account might result from placing an article, then paying me $1 per word for the 1600-word article that may help close that sale is nothing.

How did you juggle two jobs, parenthood and everything else?

I cut back my staff job to part-time and I made sure I spent lots of time with my son, but as I got busier and busier and *didn't* drop my other commitments, I ended up with the world's worst anxiety attack! Once I got a clean bill of health, I wised up, cleared the decks, and life is good again.

What skills do you feel you possess that made it easier to pull this off?

I'm knowledgeable about a highly technical and in-demand subject, I was always polite to PR reps, which meant they were happy to help me when I needed to network, and I research, organize and write efficiently and well.

Do you think writers need to value themselves more?

No question. I used to belong to a newsgroup where their most successful freelancer shared that he worked 60 hours a week and earned $50,000 a year. The other freelancers were awed at this much money, but I was appalled. If I'm going to earn $50K, it won't be for 60 hours a week—maybe 30, but not 60!

What lessons can you share with others in similar situations?

For starters, *write what you know*. Approach clients in a field you are already familiar with. Take it slowly. Starting part-time allows you to gradually build up your business and financial reserves while deciding if it's a fit. Cut out extraneous activities and take care of yourself. This career is perfect for a single mom who doesn't like to travel. I've done all of my business long distance because my clients and their agencies are scattered all over the country and don't expect to meet me face-to-face.

To journalists, I would say this—for heaven's sake, be kind to PR people! Many journalists nurse some kind of automatic grudge against PR reps, but you will need those reps to open doors for you to the corporate clients. Even if you plan on going directly after corporate clients, many will want to work through their agencies—and if a journalist has been a jerk to that agency… well, you get the picture.

Brit in Cyprus Plans Jailbreak

Russell Sleaper, a transplanted Englishman, lives in Nicosia, the capital of Cyprus, a Greek-speaking island nation and offshore center, ideally located between the Middle East and Europe. As a result, it has attracted many international businesses. He sent me this great e-mail some months back, describing his part-time progress in moving toward self-employment.

> *Middle of 2003: Sitting where I am now, doing what I'm doing now. www.wellfedwriter.com was on screen. I had a few clients, but certainly not enough to sustain myself. I bought your book, subscribed to the e-newsletter and set some goals to make my work life far more rewarding.*

January 2004: www.wellfedwriter.com is on screen again, but this time it's sharing the space with **www.thewritetrack.biz**. *I now count as clients a multinational corporation, a PR firm and a few small companies I've connected with through my designer, printer and a few business consultants. Things look bright. While I still have a demanding full-time job, I see an exit on the horizon.*

Russell shared a few smart strategies he's used to get where he is now.

1. **Use your full-time job to build your portfolio.** Specific suggestions:

   - Rewrite your company's ads or come up with new marketing headlines or tags for both your company and its competitors.

   - If you're responsible for any writing projects in your current position, create a version for your portfolio and annotate it to show clients the logic behind the structure and text.

   - Practice researching and writing commercial text about what you do. If you're a salesman, write fact sheets and press releases about each of your (and your competitor's) products. If you work in a candy store, write a brochure, ad and press release about a new Hershey bar. It will help you do your job better—I guarantee it.

2. **Use your full-time job to sell yourself.** The skills you use every day will land you freelance work. Listen to your potential client's needs and ask probing questions that reveal the full scope of the project at hand and perhaps uncover needs for the skills you have. For example, my job requires proficiency at desktop publishing, structuring large bodies of information, and managing projects and people. Had I not mentioned these peripheral skills while pitching for work, I'd have missed out on jobs—jobs which led to even more jobs.

Russell advises working sensible hours so you can retain your enthusiasm for both jobs while making the transition:

> *I cut my 12- to 14-hour workdays to a standard nine-to-six day and set aside two hours every weeknight and one weekend day for my freelance business. Soon I might have to put in a big spurt to get the extra freelance work I need to make that final break, but that's okay. When I quit my full-time job, I'll know I leave it in a better state than I found it in.*

An editorial aside about Russell's approach: I firmly believe that if you have a worthwhile dream you're pursuing, at some point, you will almost certainly have to lead an unbalanced life—at least in the short-term—to make it a reality. If you're unwilling to get uncomfortable and work some serious overtime for a while, it probably won't happen. That said, I know I can't do that for extended periods of time without going crazy—but I also know it's easier to hang in there when I'm building something of my very own, not just working insane hours to build someone else's fortune.

●   ●   ●

So, it *can* be done part-time, even if you can't (or don't want to) go cold turkey. There's lots of good strategies for making it happen. And speaking of strategies, a crucial one to move your business forward is networking—the Art of the Schmooze. Let's go work the room…

Chapter 10

The conversation started over the onion dip. I was at a party, chatting with the fiancé of a friend of mine as we scooped and munched. Inevitably the subject of work came up: He was the owner of a small but growing commercial and residential security system provider—and when he found out what I did, he chuckled and said, *Really. Hmmm. I've been working on a brochure for my company and not making much headway.*

We swapped cards and when it was all said and done, I'd completed $2,500 worth of brochure work for him and we're now talking about his Web site. All from a social contact.

Fast-forward a few months. I get a call from a friend who works for a graphic design firm. Why I never contacted her for work before is beyond me. And her first question revealed how sorry a job I'd done of letting her—and probably others—know exactly what I did for a living: *Do you do anything besides technical writing?* she asked. Huh? How about anything BUT technical writing? Bottom line, I was hired to rework huge chunks of a big (household name) client's Web site. Another $2,500.

Hidden Connections

I'd wager that 80 percent of everyone you know works for some company. Every one of them has a need—IF they want to stay competitive—to be constantly refining, improving, enhancing, growing and building on their body of written communications, as it appears in a variety of collateral materials (internal, external, print and Web-based).

Have you tapped your social network? No? As we discussed earlier, it's because you don't want to hit up your friends for work, right? Let me ask you this: If you were approached by a friend you knew was good at what he or she did, making a gentle inquiry as to possible business opportunities with your firm, what would you do? I'm guessing you'd want to help him or her out if you could. And I'm further guessing that your friends feel the same way. If you prefer warm calls to cold ones (who doesn't?), don't overlook the potential goldmine in your address book.

A few caveats on this "friend-ly" approach to prospecting. Be subtle. Remember, you should get the work *not* because you're someone's friend, but because you're competent and reliable. If you're new to the business and unproven in your friends' eyes, ask if they'd be comfortable steering you to the right person or department *and* to be honest with you if they're not.

By authentically giving them all the space in the world to say *No*, you increase the chance that they'll say *Yes*, and more importantly, preserve the friendship, regardless of their decision. If you have a Web site, invite them to check it out to boost their confidence in you. Remember, their butt's on the line if you're hired and it doesn't go well.

Be Cool

If you find yourself in a social setting—party, meeting, networking function—and you sense an opportunity, there are ways to seize the moment without being too pushy. Just introduce yourself, swap cards, get the okay to give the person a call and do just that within a few days at the most. If it is a purely social function, make a point of saying, lightheartedly, *I promise, I'm not trying to turn this party into a business meeting, but I couldn't help but overhear...* and then continue with your story (see the discussion of elevator speeches a few paragraphs ahead).

It all starts with the right mindset, one of being open to opportunities, wherever they may be. That means not compartmentalizing your life, not saying to yourself, *This is where I* work *or* socialize *or* work out, *but not where I might find business.* You never know where the next good lead will come from. And don't just react—be proactive. Think of the communities and associations you belong to—ones that include people who already know and are comfortable with you—and contact them. One reader used her university alumni directory to let her fellow classmates in the business world know what their old pal was up to. Why not? Here's a community of which she's a part and one that would be much more receptive to her then a cold contact might.

Serendipity

Anne Melfi, of Atlanta, talks about discussing the economy with an ad executive over cheese and crackers at a political get-together. When they exchanged cards, the woman noticed Anne was a writer and declared her need for marketing materials for her sideline business, a catering company. Later that month, Anne swapped contact info with a woman she met in a doctor's waiting room, gaining a paying project from "a friend of a friend of a friend of a friend."

Mary Cvetan of Pittsburgh found that even volunteer work unrelated to her writing business pays—literally:

> For the past 11 years, I've volunteered at a crisis/suicide hotline. One day, just two months into my freelance business, I was asked to evaluate some freshly trained new volunteers—a four-hour job. I grumbled but agreed and was paired with a woman named Gail with whom I had a great time chatting.
>
> A few weeks later, I saw Gail at the annual volunteer dinner and she invited me to sit with her and her husband, Tony, who asked me what I did for a living. I told him and after a few moments of silence, he said, 'I have a name for you.'
>
> Turns out Tony was the former big-wig of marketing at a huge local company. The following day, I called his former employee, who invited me in and gave me a very substantial project—one that I continue to show on sales calls today. Everyone knows the company and the piece gives me major credibility.

Utah-based FLCW Chad Nielsen underscores the power of networking to lead to both paying jobs and valuable barter:

> I've obtained two accounts from the guys I play pick-up basketball with. One's a real estate developer who's going to need PR support for at least nine months—the duration of his contract to run a 1200-member homeowner association. The other is a dentist involved with some cutting-edge technology who needs help getting the word out. I have a family of four so there will be no exchange of cash, but it's a great gig nonetheless. Make sure everybody knows who you are and what you do. Yes, even your friends!

In early 2003, Michele Ryan of Atlanta, during a conversation over margaritas and Mexican food with some of her neighbors, mentioned her new commercial writing career. A year later, she explains:

> I received a call from one of the lunch bunch who works for a local county Chamber. Several staff cutbacks, including their marketing communications person, left them with a daunting workload. My friend remembered our conversation and recommended my services. Her proposal for a steady five to seven hours a week at a healthy hourly rate was quickly and eagerly accepted.

Elevator Speeches & Verbal Taglines

Then there's the networking function. And yes, for many, the idea of striding up to total strangers, introducing yourself and discussing what you do is a positively terrifying thought. Fine. You're not doomed to failure if you don't hit all these functions (I didn't) but getting more comfortable with the process will certainly accelerate the business-building process.

At any gathering where you're making contacts—whether expected or not—a good 15-second (or less) "elevator speech" can come in very handy. For those of you unfamiliar with an elevator speech, it's a memorized—but naturally delivered—script, briefly describing what you do, and short enough to, theoretically, be delivered during the course of an elevator ride with a prospect. You might want to come up with a shorter version of your elevator speech, what might be called a "verbal tagline" for those purely social functions—a short, sweet and pithy one-line description of what you do. Here are some good elevator speeches and verbal taglines from a few business folks:

I help my clients develop clear and consistent business images to ensure their companies are perceived as they want to be in the marketplace so they can attract their ideal clients.

I help companies become more profitable by helping them craft clear, concise and effective sales and marketing messages in brochures, ads, newsletters, direct mail campaigns, Web sites or any other information-delivery vehicle.

I help my clients enhance their images and increase their sales through creative copywriting services.

I help businesses communicate powerfully and effectively through a variety of media, including brochures, ads, newsletters, and Web content. I'm also a published writer and I contribute articles on a variety of subjects to trade and consumer publications.

I'm an idiot who can't even tell you what I do very well, much less how I can solve your problem. That's because my elevator speech, though on my to-do list, has not been done. It's also because I try to be all things to all people, which isn't a great business model. But hey, what a writer I am! Call me. Third floor.

A little levity there…. But seriously, note that in all the examples—except the last one—it's not just about reading off a list of the things you do. Remember your audience. People don't really care about what you can do. They only care about what you can do for *them*. Features and benefits again. Instead of, *I write marketing brochures, ad copy and newsletters* (that's about YOU—features), try, *I help companies communicate more effectively in their marketing materials* (that's about THEM—benefits).

And at some point, with an eye toward focusing even more, you may want to take some time to figure the specific talents and gifts you bring to the market. Maybe your specialty is converting complex language into simple, accessible copy. Perhaps you're a master of creating slogans or taglines. Or a maestro of compelling direct mail campaigns. Or THE "go-to" person for effective marketing copy for the XXX industry. Over time, you'll figure out what you enjoy doing most and will naturally want to move your business in that direction. Make sure the world knows where you want to go—starting with an elevator speech.

For those of you groaning, rolling your eyes and thinking about how you've become an obnoxious salesperson, complete with a pitch and everything, let me make an observation: Chances are excellent you already have an elevator speech created for your current or former role in life; you just didn't think of it that way. But this is different, isn't it? And trickier, no? Let's probe a bit deeper here for a moment because I think it begins to get at one of the big fears of FLCWs starting out.

This Time, It's Personal

Your present (or former) elevator speech, in all likelihood, allows you to merge your personal identity with that of your employer. It's one thing to say, *I'm in software sales for IBM*, or *I'm a reporter for the Detroit Free Press*, or *I'm an English professor at the University of North Carolina*, or *I'm an attorney with Dewey, Scroom & Howe*. In those cases, you're standing behind the paternal pant legs of a larger entity. Now, you're facing the world standing behind nothing other than your own abilities. Gee, maybe it's nothing more than a garden-variety identity crisis...

Before (or presently), you linked more of your identity than you'd probably care to admit to something *outside* of you. Now, it's just you. I personally find the idea terribly liberating and empowering, but in the short run it's like we're five and we've just taken the training wheels off the bike. We're going to wobble a bit, but that's to be expected. And an elevator speech is a good way to steady our nerves and start the process of growing into this new identity of ours.

Your Chamber Awaits...

In case you nodded off during the numerous previous references, join your local Chamber of Commerce and go to the networking functions— lunches, happy hours, monthly "grip 'n grins," etc. Many even offer members the chance to get up in front of the meetings and give a little speech on what you do. At the very least, it's a regular opportunity to get face-to-face with your market—the key to landing business.

Chambers differ vastly in make up, potential and membership fees. In larger cities count on paying at least $300 to join at the lowest level, which, realistically, is all a one-person shop needs. Sounds pricey but even one job pays for it. Like any networking opportunity, it's all in what you make it. Show up, get involved, look for opportunities to raise your visibility—whether it's speaking, contributing articles to a newsletter, volunteering, etc. And as we've learned from some of the small-town folks, where joining your Chamber is even more crucial, focus on building relationships and being of service as opposed to landing work. You'll come across as more genuine and over time, the work *will* come.

And Other Groups...

Starting your own business can be a difficult and often emotionally challenging process. It just makes sense to find friends and allies on a similar path—people who want to share ideas and leads, and lend mutual support as you all move forward.

In Atlanta, as I've mentioned in my monthly newsletter on many occasions, I'm a member of a local organization called *The Freelance Forum* (**www.freelanceforum.org**). It's probably 40 to 50 percent writers, with the rest graphic designers, Web designers, photographers, illustrators, and others.

What I like about the FF is that it's not just a group of freelancers that get together and talk shop. It's an organization committed to helping members grow their businesses through, for starters, solid monthly educational programs and its *Find a Freelancer* feature on the Web site (allowing prospects to hunt for freelancers). More importantly, it's an organization that, because of its cross-disciplinary nature, becomes a place where members get work from other members. For similar organizations in other major metros, see the list in Appendix E or just ask a few freelancers in your area.

Business Network International

The November 2003 E-PUB featured a piece from Norfolk FLCW Lina Penalosa about an intriguing networking organization known as BNI (Business Network International; **www.bni.com**) with 3,000 chapters worldwide. Each chapter (typically 20 to 30 members) meets weekly and features only one member of any given profession, so you won't be competing with fellow writers within your BNI chapter.

This is a serious organization, as evidenced by its membership fees (at press time, $350 for the first year, $275 for subsequent years). In addition to sharing ideas and contacts, members are expected to deliver referrals to other members and anyone deemed to be a freeloader is punted. Their motto: *Givers Gain*.

Starting Your Own Writer's Group

There are a lot of wonderful reasons—both personal and professional—for starting your own group. And, in a smaller market, where there may be fewer organized gatherings, it's a sound strategy for creating a community that can be nourishing on many levels.

I touched on this topic in *TWFW*, but it's turned out to be such a great move that I felt I needed to give it more of a royal treatment in this book. On a Sunday morning in 1997, I welcomed six fellow writers for brunch and the kickoff meeting of an idea: a commercial writers group. When we were done eating, it was show-and-tell as each of us pulled out our portfolios and shared our work. Lo and behold, to our collective delight, we discovered we were all really good writers. Apparently, it was a good omen. Seven-plus years later, there are still six of us—five of the original crew, plus one we added when one of the founding members moved away.

I cannot recommend this idea highly enough. I feel like we were lucky, not only to find six equally talented scribes but six people who genuinely like each other. It's almost comical sometimes watching the scheduling gymnastics we go through to find a date that works for all of us—no easy feat, given six busy people. Occasionally, we have to set a date when one of us can't make it. In those cases, the missing party hates the fact he or she can't be there and the rest of us feel the absence. No kidding.

The Structure

In larger metro areas, you'll have the luxury to be choosier about whom you invite into your circle. In smaller markets it may be tougher. How to find these folks? Well, I met a few through networking meetings and freelance directories. I started with a few people I knew and liked, and trusted their judgment when they suggested others they felt would be a good fit. Honesty is key. Ask around about people and pick only those who you'd feel comfortable referring to your clients (which *will* probably happen; your name is on the line). The last thing your reputation or bottom line needs is someone who could potentially do damage, either due to sloppy work or unethical behavior. Here's a list of criteria to keep in mind.

1. **Friends First.** For starters, you've got to really like each other. That means a minimum of egos, posturing, or the need to be the center of attention. Ideally, you want a group of quietly confident individuals with strong senses of self—people who don't need to prove anything to anyone.

2. **Equal Talents.** As far as writing abilities go, you should all be at a similar level. Widely varying abilities can potentially be a spawning ground for insecurity, impatience, boredom, arrogance and worse. Shoot for parity. Just as importantly, an equally talented group makes life infinitely easier in the ways that matter: You can focus outwardly on the possibilities and potential for the group, not inwardly on its limitations.

3. **The Same Drummer.** Everyone should be an active, full-time commercial writer. Sure, you could put together a group comprised of people from many writing disciplines (magazine articles, short stories) and with varying levels of commitment. It might make for some interesting social interaction, but a more uniform profile will likely boost the professional paybacks of belonging.

4. **Keep It Small.** Our group has six members and that feels just about right. And not that it means anything, but there are three men and three women, three married and three single people. It could certainly work with a few more, but some of the benefits wouldn't be as easy to realize with a much larger group. It's also not a bad idea to include a range of expertise. In our group, we have several generalists with varying industry experience along with a few more technically oriented folks (not technical writers but high-tech marketing writers).

The Payoffs

Friendship lays the foundation of rapport and trust that makes the rest of it possible. At each of our Sunday potluck get-togethers, we eat well, talk shop, share ideas and leads, laugh and whine about clients, and have an all-round grand time. We've gotten a kick out of prospects who've called a number of us (most of us advertise in the same annual creative resource guide I mentioned earlier) for possible jobs and said different things to each of us, not having a clue that we talk. But there are also serious professional payoffs that keep us together.

EVENING UP THE WORKLOAD

Lead sharing is a key benefit of the writers group. It's a given that your workload will vary over time. When you're swamped, it's great to be able to refer work to a trusted colleague. And clients appreciate it (and value you more) when you can give them the name of a reliable writer who'll do a great job for them.

Of course, if your workload is a bit light, it's nice to know that you could get a job from one of your *compadres*, either because she's tied up with other work or the project in question isn't in her direct area of expertise. And that's another good point: Because I know folks that are just a phone call away and have extensive experience in a particular industry, I'm likely to steer those kinds of jobs to them (as opposed to struggling through a project that's not a good fit), knowing they'll return the favor when they can. Sure, sometimes I need the work and will take on something that might be better suited to one of them, but if I don't need it, now I've got options.

Needless to say, if we get referred to another's client, it remains their client. When I go on vacation, I leave contact info for two group members on my outgoing voice mail so clients have options. I've referred plenty of leads and jobs to my group and have been sent plenty in return. Recently, one member was recovering from surgery and took a few weeks off to recover. She referred a project to me, a $5000 direct mail campaign for a software firm. Pretty sweet—but better yet, my friend was happy for me.

AN ONGOING SOUNDING BOARD

One of the most important benefits is the back-and-forth Q&A that goes on regularly between us. Someone has a question about estimating a project (yes, even 20-year veterans don't have it all down pat). Or maybe it's a dilemma about pricing a new category of work. Perhaps someone's interested to hear what the others know about XYZ Company. And so we fire up the cyber-waves. In the process, we share info, ease concerns, confirm suspicions, avoid troublesome clients and so much more. It's truly invaluable on so many levels. And I think the key is the small number. If the group consisted of 25 people, one message sent out to everyone could end up being an irritation. When there's only six, it's just a few friends throwing ideas around.

THE POWER OF THE TEAM

Recently, we've taken this group idea to a whole new level: a collaborative marketing campaign. We toyed with this idea three to four years back, but our hearts just weren't in it then. Frankly, we were having too good a time just hanging out, shooting the breeze and sharing the occasional lead. And if that's all you do with your group, it will be worthwhile. But so much more is possible.

A slightly tighter marketplace and increasing competition had us thinking about how we could package ourselves into a compelling offering for our clients. We'd often heard clients complain about the scarcity of good, dependable, creative writers. Surely, we had a marketable product here: a pool of six experienced, proven, talented, strategic-minded and reliable writers who knew each other and each other's work. We could meet any client's need—individually or collectively. What a fabulous offer for the businessperson constantly frustrated with incompetent, unprofessional, and unreliable scribes (and believe me, there are plenty). How much easier would your life be, Mr./Ms. Prospect, knowing you have this resource just a phone call away?

We came up with a name for our group and have created a series of six clever direct mail postcards (we each created one) leveraging the "six-great-writers-in-one-place" theme and are in the process of putting together a simple Web site showcasing who we are and what we can provide to clients.

The postcard mailings will be spaced out according to a pre-determined schedule and sent to a list comprised of our own contacts and a list we're buying. To cover printing, mailing, list-buying and Web site expenses, we're figuring roughly $1200 each. If we each get even one modest job out of it, it easily pays for itself. Though, given our efforts and the targeted message, we're certain it'll do far better than that.

Teaming is the way of the future. See what kind of group you can put together. You have no idea where it might take you.

Suggested Reading...

I read a great book some time back—*Free Agent Nation*, by Daniel H. Pink (**www.freeagentnation.com**). If you're already successfully working as a "free agent," you'll find tons of great ideas to incorporate into your own business while reaffirming all the glorious benefits of the independent life.

If you're still part of the salaried world but plotting your "jailbreak," the book will give you a ringside seat to an exciting revolution that gathers more recruits every day. And it might help you see yourself less as some intrepid pioneer alone against the world, and more as a new player in a dynamic and rapidly expanding business sector that boasts an extensive network of support industries—with the power of a new consciousness on its side.

In the book, Pink discusses the vastly different paradigm of collaboration that exists in the salaried world vs. that in the free agent arena. In the world of full-time employment, you're thrown together with people you did not choose and might very well not have chosen to work for or with. That reality, coupled with the dog-eat-dog hierarchical structure of Corporate America, can explain why the average workplace environment often brings out the worst in people.

By contrast, in the free agent arena, you build looser, more shifting alliances based on mutual trust, support and complementary skills. And those partnerships are absolutely by choice. You stay allied as long as both sides derive benefit from it. Should someone betray that trust or prove unreliable, you simply sever the relationship. You're not stuck with anyone. And that's how it is with my writer's group. We don't have to be together but we choose to because we're all getting so much out of it.

●　　●　　●

Okay, you've got your marching orders on how to get more plugged in—anything to make fewer cold calls, right? Let's now turn to a topic near and dear to so many hearts out there—the economy—and dispel a few myths…

Chapter 11

There's a great story—reportedly true—that's often used to make a point about human potential:

A young college student sits in Physics class listening to the professor drone on. Being one of the sharper students, he considers the material to be very basic, so he dozes off, waking only to find the rest of the class filing out of the room. As the professor's habit is to write homework assignments on the board, the student glances up and quickly copies down the two problems he finds there.

That night as he works on the problems, he finds himself uncommonly challenged. Typically he would finish quickly, but these two are exceptionally difficult. While he finally manages to solve one, he can't unravel the second. Disturbed by this, he seeks out his professor prior to class the next day.

After hearing the student explain he could only solve one problem, the professor asks to see his work. With shaking hands, he looks at the homework paper—and what he sees leaves him completely flabbergasted. What the young man has done is to solve what Albert Einstein had dubbed one of "the world's unsolvable problems." And all because he'd mistaken this "riddle-of-the-Universe" for homework.

The story is an incredible testimonial to what we can accomplish (or NOT accomplish) if we convince ourselves that something is so. Basically, the mind believes what it's told and then acts on it blindly.

A Common Question

Virtually every day during the dark economic times, I'd get an e-mail asking the same question, *Given the current recession, is freelancing still a viable opportunity?* Whether or not all the financial doom and gloom is behind us as you read this, you can apply the point I make in this chapter to virtually any limiting belief your mind can entertain. Let me tell you another story—one that appeared in the E-PUB some time back.

Earlier, I discussed my first grueling months of business startup in 1994, when many people I cold-called asked me which ad agency I'd worked for (the assumed background for this field.) Upon hearing that I had no agency experience, many told me what a hard time I'd have getting established. I ignored them, pressed on, and after starting out with an income of $0 on Day One, was paying all my bills within four months.

Fast-forward three years and I'm walking down a cubicle corridor in the offices of one of my biggest clients. I see a familiar name on one of the nameplates. If my memory served me correctly, she was one of the folks who, way back when, told me what a tough row I had to hoe. I poked my head in and asked if she used to have an ad agency here in Atlanta? *I did,* was the reply, *but thanks to the huge recession in the creative industry in 1994, I had to shut my doors.*

Huge Creative Recession?

Where was I? I'll tell you where I was—smack dab in the middle of it with my blinders on, building a livelihood in a field in which I had no industry background, no prior paid experience and virtually no contacts. Others have since verified that said recession did exist, but apparently what I didn't know didn't hurt me. Yes, a recession would increase outsourcing among lean-running corporations and that undoubtedly contributed to my relatively quick start-up. But, by the same token, I had not a hint of the usual profile or resume of a typical candidate for this field.

Today, what I'd wish for you is a bout of amnesia that allows you to forget everything you know about an "economic downturn." If you're going to believe anything, believe that there's plenty of work and plenty of companies needing writing help. And frankly, that's a lot closer to the truth. *If you think it's a good time to build this business, you're right. And if you think it's a bad time, you're also right.* (See Wendy Knerr's story in Appendix B about building a thriving biz in a new city and a crashing economy.)

Perception is Everything

It's all perception. Take the stock market. What's at the heart of the Dow Jones or NASDAQ numbers we see flash across our TV and computer screens? Isn't it just an aggregate reflection of the opinions of all investors as to how good or bad they think the economy is now and will be?

Think about the high-tech boom a few years back. For several years, many companies that showed zero profitability were in fact valued in the billions. How did that happen, except as a result of perception? And in fact, that perception, flawed as it was, created real wealth for many people, wealth that many people took and ran with. It wasn't based on anything, but because people thought it was real, that's all that mattered. Of course, when the perception changed, the whole thing came crashing down.

While I'm certainly not trying to pretend that business cutbacks and layoffs, past or present, are just mirages, I will assert that the overall national economic situation is totally irrelevant to ONE person's quest for financial self-sufficiency as a writer. The effects of a downturn, I assert, are too far removed from the level of the individual to be able to make a deep impact on ONE person's efforts to make a living, *assuming* that person is out there beating the bushes. Remember: You need an absolutely infinitesimal percentage of the available universe of work out there to make a *very* handsome living.

A Diversified Portfolio

Ask any financial planner the key to successful investing and the answer is likely to include the advice, *Diversify.* And the logic is sound: A diversified portfolio diffuses risk, spreading it out over multiple industries and sectors of the economy. Not a bad strategy for your work "portfolio" as well. What makes more sense: to get all your work from one client (i.e., a full-time job) or to get a little work from a lot of different places (i.e., freelancing)?

It's precisely *because* we're diversified, drawing our business from a broad base of customers, and *because* freelancers make more sense to companies that are scaling down than do full-time employees, that the economy has far less power to affect us than we imagine it does. More to the point, after the events of the past few years, is there anyone out there who believes the financial experts paraded around by the media have the answers when it comes to the economy?

But, you say, *the economy IS down.* Yeah? So what? Does that mean that all companies have stopped operating, advertising, promoting or moving their businesses forward? The very notion is positively ludicrous. If anything, they'll be (or should be) doing more of it.

Quantifying Irrelevance

And what does "downturn" mean in real terms? A 10 percent reduction in gross domestic output would be absolutely huge in dollar terms *and* front-page news. Let's assume for a moment that it results in a 25 percent reduction in writing jobs. How you'd even begin to calculate something like that is beyond me, but while we're mentally meandering anyway, what the heck? I don't believe for a moment that it would actually get anywhere near 25 percent, but let's get downright gloomy for a moment.

Okay, so of the vast, gargantuan, colossal, mammoth volume of possible writing work that makes up the whole, 75 percent of it is still intact. What difference does that make to you, the solo operator, who only needs relatively few crumbs to make a good income? Not much. Yes, the downturn has affected freelancers, but in my experience, it's affected them much less than it has salaried employees—and again, that's precisely because we have a more diversified portfolio.

It's not always easy, but try to view economic news as mildly interesting stuff that has very few negative—and often quite positive—influences on your life. If we keep marketing ourselves, getting the word out and doing good work for our clients, we'll always eat well. Am I saying we won't have to work harder in tougher times? Absolutely not. We definitely will. I'm saying the work is there—and hopefully, in the preceding pages, we discovered some new and unusual avenues worth pursuing.

Learn From Technical Writers

In recent years, the technical writing arena (arguably the quieter, more studious and hard-working cousin of commercial writing) took a big hit, thanks to the dot-com crash and the general economic downturn. Technical writers have historically put all their marketing eggs in two baskets: the technical staffing agencies (that place them in long-term contract jobs) and the online high-tech job boards.

For a long time, those two sources of work had consistently come through for them. It was like having one or two huge repeat clients. And then one day, they both dried up. And because these folks had never really learned the discipline of marketing themselves (they didn't generally have to, given that many of their contracts went on for six months at a time), many of them ended up dead in the water.

Try Less-Traveled Roads

We commercial writers, on the other hand, because projects generally have a much shorter time span *and* because they come from so many possible arenas, have to get good at the marketing game if we want to stay well-fed. That said, I think all commercial writers (including yours truly) can get complacent when things get cushy. Much of our work has come from the usual suspects: the big corporate end-users and the popular middleman categories like ad agencies, graphic design firms, etc.

These two sources have been good to us for a long time, but it's just not smart to hitch our fortunes to these horses alone. And because people will be reading this book at very different points in time, I hesitate to make predictions as to the relative fertility of certain traditional sectors. That said, my sense, given my observations and the empirical evidence, is that the middleman sector, including ad agencies, will probably get stronger. At the same time, while I see some evidence of larger end-users pulling some traditionally outsourced projects back in-house, I think the small-to-medium sized end-user market segment (companies of 25 to 100 employees) is ripe and plentiful.

More to the point, if *everyone* is knocking on the same doors, it's never a bad idea to bark up another tree. Yes, I know, there's a perverse glee in finding company in your misery, but just because a bunch of people are sitting around agreeing that times are tough doesn't necessarily mean that's the whole story.

Not IF It's Viable, But Rather...

Many ask, *Is this still a viable opportunity?* That's the wrong question. In many ways, it's self-evidently viable. For starters, it can and *is* being done around the globe by people from all backgrounds, industries, experience levels, ages, and races. Successful FLCWs include retirees, recent college grads, career-changers, former journalists, former corporate staff writers, English professors, marketing professionals, attorneys, scientists, healthcare managers, teachers, single Moms, and about a zillion other profiles too numerous to mention.

Moreover, the freelance model will always be a highly advantageous one for any company, regardless of the economy. Think about it—the corporation doesn't have to hand out a salary, vacation pay or benefits; it can buy what it needs only when the service is needed. In many ways, it's about the evolution of the corporate business model vis-à-vis resource allocation. Certainly, some companies will boost their staffs in a strong economy (though that doesn't preclude temporary overflow work beyond the capabilities of that staff). Many others, however, including some top

Fortune 500 companies have come to love and lean on the freelance model after years of seeing firsthand the clear and distinct advantages to the approach.

Building your own business is not easy, and if you're somehow convinced that it should be, then you probably aren't cut out for this line of work. We all have our relative tolerance levels for risk, discomfort, hard work, uncertainty, unpredictability and lack of routine. If even a little bit of all those things upsets you, then you can want to be a commercial freelancer till the cows come home but you'll end up sabotaging yourself all along the way.

As mentioned, by the time you read this, we may well be back in deep clover. Meaning that the *Is this a good time…* question will have been replaced by *Now that the economy's so strong, won't there be a lot of people jumping into the field, increasing the competition?* Sheesh—I can't win...

●   ●   ●

So, that's my two cents on *that* subject. Now, let's relax, get away from all this bothersome marketing talk and discuss the craft of writing…

Chapter 12

The business of writing. The craft of writing. It's no secret which one I've focused on in both my books. And for good reason. There have always been a lot more "how-to-write" books than "how-to-start-and-grow-a-TRULY-profitable-writing-business" books. Yet I've always been intrigued by the writing process and the subtle differences that make one person a better writer than another. Fact is, those who write more intelligently, creatively, effectively and engagingly make more money than those who don't. No newsflash there.

I believe anyone can improve their writing ability if they follow a few simple guidelines. Sure, some people are inherently gifted with an almost sixth sense when it comes to crafting copy or just knowing instinctively which word to choose, but wherever you see yourself on the spectrum, the ideas that follow should nudge you a little further along.

In several cases I support my points with examples; some are excerpts from actual pieces I've seen and others I simply made up. Many of them are extreme, in order to leave no doubt as to my point. And if you learned anything from our earlier discussion of the Features/Benefits equation, you'll also notice that many of the bad examples below could be improved by an increased emphasis on benefits (what's in it for the customer) instead of features (facts about the product/service and the company who provides it).

Not surprisingly, given the nature of writing, there is some overlap in many of these. Suffice it to say, in the aggregate, they're all about making your writing more concise, clear, conversational, coherent and compelling.

175

One final caveat: We can't put all these ideas to use in every case. Depending on the scenario, some apply to certain types of projects but not others. But the more you keep these in mind, the better your writing will be.

• Write Like You Talk

For some inexplicable reason, many articulate people, even aspiring professional writers, when they pick up a pen, often seem to be taken over by some alien power that compels them to adopt an awkward, stilted tone. In an article written for a graphic designer's newsletter, my valued Atlanta colleague (and former mentor) Paul Glickstein nicely raised this point while underscoring what good writers do instead:

> Some people can't shake that stern English teacher who wouldn't give it up about sentence structure, grammar and the like. So they write (for the most part) **correctly**, but maybe not **effectively**. Professional writers, however, never forget that our work is about selling—and that "correctness" has more to do with audience, message and objective than it does about rigid textbook rules. And while we rely on our skills and experience to develop copy, we rigorously evaluate it from the customer's point of view. Ironically, not knowing everything about a business can be a benefit. It can help make us better advocates for our customers.

[handwritten margin note: USE THIS FOR "WITH USE" A FREELANCE COPYWRITER]

I assert that when people read anything, a voice in their mind is narrating those words to them. Are you hearing these words as you read them? (If you're not, for the sake of your writing, pretend you are.) That being the case, read everything you write aloud and make sure it has an engaging, conversational tone (within reason, depending on the subject matter). If it doesn't, work it till it does. I promise it'll be stronger.

You can picture the following sample being read by an android. In fact, run all your copy through the Android Test. If it comes up positive, sharpen that pencil, oil those joints and loosen it up some.

We Can Help Get Your Business in Focus

Let Maximum Video Production help you bring your business into focus. Call on us for all your specific video production needs, whether they be industrials, training videos, video news releases or any other pressing projects needing immediate attention. We will be happy to show you our work and explore how we can help meet your needs.

This breaks beaucoup rules, not only *Write Like You Talk*, but others to come like *Give Your Audience Credit* and *Make Every Word Pull Its Weight*.

Don't be afraid to use plenty of contractions—they'll make your copy infinitely lighter more conversational. Why say, *You simply will not find a better accounting program on the market*, when *You simply won't find…* just sounds better to the ear. Or, *What if you have changed your objective from service to sales?* vs. *What if you've changed…* There's simply no reason to be so formal.

• Lose the Weak Words & Tone

The headline above, *We Can Help Get Your Business in Focus*, came verbatim from a piece I helped write for a video production company years ago. They insisted on the headline, but it wasn't mine. What might you do differently? How about losing the *We Can Help* part? In my opinion, *Get Your Business in Focus*, is a lot stronger. And don't say you "may" or "might" or "should" be able to do this or that. Tell people what you *will* do and say it with conviction.

People want to do business with people who are confident and who tell them what they can expect, not what "possibly might happen if everything goes right on a good day." Sure, they may take that conviction with a grain of salt, knowing that it's partly marketing bravado, but they'd much rather hear that than shell out money to someone who doesn't even seem to have convinced himself he can get the job done.

• Give Your Audience Credit

I'll put it another way: don't overwrite. We all know the good feeling we get when we're at some gathering and someone's talking to us as if we "get it." Want to win over readers and keep them reading? Assume they're bright enough to catch on without spelling it all out like you would to a ten-year old. It'll flatter them, and a flattered reader is an interested reader. Sure, there are times when you have to write to a lowest common denominator, but that's a question to ask of your client. A particular subject may be new to you, but if it's old hat to your audience, you can make more assumptions in your writing. Here's an example:

> *The billing systems we create for our clients are customized, easy-to-use, and designed to be responsive to the needs of their customers. That in turn inspires a high level of confidence in those customers because they recognize that our clients are capably handling today's challenges and consequently, can be expected to deal effectively with those that come in the future.*

Why the need to explain the full train of logic? People can figure out that if their customers are pleased, it reflects well back on them. These things are understood. And another thing: Talk *to* someone, not *about* someone. I adapted this copy from something that had been written for prospective customers, but it keeps talking about "our customers." Why not be a little assumptive and say "you" and "your" instead of "our customers" or "our clients." If the piece is targeted to prospective customers, talk to those people as if they already are customers; put them in the role and they're more likely to feel like they belong there. And by the way, all this means trimming a lot of fat. How about this:

> *Our billing systems are customized, easy-to-use, and designed to be responsive to the needs of your customers. Translation? We'll make you look good and that spells customer loyalty.*

Here's another pretty obvious example of what not to do. I came across a Web site that featured samples of the company's work. I clicked a "Portfolio" link and ended up on a page that read:

> *This section contains various samples of our work from the past and present. Take some time to look them over and if you like what you see, then get in contact with us by phone or e-mail.*

Totally unnecessary. If visitors click on "Samples" or "Portfolio" and get taken to same, I promise, they'll know what to do once they get there. And assuming you have a "Contact Us" link somewhere on the page prominently displayed, they'll also know what to do once they're finished if they've liked what they've seen.

• Make Every Word Pull Its Weight

Lose the fat. While this may seem to echo the previous tip, it's actually less about assuming your audience is intelligent and more about just writing economically. I once heard an exceptionally useful writing tip: If a word doesn't move the story forward, cut it. Words should not be used to showcase your ability to fill up white space or as a forum for flexing your linguistic muscles.

Words are the building blocks of the case you're making for a company's products or services. Last time I checked, a brick wall was composed of bricks, not a motley mix of bricks, rags, chunks of balsa wood, a few bird's nests and some aluminum cans. Don't have words just parading around, impressed with themselves, leaning on their shovels watching other words work, or in some other way, taking up space (like I'm probably doing here...).

At the risk of overstating the obvious, check out the following sentence pairs, the clunky, bloated *Before* version, followed by the attenuated *After*:

> Like many authors I know of who are just starting out...
>
> *Like many authors just starting out...*

> It's a great field to go into for those of you who do not want to wake up that early.
>
> *It's a great field for those who don't like waking up early.*

> When I told him about my decision to leave and become a stuntman in the circus, he told me that he wasn't going to let me leave until I'd spent some time thinking about it.
>
> *When he found out I was leaving to become a circus stuntman, he refused to let me go until I'd thought about it.*

> When it comes down to deciding which plumber to hire for your everyday household needs, by doing your homework and research beforehand, you'll save yourself a lot of hassle and heartache down the line.
>
> *When deciding on a plumber, a little research now saves a lot of hassle later.*

The following ghastly copy comes verbatim from a piece I helped rewrite a few years back. If you can't figure out how to improve this, not only by saying it in far fewer words, but by cutting out things that are implicitly understood, you probably need to find a new line of work.

> *You are most welcome to call our offices, toll-free, for any assistance you may need. We have staff members who have placed orders for millions of dollars of materials and they will be glad to make an effort to provide information that would be helpful to you.*

Any questions?

• Make Your Writing Disappear

I want you to consider your job as a writer differently than you're accustomed to. When you write something, your goal should be to disappear from the process of information dissemination. Let me explain. While I'd obviously hate to have someone read something I wrote and say, *That's lousy writing*, I also don't really want to hear, *Wow, that's really good writing*. Sure, my clients better feel that way, but ideally, the ultimate reader of my words should just get the communication, without even noticing the words.

Words should be the vehicle of a thought or idea but they shouldn't be a distraction. Think of two people with different working styles—one quietly and effectively does his job without drawing attention to himself while the other makes a big show of what he's doing, and since he's more focused on having everyone aware of what he's up to, he ends up doing a half-assed job.

Read the following paragraphs. The first is bloated, overdone, pompous and preening. The second, which covers the same ground, effectively conveys the same points without getting all full of it itself like Version One.

> *When you're pondering the quality of life in a residential community, there's a demonstrable difference between just a good property and one that's truly superior. And that difference is found in the details. At ABC, we've gotten quite proficient at transforming those seemingly unexceptional details into lifestyles that are not only high quality, but affordable as well. And as is true in so many things, there are those not-so-obvious components. Things like greater reliance on brick when crafting the building exteriors. And Hardee Plank siding—as opposed to vinyl— which, happily, delivers both durability and attractiveness. Plus the fact that we journey that extra mile and follow stricter-than-required energy codes, which results in units that are significantly more energy-efficient. In the long run, it all pays off: These details end up delivering an exceptional living experience for residents, dramatically reduced maintenance costs, appreciably enhanced property value and minimal investor risk.*

When doing non-client writing examples for your portfolio, use something like "ABC" for the Co. name

I need a nap. How about this one?

> *The difference between good and superior quality of life in a residential community lies in the details. At ABC, we've gotten good at turning those details into high-quality, affordable lifestyles. There are the not-so-obvious things.*

Greater use of brick in the building exteriors. Durable and attractive Hardee Plank siding (vs. vinyl). Following stricter-than-required energy codes, resulting in more energy-efficient units. In the long run, these details deliver an exceptional living experience, reduced maintenance costs, enhanced property value and minimal investor risk.

• Cadence Is Everything

Good writing has a rhythm to it that bad writing usually lacks. This is a subtle distinction in that readers with an untrained eye may notice something doesn't quite feel right, but they may not be able to put a finger on what it is. As professional writers, however, we can't make that excuse. Look at the following paragraph. Don't focus on the choice of words themselves (I grant you they're not so hot either.)

The first step of our business process is to understand your goals. We follow that by determining the best avenue to get there. Our solutions always end up being simple, direct and effective. And the feedback we've received has been uniformly positive. Give us the opportunity to meet your needs. You won't be disappointed with the results.

Something's off, but what is it? How about this: all the sentences are roughly the same length. Big problem. Very mechanical. And clearly not how people talk. Mix up your sentences, alternating short and long, exactly like I'm doing here. And no, a freeform, casual style like this isn't appropriate in all cases—though it certainly does lend itself nicely to writing ad copy, direct mail and other more creative content. Just know that the example above is never appropriate in *any* case.

• Start in the Middle

This device has become completely second nature to me. And given how easy a way it is to make writing more interesting, I'm not sure why it's not used more than it is. Use it when writing articles—for newsletters or publications—or even marketing brochures.

Most writing jumps right into the "sell" copy or the point of an article:

Since 1989, ABC Digital has been offering state-of-the-art services for the creative industry...

Atlanta boasts some of the best restaurants in the Southeast and when it comes to desserts...

Instead, drop the reader right into the middle of the story *with* a story:

> *It was 1992, and Joe Collins was miffed. The CEO of ABC Digital was in the midst of phone conversation with a client when he had an epiphany…*

> *I'd heard about this crème brulee. Unforgettable texture. Unfathomable flavor. Unbelievable aroma. No, my hand wasn't shaking as I steered my spoon toward paradise. At least I don't think it was…*

Then, once you've earned the reader's attention, you can continue on with a more conventional approach. It's more effective, it's more interesting and it's a heckuva lot more fun to write. I don't care how boring you think the topic is. There's *always* an intriguing angle that will spice it up. What's so interesting about, say, plumbing? Well, do a little research on the trade. Who knows what trivia you might unearth? Or find out about the owner's roots. The human angle can often dish up compelling anecdotes.

A reader and budding FLCW sent me a piece for the E-PUB sometime back. Here's a trimmed-down version of what she sent:

> *I have been writing virtually all my life and developed these talents in different jobs over time. About 16 years ago, after deciding to stay home with my kids, I quickly discovered I could share my passion for writing in return for purely intrinsic rewards. When the PTA discovers you're more than mildly coherent, your phone rings off the hook with requests. Now that I'm pursuing commercial freelancing for real money, my greatest support comes from my children.*

> *My middle school-aged son recently caught me completely off-guard when we were hanging out in his room, he listening to music and me brainstorming over some marketing copy for a client. As I frantically scribbled, muttering to myself, I noticed John staring at me in amazement. "Wow, Mom," he said, " you're really into what you're doing. That's cool!"*

> *Another wonderful testimony comes from my 15 year-old daughter…*

I wrote her back and made a simple suggestion for instantly making the piece more interesting and compelling—something she could do in five seconds. Any guesses? Just reverse the first and second paragraphs.

• Avoid $50 Words That Cheapen Writing

Let us ponder fine literary fiction for a moment, books like *The Grapes of Wrath* and *To Kill a Mockingbird*. Obviously, many factors contribute to the making of a classic. Yet to my mind, one of the most important is the use of ordinary, unadorned words and phrases—the building blocks of everyday speech from everyday people—to create an extraordinary story. And really it's not much different from any other kind of writing, including our own humble field of commercial writing.

We got a taste of this tip in "Make Your Writing Disappear" above with comparisons of overblown vs. spare examples of writing.

Read the following paragraph, from a brochure I did for a hospital community outreach program some years back. Could be improved, I imagine, but I think it works in conveying a story, without drawing too much attention to itself. I'm describing the activities of a woman who works with the outreach program.

> *Martha Graves walks the world of the forgotten elderly—*
> *people who are often alone and grieving. They grieve for*
> *the loss of a lifelong spouse, the loss of independence, and*
> *most of all, the loss of their self-worth as a vital member of*
> *their communities—which have moved on without them.*
> *It's not glamorous work, and there are few "success stories."*
> *Yet, Martha Graves knows the difference she's making.*
> *Whether it's a smile coaxed from a timeworn face or a*
> *thank you from a friend who needs so little—but needs it*
> *so much—her rewards come in small, sweet packages.*

• Be a Storyteller

Tell me a story. Kids have been using that line on their parents since it all began. And why not? Our sense of wonder and our capacity for delight are so acute when we're young. But no matter how old, jaded or cynical we get, we never lose our desire to be entertained, moved, touched, amused and transported to another place—in other words, to hear a good story.

Your marketing brochures, newsletters, Web sites, executive case studies, video scripts and most any other commercial writing projects can almost always be dramatically improved through storytelling techniques. A "story" can be a testimonial or a case study (a narrative about a client, the challenge they were facing and how a specific product or service solved that problem), or even a fictitious scenario of a customer using a product, written in a way that allows the audience to imagine their customers happy because of it.

In the case study I shared in Chapter Two on the medical software, I offered an example of using stories. Here's another from the same piece, showing a real-world scenario instead of just talking about how the software works:

> It's 9:30 p.m. and Mrs. Wilson is paying bills, but has misplaced your invoice. Thanks to **In-Vox**, she calls the office and using her confidential PIN, accesses her account balance. Pressing another keypad button gets her the office mailing address while a third allows her to confirm the correct date and time of her next appointment.

Remember: When working on a commercial project, you always have a choice—just the facts, or a couple of good stories plus the facts. Overwhelmingly, most writers opt for the former. Be different. Tell a story. Your work will stand out. And you'll stand out.

• Focus on the Reading, Not the Writing

This is an over-arching suggestion, under which arguably, all the other tips fall. And it has several meanings. The first of course, is a literal one—to focus on the sound and flow of the piece as it's being read so that it reads naturally, free of excess words, awkward syntax or robotic rhythm. The second interpretation is more global—and it's one I've been beating you over the head with all throughout this book and the last one. Always write with the reader in mind and try to appeal to *that* particular reader; don't just focus on the words for their own sake.

•   •   •

Clip 'N Save

Bay Area FLCW Kathy Steligo (**www.thewordcompany.com**), who shared her great Web site to-do list in Chapter Six, sent me this exceptionally helpful and meaty list. Follow this and you'll ensure your writing is fresher, easier to read and more engaging.

THE WRITERS' SELF-CHECK LIST

1. Double check all facts and dates
2. Don't rely on computer spell-check to catch all errors
3. Verify all contact information and Web site addresses
4. Verify spelling of proper nouns
5. Use the "Find" command to locate words used repeatedly on the same page
6. Be sure statistics, quotations and other facts are credited
7. Secure permission for all copyrighted material
8. Condense and tighten wording where possible
9. Include cross-references to related materials in document
10. Define unfamiliar or unusual terms
11. Spell out the entire name or term before using an acronym
12. Check for consistent headings, font and format
13. Make smooth transitions between paragraphs and between chapters
14. Give each paragraph and chapter a beginning, middle and end
15. Search for all instances of "that;" most can be eliminated
16. Break down run-on sentences
17. Mix sentence lengths
18. Use an active voice
19. Replace worn verbs with powerful, descriptive verbs
20. Don't overdo metaphors
21. Check for correct use of "its" (possessive) and "it's" (it is)
22. Tailor the work's personality to the subject

Writing for the Web

Consistent with my approach to the rest of this book, since I'm not an expert on this subject, I've gone looking for a *bona fide* pro—someone who's done a TON of Web writing. Boston area FLCW Andrea Harris (www.minerva-inc.com) has learned over time what works, what doesn't, and how to avoid the common mistakes. Here, she provides us with a solid overview of the basics.

The Well-Written Web Site
By Andrea Harris

While Web sites are plentiful, those that are well written and effectively structured are rare. And that's why it makes sense to add Web writing to our repertoires. In many cases, clients need to be educated as to the crucial, image-building importance of their Web sites. It's not enough just to *have* a site, even if it looks gorgeous. It needs good copy to help it *work*. No amount of pretty graphics will hide lousy content for long. As soon as customers get frustrated because they can't find the information they're looking for, they're likely to leave and not come back. And the worst part? The company will never know.

The easiest way to pick up Web work is through an existing client. If you're already writing print projects for them and they like your work, it's a natural segue into writing for their site. If your specific client contact doesn't have responsibility for Web content, why not ask to meet the person who does?

Just as with print, aligning with Web designers is one way to land work. Position the alliance to their advantage: By adding copywriting to their list of services, they become a complete solution, not just a Web designer.

Fees

Price Web writing by the hour or by the project and at similar rates to what you charge for similar print work. If you charge per project, either:

- Bid on each project individually (after scoping it out) OR
- State a per page rate

Before you state a per page rate (anywhere from $200 to $600), remember a Web page can go on almost forever, so set a limit upfront on the length (typically, 300 to 400 words). Fail to do that and you run the risk of a client expecting five screens worth of text for a set per page amount.

How is Web Content Different?

Take the most compelling brochure copy in history, stick it on a Web page verbatim, and it'll likely make peoples' eyes glaze over. You have to change your writing style to accommodate differences in the medium. While less is always more in *any* kind of writing, it's even more crucial in Web writing.

Web copy, like direct mail copy, is almost always trying to get the reader to do something now, such as:

- Read a product description or article
- Click to initiate a purchase
- Enter an e-mail address in a subscribe box
- Travel deeper into the site
- Fill out a survey or form
- Request a quote

People don't read on the Web; they scan. They expect a more informal tone. Some of the more common Web writing guidelines include:

- Highlight keywords with bold type
- Use meaningful (not just clever) subheads
- Include lots of bulleted lists
- Write short paragraphs—just one main idea per paragraph
- Use half as many words as you might in a brochure
- Put the most important items first on the page

Why Should It Be Different?

People interact with a Web page differently than they do with a printed piece. A Web site is fluid while a printed piece is fixed. Because the Web reader can "change the channel" much more easily and is constantly distracted by other links, new e-mail, moving graphics, etc., short paragraphs, intuitive subheads and return links help users resume their place on the screen and keep them on the desired path.

The Mechanics

Good news: You don't need to know HTML to write for Web sites; the designers will almost always handle all the techy details. Even if you never learn HTML, however, you need to think about how a Web page is going to be used. Some things to consider:

- **Page length.** For long articles, consider providing links at the top to the sections below. You may want to break a long article onto multiple pages. Either way, provide the Web designer with the verbiage for those links.

- **Links.** Make links consistent. For example, a link to an article could be handled one of two ways:

  Words Make Your Web site a Success, Jerry McGovern (Oct-02)

  Words Make Your Web site a Success, Jerry McGovern (Oct-02) **more**

- **Page design.** Ask about the layout of the pages in case you need to supply copy for sidebars or call-outs, and to make sure you stick to any page length restrictions.

Print Material on the Web?

If something you've written for print is slated for your client's Web site in its unedited form, some formatting changes may be in order. If it's more than a couple of printed pages, suggest ways to make it easier to read online.

If the document has intuitive subheads that actually describe the text to come, suggest listing the subheads at the top of the page like a mini-table of contents. Each one (called "anchors") would be hot-linked to the actual subhead lower down on the page. The reader gets to see at a glance what the article's main topics are, and can choose to jump right to a relevant topic rather than read through the entire article. If you're going to do this, make sure the subheads aren't just clever, but descriptive enough to be meaningful.

Writing for E-Zines

More and more businesses are using e-zines as a way to showcase their expertise and nurture relationships with their customer base. Far from spam, these are permission-based, opt-in pubs with strong, value-added content to help them stay competitive in the marketplace (like THE WELL-FED E-PUB!).

Internal newsletters are another huge and growing segment, as companies create Web-based communications vehicles to keep the crucial lines of communication open. Small firms might create one for the whole company, while larger companies would generate multiple ones, each focused on different divisions (i.e., a sales force, customer service staff, technical support people, field service reps, etc) within a larger corporation.

The e-mail message might contain the entire e-zine article or just a synopsis and a link the reader can click on to read the entire article on a Web site. They need to be short (about 400 to 700 words) and customer-focused.

Frequency can be daily, weekly, monthly or even quarterly. The more frequent, the shorter they should be. Like any newsletter, e-zines can be a nice steady source of work.

Writing for Search Engines

Web pages are worthless if they aren't seen. And if they don't show up on the first three pages of search engine results, they may never be found. By far, the most powerful tool to help a site rank high in the search engines is the copy that appears on the page. Knowledgeable search engine optimization (SEO) experts work with skilled copywriters to write their clients' Web pages—but a copywriter has to learn how to write in a way that attracts the search engines *and* appeals to real people once they find the page.

The first step is knowing what terms and phrases ("keywords") a potential site visitor would type into a search engine. Only then can you write a keyword-rich Web page that search engines will rank highly. You may be asked to "patch" an existing Web page with keywords in an attempt to increase its rankings, but you may find that the only way to make the copy flow is to go back to square one and write it from scratch.

Search engines like pages with at least 250 words, so determine the best balance between brevity and the need to rank high. Short paragraphs, dual columns, sidebars, frequent headers and bullets can help make that long (but perhaps necessary) copy more readable. Your goal is to get the all-important keywords into the copy enough times to attract the search engines without overusing them to the point where the copy sounds ridiculous.

Writing for search engines is an art, and it's best to read some articles on it if you're asked to write "optimized" copy. See the Web resources in Appendix E.

As more and more company executives figure out that pretty Web sites need compelling copy, they'll be calling on Web copywriters. Learning how to write effective Web copy (and search engine optimized copy) can keep you at the top of their vendor lists.

PB: If you're pondering Web writing, why not check out the best Web sites out there? Certainly, the quality of the sites that appear on those "Best Of" lists varies according to the award criteria (i.e., best info sites, best articles, best design, best navigation, etc.) but you could no doubt pick up some overall impressions about what makes a site stand out. To that end, check out this *very* partial list:

www.webbyawards.com   1 - The Webby Awards

www.pcmag.com	2 - PC Magazine (look for their annual Top 101 list)
www.btobonline.com	3 - The Annual Net Marketing 100: Best B-2-B Web sites
www.webaward.org	4 - Web Marketing Association (click "Winners")
www.web100.com	5 - The Web's Best Sites
www.thebestdesigns.com	6 - Showcases top Web designers

The Stakes

Given the title of this chapter—*Write Better, Earn More*—thought I'd wrap up with a little food for thought about the kind of money that good, talented, strategic writers can make in this business. I got these comments from Cameron Foote, author of the best-selling book on creative business startup, *The Business Side of Creativity* (**www.creativebusiness.com**). Cam took issue with my assertion that rates in this business range from $50-$125+. Here's a case where I certainly don't mind being wrong. He writes:

> *"My experience as both a former freelance writer (15+ years) and editor of* Creative Business *for the last 15 years is that the hourly pricing range for viable freelance operations is currently $75 and up, below which it's impossible to make it in the long-term. The successful (versus dilettante) writers I know all charge more than $100 per hour, some double or triple that. And the key to doing that is to go after the clients that can afford it, and forget all the others. And they're out there."*

Hey, listen to the man.

•   •   •

Well, believe it or not, we're just about done here. All that's left is for me to get all lofty, passionate and philosophical with you before we wrap it up. Wouldn't want to miss that. Thanks for hanging with me...

Chapter 13

First Steps: The Bigger Picture

It was just a moment, a snapshot in time. Nothing life-changing or terribly profound had happened. But suddenly, I saw it all in perspective—from the 30,000-foot view—and everything took on a deeper, richer meaning.

I'd been referred to a woman who books speakers and entertainers on cruise ships and we were in the process of negotiating a nice trade-out arrangement. As a speaker, I'd pay a few hundred bucks for my seven-day cruise, in return for delivering four 50-minute lectures. Good deal.

In our conversation, she asked which four subjects I could speak on. I mentioned commercial writing, self-publishing, the joy of self-employment (my lifestyle for most of the past 18 years) and the whole idea of finding your passion in life. I'd spoken on the first subject many times, the second only twice and the last two not at all. But nonetheless, I suggested all four without a moment's hesitation.

Big deal, huh? Actually it *was*. A little history...

Roughly ten years ago, as you all know by now, I was working for a video dating service in sales—a going-nowhere job if ever there was one. It was the latest in the string of dead-end sales jobs I'd held while trying to figure out what I wanted to be when I grew up. Something, incidentally, that was looking more and more remote with each passing day (growing up, that is). I was in a rut.

Well, you know the rest of the story. I decided to become a freelance writer, was making ends meet in less than four months, and never looked back. And that was just the beginning...

The Peak-to-Peek Principle

Nearly 20 years ago, I read *The Peak-to-Peek Principle*, by Dr. Robert Schuller, the world-famous minister, creator of the weekly inspirational *Hour of Power* TV show and the force behind the Crystal Cathedral in California. I've never been a conventionally religious man, but Dr. Schuller's non-preachy message of "possibility thinking" has always resonated with me. I stumbled on the book again a few years back, when I was well into my writing and publishing careers. And it all came together for me like it never had initially. When I'd first read the book, it was theoretical. Now, it was my life in retrospect.

The essential message of the book is this: When you set a goal and begin moving toward its realization, it's like being at the base of the mountain looking up at the summit. All you can see is the mountain, and if it's cloudy, you may not even see the top (mmmm…all these great metaphors…)

When I launched my commercial writing career in 1994, my "peak" was simple and modest: to work full-time as a commercial writer and be able to pay my bills. Nothing *too* lofty, but for that point in time, a good and worthy goal. And I quickly reached that peak, from which I now had a peek at other mountains, other possibilities—ones I hadn't been able to see from the bottom and that *were now only visible because I was higher up on the mountain*. For me, the next peak was to make a lot more money than just what was needed to pay the bills.

New Peaks, New Possibilities

From there the peeks of new peaks came faster, and as my confidence grew from each passing success, each new mountain seemed less daunting and more exciting—less of an obstacle and more of an opportunity. I know I sound like so many self-help gurus and that's not my intention, but this really *was* how it felt.

As I reached each peak, the next one came into view. Hmmm... maybe I could write a book... then, maybe I could self-publish it... then, maybe I could beat the odds and make it a success... then, I could build a name and reputation... then, perhaps I could do seminars around the country... then, maybe a monthly e-zine... then, maybe a CD series... then, paid mentoring... more books... more speaking... and on and on till the day I got on the phone with this booking agent discussing the fun and novel idea of leveraging my "Expert Author" status to speak my way to a practically free cruise.

I'd climbed a lot of peaks to put myself in this position. Not that speaking on a cruise ship was some pinnacle in and of itself. It's just that this whole wonderful journey I've been on over the past decade seemed to pass before my eyes as I spoke to this woman, culminating in my unhesitating confidence in my ability to deliver an entertaining lecture to a small crowd of people on several subjects I'd never spoken on before.

This underscores one of the key components of the peak-to-peek principle: the growing sense of your own self-worth and unmet potential that comes to you as you reach these successive milestones along the way. As Schuller puts it, *Face your mountains and you'll gain a grand new perspective of what you can do and be.*

The Self-Esteem Movement

My sister has a clipping on her refrigerator containing a list from an old Ann Landers column: *Ten Rules Kids Won't Learn In School.* Far and away, this is my favorite:

> *Your school may be "outcome-based" but life isn't. In some schools, you're given as many chances as you want to get the answer right. Standards are set low enough so nearly everyone can meet them. This, of course, bears not the slightest resemblance to anything in real life, as you will soon find out.*

Allow me a little editorial aside. Over the past two decades, there's been a well-documented movement in education on fostering self-esteem in young people. While I can certainly understand the desire to want to remove some of the overly competitive "win/lose" orientation from the equation, especially when kids are younger, it has arguably been taken to extremes. The cardinal sin? Making kids feel bad about themselves by highlighting the superior achievements of some in contrast to the lesser accomplishments of others. The strategy in many cases has been to equalize all accomplishments, let everyone "win" and, at all costs, avoid rankings-based systems. The whole philosophy is built on a well-intentioned but misguided myth: *The Myth of Equality.* I can hear the gasps echoing across the land.

While everyone is absolutely entitled to an equal shot at success in life, not everyone *is* equal in terms of the skills, abilities, intelligence, talents and relative levels of ambition they bring to the table. It serves neither the individual nor the truth to foster such a premise, which, in the face of a veritable mountain of empirical evidence, just isn't so. Some people are just plain smarter, sharper, more ambitious and more talented than others. To pretend otherwise is both crazy and cruel.

And kids are smart—they see what's going on when either superior accomplishments are downplayed to protect someone else's feelings or inferior ones are being pumped up to create the illusion of being on the par with more noteworthy ones. If it's indeed true, as I assert, that kids aren't really being fooled, then despite what those in charge may think or say, they're not really doing it for the kids at all. They're doing it for themselves—as a way of bringing their environment in line with their overarching worldview: *Everyone is equal in every way.*

You don't build self-esteem by having someone bestow it upon you. Regardless of the circumstances, that's a counterfeit self-esteem. It might last a few hours or a day but it's an ice castle. The next dose of reality will melt it away like a Popsicle in Phoenix in July.

The Genuine Article

You build self-esteem by stretching yourself, by reaching beyond what's comfortable, by taking chances and ultimately succeeding at something. And then doing that over and over again. That's real. And more importantly, it's a foundation you can build on. Whatever you feared, you faced and overcame. That fear can never wield the same power over you again. On to the next obstacle—face it and you step up higher yet, rising up on the backs of your slain dragons. And it's from fears vanquished through achievements that the clouds of doubt clear and greater peaks (possibilities) come into view. And it's from repeating this process again and again that we build a life worth living.

That's the lesson we should be teaching kids. Instead, too often, we hobble them with the notion that all life's riches can be theirs and all life's doors will open for them simply because they're good and worthy people. Compared to the story of how one builds the foundation of a solid, confident, clear-eyed, capable adult, that's pretty weak stuff.

And here's one for those folks who've struggled with low self-esteem all their lives. Like *me*, for instance. No kidding. Ever seen a quote from someone successful who shares that they've always wrestled with low self-esteem? What does that tell you? *You don't have to have licked the self-esteem thing to be successful.* You may never have high self-esteem, but there's not a reason in the world that it has to stop you.

One thing is certain: You're *not* going to suddenly develop self-esteem by declaring you possess it, from reading some book about developing it, or from reciting mantras. You'll develop it by doing things. By accomplishing things you doubted you could. By stretching. For a prime example of this, check out Wendy Knerr's great story leading off the *Well-Fed Success Profiles* in Appendix B. But, off my soapbox...

Destination Unknown?

When you start out, chances are, you won't have any idea where the journey will end up. I certainly didn't. I never dreamed it'd end up here. I didn't have to know it all or have it all figured out. It was enough to just start with that first goal in mind. All I knew and chose to focus on at that point was making this freelance writing gig work full-time. Period. I didn't care about and wasn't looking at anything past that. And incidentally, in many ways, this flies in the face of much of the self-help literature that focuses on goal-setting.

Heaven knows, I've read enough books on the subject and so many of them talk about those people—famous personalities, actors, athletes, etc.—who knew from waaaaay back where they wanted to end up, and with their eyes fixed on that ultimate prize, slowly, methodically but inexorably moved toward it. All these inspirational stories—complete with a full orchestra in the background—were enough to leave you feeling that you too should have this incredible, fabulous, grand objective in life. And fueled by some newly-realized passion (*This is me! This is what my life will be about!*), you'll launch this wondrous journey, leading to this crystal clear summit.

Isn't *That* Special?

Hey, more power to you if you're one of those lucky ones who figured out the whole journey before taking the first step. But what if you haven't zeroed in on that blissful life direction that calls to you like nothing else in the history of the world? Does that mean you're out of luck until that day when the Bliss Fairy finally gets around to paying you a visit? Not hardly.

More importantly, for every one of these "pre-planned" winners we hear about, I'd wager there are several others who—like yours truly—will freely admit they had no idea things would end up where they did, that they *never* originally set out to accomplish what they ultimately managed to. And frankly, I think that's a much more fun and exciting way to live. Move forward, know your general direction and be open to what may unfold—unencumbered by a rigid plan that could, very realistically, prevent you from seeing other possibilities.

Waiting on the Rapture?

What prevents or delays people from moving toward a more enjoyable overall life experience? I say it's an attachment to finding that one perfect magical life direction, one in which one loses oneself and where work becomes play, blah, blah, blah. Oh sure, we'd all love to have that and I'm not saying it's not a desirable outcome, but to somehow imply that anything short of that scenario isn't worth the effort is tragically dumb. I'd venture to guess that for, oh, roughly 95 percent of people, finding something they "pretty much like to do most of the time" would be a 100 percent improvement. You know who you are.

So, if you can come up with a short-term plan that sounds fun and worthwhile, go for it—without having to know how it's all going to turn out before you start. I can't tell you how many e-mails I get from people who ask every possible question under the sun, trying to plan for every contingency, wanting to have the "right" response to any conceivable question they might ever be asked and wanting to know how to do everything they might ever called on to do—all before taking the first step. Not only is that impossible, it's also crazy, totally anxiety-producing and, frankly, no fun at all.

These are people who are deathly afraid to, 1) make a mistake, 2) look stupid, and 3) just let things happen. A really bad combo. Even after more than a decade in this business, I'm still not experienced enough in some arenas to land work there. So what? I've got enough confidence in my abilities that I know I *could* take on a type of project I've never tackled before *if* I were so inclined and the client gave me the green light to proceed. That confidence wasn't there on Day One, but after plenty of successes, it's there now.

Take the First Step

The toughest part of any process is the beginning. I've heard from plenty of folks who've said, *Gee, I put off starting forever, making it out to be this big scary thing. Once I finally took the plunge* (in all their trembling, knee-shaking glory, no doubt), *it wasn't nearly as difficult as I built it up to be.* Well, guess what? It almost never is. Real life can rarely compete with our over-active imaginations.

And where might that first step lead? You have no idea and that's okay. In fact, that's preferable. Why? Because then, as things unfold, instead of feeling bound to some plan that may no longer feel completely right, you'll naturally start moving in the direction of your interests, passions and fascinations. But, the first step is... the first step. Life really can be an adventure. Make it your own.

Appendix A

To Those Who've Read TWFW...

While I've added some up-to-date goodies here, you could get away with a good skim. Obviously, this section is primarily to give those who haven't read the first book (yes, hard to fathom…) a good context for understanding this one.

To Those Who Haven't Read TWFW...

While this section offers a rough encapsulation of the first book—to provide a good context for this book—12 or so pages simply can't provide the same detail as 300. Needless to say, I'd strongly recommend you read TWFW, as it includes tons of stuff you won't find here: types of clients and projects, how to write them, client meetings, what to charge, how to estimate projects, sample contracts, brochures, direct mail pieces, and pages of actual projects to give you a feel for the ballpark caliber of writing expected. It'll make this book mean that much more.

Could You Get Used To This?

True story: The marketing communications firm, a regular client, called me on a Thursday—in a bind and a bit frantic. They needed an 800-word article for *their* client by Monday and provided the source material and contact for one interview. My fee: $1000, including a 25% rush fee (that was a few years ago; I'd charge more now).

Over the next five weeks, I worked on a long list of projects for them, all focused on two key initiatives: the launch of a new Internet/Intranet presence and the introduction of revamped benefits programs for two distinct audiences. Four

197

more articles, averaging 800 words and approximately $850 each. Promotional posters and flyer copy for $950. Two roughly 24-page benefits guides averaging $3300 each. Step-by-step "walk-through" sales sheets for their Internet sites: $850. Six sales letters: $1500.

Plus a 17-hour job for another client in the midst of it all. I tried to discourage them by bumping my then-$85 an hour rate to $95. *Fine*, they said. When it was all said and done, I'd earned close to $16,000 in 6 weeks. Is that typical? No, probably not typical. Is it rare once established? No, it's not rare either. That's the potential of this business.

I did most of this work while comfortably ensconced in my sunny home office or sitting on my deck, cold drink and phone nearby. Or perhaps at my other "office"—a picnic table at a nearby state park overlooking the river—office phone forwarded to my cell.

A Lucrative and Growing Opportunity

In the last decade, the twin trends of downsizing and outsourcing have permanently altered the business landscape. Corporate America is doing more with less—fewer people, less resources, smaller budgets. Marketing and communications departments are being scaled back or eliminated altogether. Ad agencies, graphic design firms, marketing companies and others (more on them later) stay lean and nimble by rarely staffing writers. Ad agencies typically are more likely to have in-house writing talent but even that's starting to shift for the same reasons.

As a result, many organizations rely heavily on well-paid freelancers to get their work done—and for some good business reasons: They provide no salaries, benefits and vacations. They pay only for what they need when they need it. They get a broad range of talent. They enjoy fresh "outsider" perspectives.

And yes, when companies scale back, projects can scale back as well. Companies who used to hire a lot of freelancers might choose to pull more projects back in-house instead of hiring anyone—freelancer or agency. But just as likely, downsizing means fewer (and overworked) employees. And as budgets shrink, the same company who couldn't afford to keep on full-time staff or hire an expensive agency or design firm may now find the freelancer option a lot more economically attractive.

What You Don't Know...

But what if you find yourself it a tight economy? Wouldn't that be a crazy time to start a writing business? Well, I did just that and it turned out smashingly. Check out the story in Chapter Eleven (*It's NOT the Economy, Stupid!*).

WHY PURSUE COMMERCIAL WRITING?

You Like To Write and Are Good At It

Just making sure…

The Time Is Right For Freelancers

Downsizing, outsourcing, etc. (see above).

Easy, Low-Overhead Start-Up

As writing fields go, commercial writing is one of the easiest to break into and, for even a moderately talented scribe, one of the most lucrative. Given that you're probably already set up with a computer, fax and Internet access, the overhead is one of the lowest around.

No Special Skills

My major in college? Russian Studies—not English or Journalism. I'm a good writer. I'm only a passable grammarian. Remember, I had no writing background whatsoever. You don't need special credentials. Clients want good reliable writers who are creative, strategic, competitively priced and who will deliver good work—on time and on budget. They don't care what your work background is, unless it's relevant to the specific project.

Brilliant Writing Not Required

You *do* have to be a good writer. Mediocre talent isn't enough, but incredible talent isn't necessary. There are plenty of industries, such as healthcare, banking, manufacturing, insurance, high technology and many more that need oodles of clear, concise copywriting that effectively conveys information but simply doesn't have to be a work of art. If you are "crackerjack," you'll get into the fun, creative arenas like ad copy and direct mail writing, amongst others.

High Demand For Talent

Check out my Web site (**www.wellfedwriter.com**, then "Testimonials") for comments from corporate writing buyers about the demand for good writing talent in this field.

Unlimited Work

Marketing brochures, advertisements, newsletters, direct mail campaigns, corporate image pieces, speeches, industrial video scripts, trade articles, press releases, case studies, executive profiles, educational/industrial CD-ROM scripts, radio spots, TV commercials, event scripting, business letters, sales promotion material, marketing manuals, corporate profiles, annual reports, product spec sheets, proposals—shall I go on? Every single one has to be written by someone.

A manager with a Fortune 500 firm in Atlanta noted, *Most people would assume a company our size would do the bulk of our writing in-house, and they'd be wrong. It's amazing now much writing we outsource. My writing needs are pretty steady, and I pay anywhere from $65-85 per hour, depending on the writer's experience.*

There are three main arenas of work: B2C (Business-to-Consumer; the things you see as a consumer); B2B (Business-to-Business; which you usually don't see, except as an employee of a company); and *internal communications*—projects that exist within the four walls of a corporation and for their eyes only—a *huge* segment.

To see samples of the types of projects you might be doing (and get some ideas about putting your own commercial site together), visit my site at **www.writeinc.biz.**

Be Your Own Boss

In the nine-to-five working world, you've pretty much got to march in lockstep with the rest of the troops. If you're a night owl, your time has come. Want to sleep from two a.m. to nine a.m.? Go for it! Of course, in the beginning, you'd better be meeting clients when and where they want.

Sheer Variety Of Work

Over the years, I've written about UPS' Canadian operations, BellSouth's product line, Coca-Cola's alliance with The Boys & Girls Clubs of America, how one company would design an entertainment pavilion for the Olympics, the charitable activities of a prestigious Chattanooga hospital, and on and on. Every day is different, so if you lean towards ADD, rejoice!

Finance Your Writing Bliss

Maybe you're thinking that there's something terribly mercenary about writing for Corporate America. But, what's the point of writing books and articles if you end up moonlighting to make ends meet? Or working full-time at a job you can't stand? Writing for rates that start at $50 will give you the time and space to pursue your "bliss"—that future Oscar, Pulitzer, Emmy, or Tony-award-winning masterpiece.

Healthy Income

If you're moderately intelligent, capable and ambitious, you can easily make $30,000 a year early on. If you're good and reasonably aggressive about getting the word out, $50,000 is very doable. Build a good reputation, start getting referrals, and who knows? A healthy number of commercial writers gross $100K a year. Interested in part-time? Once established, $2000 a month is quite possible.

And no, it's not always as easy or rosy as the "$16K in 45 days" scenario described earlier. You'll have your share of $500 weeks and in the beginning, you'll be working a lot more for a lot less. This is not a get-rich-quick scheme. But, develop the right work habits early and you'll be surprised at how soon you'll be having some pretty lucrative stretches. And by the way, most projects are done within a few weeks, you're generally paid in 30 days, and chasing your money is the rare exception, not the rule.

Use Your Background

What's your industry background or work experience? High-tech? Finance? Healthcare? Retail? Telecommunications? Advertising? Wherever you come from, approach that industry first. Chances are excellent you'll find writing projects—and, as someone who knows the ropes, you'll be especially valued by your clients.

A Nice Life

Good money, flexible hours, stimulating work. Go to bed when you want, get up when you want (most of the time), wear what you want, take vacations when you want, shower and shave when you want. Yes, getting established takes some effort, but it's not nearly as difficult as you'd think and depending on your present situation, you could be halfway there right now!

WHERE'S MY PORTFOLIO?

So, how do you get work when you have nothing to show? Start with any projects you've done in a past or present job: marketing manual, brochure, press release, newsletter, sales sheet, speech, article, etc. If these are lean, try doing some *pro bono* work for a charity or start-up. It could be the Arthritis Foundation, a hospital, a group like The Sierra Club, a political organization, a small theater group, etc. For more specifics on starter portfolio creation, check out Question 5 (*How Do I Create a Decent Portfolio?*) in Chapter Four (*Let Me Clarify…*)

WHO WILL HIRE YOU?

The Basics: EUs & MMs

For the most part, you'll be dealing with two types of clients: the **End-User (EU)** or a **Middleman (MM)** who's dealing with the end user. EU means any company from small to Fortune 100, while MMs include, but aren't limited to, graphic design firms, ad agencies, marketing companies, Web designers, PR firms and event production companies. Except for larger ad agencies and PR firms (and that's starting to change), MMs rarely staff full-time writers, and as they hunt business for themselves, they'll find work for you.

One big advantage of dealing with EUs is that there's just one layer of communication and copy approval, as opposed to two with MMs. And EUs that work with MMs are also used to paying inflated rates for copywriting—a normal rate plus the MM's premium, so that'll work to your advantage when approaching EUs.

Small Companies, Big Market

Both EUs and MMs, if established, need little educating about the process, though you may have to "educate" more with smaller firms doing their first formal brochure, ad, or marketing campaign. Which is even more reason to partner with graphic designers—not only so you can offer "end-to-end" solutions but also because an experienced designer will typically manage the project and be a great resource for the novice writer.

END-USERS (EUs)

Corporations

EUs (the end-users of the writing you create) mean Corporate America plus companies of every size. The larger the company, the broader the spectrum of work. UPS, The Coca-Cola Company, BellSouth and many other giants have countless departments and a wide range of potential needs. And while every company is different, in my experience, much of it gets outsourced.

FIRST STOP: "MARCOM"

Also known as Marketing Communications or Corporate Communications. This department—essentially an in-house agency for the corporation—turns out a wide array of projects like the ones described above.

In the absence of a MarCom department, contact the marketing department, sales, or, when all else fails, human resources (it's always smarter to go to those with the specific needs, as opposed to those who serve them).

After one or two successful projects, always ask for referrals—to other divisions of the company or elsewhere. A "warm call" is *always* preferable to a cold call.

MIDDLEMEN (MM)

Possible contacts at MMs are Creative Directors, Assistant Creative Directors, Project Managers, Account Executives, Producers and others.

Graphic Design Firms

I've gotten a huge chunk of my business over the years from graphic design firms. The good firms are smart and creative with a strong grasp of marketing strategy. Most have added Web design to their repertoire. Get to know the talented designers at a particular firm; they'll eventually go off on their own and, if they like you and your work, you'll have a client for a long time. Speaking of which...

DON'T IGNORE THE "LONE RANGERS"

Make a point to forge strong alliances with three or four talented one-person design shops. These relationships are likely to be much more long-term, stable and lucrative than ones you develop with larger firms, where things and people always change. Midway through one year, my top account in billings was a one-woman design shop. Don't let size fool you.

Advertising Agencies

Unless you have extensive agency experience, the average freelancer is unlikely to land the juicy, high-end, big-name Fortune 100 advertising work for the big agencies. Your best bet with ad agencies is "collateral"—brochures, internal campaigns, and other peripheral supporting projects.

BIGGER OPPORTUNITIES WITH SMALLER FIRMS

Try smaller agencies for better opportunities to do fun, creative concepting and headlining projects. Because they're more likely to view you as an expert (not just "hired help"), you've got a much better chance of having your efforts see the light of day. That means more job satisfaction and creative fulfillment.

Web Designers

A fast-growing category. As a rule, pure Web designers have technical roots, and as such, have a stronger grasp of the inner high-tech guts of Web creation (a factor in issues such as search engine optimization) than pure graphic designers. Neither, however, writes good copy nor is likely to have writers on staff.

Marketing Firms

While these entities often specialize in a particular industry (high-tech, healthcare, real estate, etc.), occasionally they're broad-based. A marketing firm might help a growing company that's made its mark locally but is looking to have a national presence. It might mean designing a comprehensive strategy involving ad/media campaigns, public relations, direct mail, Web sites, etc.

Public Relations Firms

PR firms, like ad agencies, span the gamut in size, with a healthy number of huge ones in any large market. As with ad agencies, freelancers may not see too much of the high-profile work, but collateral work can be plentiful. As mentioned, the larger ones may staff writers but even these may be leaning more toward fewer on-staff resources.

Event Production Companies (EPCs)

Located in major convention cities, these entities work with large corporations to produce annual conferences, trade shows, product launches, etc. Most handle design and construction of all exhibits and printed literature—before, during, and after the show—conference signage, speaker support (helping speakers craft their remarks), meeting rooms, catering, entertainment, shipping and more. Try the Yellow Pages or call the management of the big conventions that come to your area and ask who's producing the event.

GETTING STARTED

Build Your List

Especially with MMs, start with the Yellow Pages (or online versions like **www.switchboard.com** and **www.theultimates.com/yellow/** that allow you to generate extensive lists of prospects, broken down by city and category) to build a calling list of companies, looking up categories directly: Advertising Agencies, Public Relations Firms, Graphic Designers, etc.

Another great source for prospects is the *Book of Lists*, published by your city's weekly business publication (check out **www.amcity.com** for complete listing). Also, check with your library for other local business listing directories.

Ready, Set, Dial...

Okay, you have your list, and it's long enough to keep you busy for a while. You don't want any excuses to stop calling (except maybe that it's Saturday or something). A few tips for successful prospecting:

DUMB DOWN. Check the analytical side of your brain at the door—the side that filters and second-guesses every name on the list, asking pointless questions, beginning with, *Should I...*, *Would they...* and *I wonder if...*

REALITY CHECK. 75 to 80 percent of the people you talk to won't be interested in your services. That's four out of five. They're almost invariably nice about it.

YOUR SCRIPT. Know exactly what you're going to say, write it out word-for-word on a 3x5 card and keep it in front of you. It's a highly effective tool for staying focused and reducing anxiety. (See Chapter Five for specific phone scripts and lots more advice on phone prospecting.)

HOW TO TALK. Speaking slowly, clearly and evenly allows your prospects—who weren't expecting your call—to switch gears and catch up.

GET YOUR MIND RIGHT. Set a goal to simply have some nice conversations and gather some good information. If you feel there's less at stake, you'll come across to prospects as relaxed and confident—a great attitude to project.

KEEP A LOG. Keep track of your calling efforts with a printed log or good contact management program.

HARNESS THE LAW OF AVERAGES. It absolutely, positively works. Make enough calls and you'll find the business. Making 50 calls a day (*not having 50 conversations*) for a month is 1000 calls. It may sound scary but I can't think of a single better way of kick-starting this business. When I started my business, I made close to 700 calls in a month. That's called critical mass. Make that many calls, and something's bound to happen.

BE READY TO PROVIDE SAMPLES. There are three main ways to provide samples to a prospect who's said she has occasional or ongoing needs for writers: 1) via an online portfolio on your Web site (highly recommended); 2) by fax (text only or copies of samples) or e-mail (text-only or PDF files); and 3) by copying and snail-mailing clips along with resumes/cover letters. *Never* send a package to anyone who isn't expecting one. Whichever strategy you use, the next step is always the same: follow up, follow up and follow up some more.

Is Cold Calling the Only Way?

While you should count on doing some cold calling, if you have an extensive network of industry contacts from past jobs, you may get away with few cold calls. Couple that with fiendish networking through professional associations, Chambers of Commerce and the like and you could build a business without the pain of calling strangers. E-mail marketing and direct mail strategies are other ways of keeping the cold calling beast at bay. We'll explore all these in the coming pages.

Get Out And Meet Your Market

Early in my career, I heard this statistic: You'll be hired by one out of ten prospects to whom you send information but by one out of three who actually meet you. *Always* try and get a face-to-face appointment, even if you're also sending samples. Now, that's what's worked for *me*. On the other hand, Bob Bly, the freelance writing icon, doesn't believe in meetings (he feels they're a time drain). And given the wired world in which we live, you certainly can get the job done without them. That works for him. Putting faces with voices has always worked for me.

THE SYSTEM IS THE SOLUTION

Simple Repeatable Systems

To get the business, you have to get your name (and usually yourself) in front of a lot of people. Cold calling, sending out information (mailed, faxed, e-mailed or steered to a Web site), networking and follow-up has to happen. Make the process simple and you'll do it.

Follow-Up & Cover Letters

Every time you talk or meet with prospects for the first time, send them something to remind them of you. Sit down and create a series of form follow-up and cover letters to apply to different client meeting scenarios — i.e., pending work, no pending work, long shot, contact by an assistant, etc. (FYI, I provide samples of these letters in TWFW.*)*

Résumés

Create multiple versions of one-page *résumés*. I have versions geared toward ad copy writing, video/CD, technical projects, brochure/collateral work, speeches, articles/editorial, PR, as well as several general versions. This is the format I use:

PETER BOWERMAN
(770) 555-6543

SELECTED FREE-LANCE WRITING CREDITS

1) CLIENT: **ABC Corp**. - Atlanta, GA

PROJECT: Corporate Sales Brochure, Rate Book, and Customer Newsletter for Mexico Sales Operation

2) CLIENT: **The Biggie Snack Company** - Atlanta, GA

PROJECTS: Program Guide for Boys & Girls Club/Biggie Snack Alliance,

Concepting Projects (Est. 35+)

Misc. Product Marketing Brochures

Direct Mail Postcards

Unless you're blessed to be in a market bursting with work, you'll probably have to periodically remind your prospect base that you're out there. Yes, you'll be following up with calls, samples and links to your Web site, but a simple direct mail campaign two to four times a year can effectively and inexpensively keep you in front of your market. (See Chapter Six, *Touching Your Market—By Direct Mail, E-mail and Fax,* for specific direct mail strategies.)

WHAT SHOULD I CHARGE?

While you'll ultimately be pricing most of your work by the job—i.e., a flat rate—you first need to establish your hourly rate. For creative writing such as marketing work, ad copy, descriptive collateral, the range is about $50 to $125 an hour with $60 to $80 the average in good-sized metroplitan areas.

I started at $50 per hour. You won't make anyone flinch—except yourself—with a $50 rate unless it's someone who's never hired a writer before. In fact, $50 is actually going to sound too low to seasoned copywriting buyers. As your portfolio and reputation grow, periodically bump your rates up $10 per hour.

If You're Fast, Go Flat

If you know you work fast, work on a flat rate. If the client signs off on a flat fee bid and it takes you fewer hours than you figured, you earn more per hour. Unethical? Not at all. It'd only be wrong if you quoted a number of hours, used less, but still charged them for the original higher number.

Contracts? (Use the "Bid Letter")

In nearly a decade in the business, I've only signed about six formal contracts, most of which came from the client side. What I have used a lot more often (but by no means on every job) is what I call a "bid letter," (copy provided in *TWFW*) where you spell out the details:

- *The specific parameters of the project*
- *What fee you're quoting (a range is acceptable; i.e., $1500-$1700)*
- *What's included: meetings, background reading/research (if any), copywriting, revisions (I include two rounds; additional billed at my hourly rate)*
- *Time frame for delivery*
- *Up-front deposit (usually one-third to one-half for new clients and big jobs)*

You have your client sign it and fax it back to you. Posterior covered.

Keep Your Word

Woody Allen once said something to the effect of, *90 percent of success in life is about showing up*. You don't necessarily have to be the best, brightest, fastest, or sharpest. But *do* show up—that is, do what you say you're going to do. Be where you say you're going to be. Make your word count for something. Deliver more than you promise. Put this simple no-cost strategy to work and you'll put yourself ahead of about 95 percent of the pack. No kidding. The work is out there.

Final Advice

Don't put these big brand-name EUs or marquis MM clients on a pedestal and think you're not good enough to work with them. You'd be surprised. They're just people—usually overworked and often ill-suited to their roles. If you're good and reliable, I promise you, they can use your help.

Appendix B

As I'm sure is abundantly clear by now, "well-fed writing" takes many forms and is being accomplished in many different settings by individuals with wide-ranging backgrounds, education levels and life circumstances.

As mentioned in the introduction, in *TWFW*, by definition, I could only share *my* experiences in building a freelance commercial writing business. There are so many other takes on it and I wanted to share a few of them in more detail here.

While all these folks received the same basic questionnaire from me, each chose to tell their story in a different way: some stuck to the questions, some wrote narratives, some did a hybrid. Rather than forcing them all into some set template, I chose to leave them as they were when I received them. Regardless of how they chose to craft their replies, I'm confident you'll find them as interesting, entertaining and informative as I did.

(*NOTE*: To help you zero in on specific points of identification or interest—i.e., smaller market, niche offering, journalism background, etc.—I lead off each profile with 3-5 themes present in that profile. And where I wanted to highlight something about the individual(s), I included my own intro.)

Themes:

From Publishing to FLCW
High-Tech w/NO High-Tech Experience
Brand-New City
Built Biz In Crashing Economy
First Cold Call: 9/11/01

Name: Wendy Knerr

City: Austin, Texas

PB: This is such a great story I just had to include it. In February 2000, I contacted Writers Digest Book Club to see if they'd be interested in taking on my title. I called the editor, a very warm and upbeat young woman (29 at the time) named Wendy Knerr.

When I described my book—still five months from publication—she was cautiously enthusiastic. She asked me to e-mail her a few chapters and much to my delight, I soon got a note from her telling me how much she enjoyed it and to please send more. Only too happy to comply, I continued to feed her more chapters over the next several weeks.

Ultimately, of course, the book club decided to go with it and it ended up being an exceptionally successful title for them (second best-selling Featured Alternate selection in over two years. Yeeha.). When the book appeared in the July 2000 catalog, Wendy included a mock sticky-note on the write-up, telling them how much the book had changed her thinking about writing. The last line read:

> *I've always heard that you can't make a living as a writer.*
> *The Well-Fed Writer has convinced me otherwise.*

Apparently, it truly *had* convinced her otherwise. Over the ensuing months, Wendy and I discussed the opportunity in more and more detail. It quickly became clear to both of us that she was seriously considering the field for herself. To make a long story short, in early 2001, Wendy quit her job at the book club. Not feeling entirely comfortable about jumping to freelance immediately, she went to work for an ad agency in Cincinnati for six months. In July 2001, she quit the agency and moved to Austin, Texas—a city she'd visited only once and where she had no business contacts—to start her own freelance commercial writing business.

In her first year in the business, she made twice as much money as she'd ever made in her life and was enjoying a level of freedom and flexibility that was still, in many ways, unbelievable to her. First and foremost, Wendy is committed to quality of life and to the idea of working to live, not living to work.

•   •   •

Looking back after a year, what were your keys to success?

The primary key to success is remembering, first and foremost, that this is a business and that professionalism counts even more than experience and connections. Sure, I can make phone calls to clients wearing my PJs or take a nap in the middle of the day, but when I answer the phone, you'd never know it because I always act as if my biggest client is on the other end of the line. And when I meet with a client, I always err on the side of being over-dressed and over-prepared. This professionalism extends into all aspects of the business. I don't send anything to clients without triple-checking it, and I do a thorough job on every project—even if the pay stinks—because you never know how doing a bad job is going to affect you later.

My college degree is in sociology, not English or marketing. When I got my job as an editor, my only writing experience was as a volunteer editor for a non-profit group in town. I knew I wanted to work with writing somehow, so I did free work for that group because they didn't expect me to have a big editing or writing background—they just needed someone to put their newsletter together. I found out later that when I got the paid editing job, my new employer wasn't impressed by my writing or editing background (or the lack thereof), but by my professionalism and maturity. Same is true with freelancing—be professional and you'll put yourself ahead of 90 percent of the competition.

How important was your six-month stint at the ad agency?

Working for the ad agency exposed me to some very specific types of copywriting jobs and it gave me some personal confidence that I needed to take the plunge into freelancing. But since going out on my own, I haven't worked with a single ad agency and I've rarely done the kind of writing that I did for the agency. Essentially, working for the agency showed me that I already had the skills to be a freelancer, and with hindsight I realize that I would have been just as successful in this business without that experience.

How did you get started building the business in Austin?

I've never been a big risk-taker, but something clicked while I was working at the ad agency job and I just knew I had to do something to change my life. Starting this business was the biggest risk I've ever taken and it's been one of the most satisfying experiences of my life.

I moved to Austin in the summer of 2001 without a permanent place to live and without much money set aside. I had one friend and no business contacts. My initial goal was modest—to be able to survive for six months and go on a month-long vacation to New Zealand that I'd planned and paid for long before deciding to quit my job, move and freelance. I spent the first month getting settled. Then I prepared everything I needed—business cards, portfolio, form letters, etc.—before making my first calls. On September 11, 2001, to be exact.

As you can imagine, the response was not great. The economy was plummeting, and I began to worry. But in my second week of making calls—after about 150 total—I got my first job. That client gave me enough work to live for several months and go on my trip.

When I got back, I was concerned about how the break in my momentum would affect my business. Funds were low and my spirits even lower as I made calls and didn't get immediate results like I had previously. After nearly a month of calling and two low-paying jobs, I began to panic. I looked at my finances and decided I could live for three or four more months without income and then I'd have to get a job. The next day, three clients called me. Two more called later that week. Within three months I had surpassed the income goal I had set for myself and was getting regular calls from new clients a few times a week.

What was it like being backed against a wall financially?

Scary! I don't deal well with financial uncertainty and that was my biggest fear going into this business. But it helps to be hungry. If you've got someone paying your mortgage every month, you don't have the same motivation to make it happen. I never thought that I could work under those kinds of conditions, but I really surprised myself, which is one of the blessings of going out on my own—I'm constantly challenging my ideas of what I'm capable of.

What kind of work have you gotten for the most part?

I've done quite a few Web sites for high-tech companies, along with technical papers, interview-based company profiles and brochures.

Did you know how to do this work when you started?

No. Austin is a high-tech hub, and I didn't have a tech background at all. My first client was a web developer who was looking for a technical writer to write a site for a microchip manufacturer. The site required the use of technical language—which I was completely unfamiliar with—but as it was intended for consumers, it needed a marketing spin. The client knew I didn't have a technical background and they had to decide between a tech writer with no marketing background or a marketing writer with no tech background.

I did my best to convince them to go with me, and as it turns out, I happened to cold-call them on the very day they were looking for a writer.

I also gave them a slightly lower rate than I had hoped to charge because I wanted them to take a chance on me. Since that first project, they've given me five more Web sites, a few other jobs and more down the road.

The numerous technical papers and company profiles I've handled require interviewing engineers and other technically trained people. I had never done this type of work before, but I put forth extra effort to teach myself the language and technical needs for these projects. It's paid off because every one of these clients has given me multiple projects of the same type and it gets easier to do every time.

How did you get clear about what you were offering to businesses?

I did it by creating my business card and brochure, which list the types of work I do. I rarely use my brochure now, but it was a great tool for forcing me to get focused about the kind of work I was going to pursue.

I have some design experience and can do any type of writing, but I didn't want to say to a client, "I'll do anything!" I think most clients appreciate when a writer is focused and clear about who they are and what they can offer. For example, I don't enjoy traditional ad writing, such as snappy one-liners for billboards. I'm more comfortable doing writing that educates readers, like brochures and web pages. So if I meet with an ad agency, I tell them this up front and they're always pleased to know that, among freelance writers, I'm the one to call when they need a more informative piece written.

And when people ask if I can do highly technical software documentation or if I can do design work, I tell them I could but that there are other people out there who can do it better and faster than me. I don't recommend selling yourself short and avoiding new things, but if there's work that's going to drive you crazy, be honest about it and focus on the work you enjoy.

Ten months into this career, you have a great income, lots of happy clients, tons of freedom. Is it a little hard to get used to?

I find myself shaking my head at my new life. I can't believe—and this is how it feels—that I'm getting away with this! I shouldn't be able to do this job where I'm charging $75 an hour, living a life with incredible freedom and flexibility, going for a swim in the middle of the day, knocking off early, and making more money than I've ever made in my life. It goes contrary to what we believe is the way things should be. After all, you're supposed to be in a job that you don't like and that has you working way too hard, a job that doesn't give you enough time off or even enough time to get your basic personal things done, right?

I'm living a life that many people would envy, yet I feel guilty, feel like a slacker sometimes. But then I stop, think about it and say to myself, *You created this life. You really, truly created it out of nothing and it works (laughing).* And then the other side says, *What?! How can this work? How can this be? This isn't the way life is supposed to work.* As long as a small part of you believes it can work, that's enough to keep you going when things get tough.

So much of it is attitude and working smarter. Here in Austin, I run into a lot of out-of-work technical writers, victims of the high-tech downturn, moaning and groaning about how tough it is. And here I am, a lot newer to the business than they are, brand new in town, and yet I've got plenty of work. It's certainly not a matter of me being smarter or more experienced than them, but clearly I'm tapping different avenues. I'd just encourage people to look past what they're used to and what's comfortable. There's always another avenue to pursue.

What's the most important thing you've realized this past year?

I guess it could be summed up in a quote I have on my wall from a guy named Gerar Toye: *Limitation is a creation of the mind.* I've wrestled with my own limiting thoughts over the years and especially over the last year as I built my freelance business. In my past jobs, I developed a fairly "no-risk" mindset for my life. I played it safe, didn't take many chances, and didn't even realize I was doing it. But your book opened my eyes to something I didn't think was possible. But it required that I take a big risk, and that was scary. This last year has been all about risks, taking chances, moving to new cities, you name it.

I never realized that my limitations were self-imposed, or that they were even limitations, until I stepped into this new life and saw who I could be. Turns out, I like this new me a lot.

●   ●   ●

Name: April Terrell

City: Philadelphia, Pennsylvania

Background: Recent college graduate, physics major. I had one year's professional experience in the field of technology transfer before becoming a freelance writer in this field. I had no previous writing experience other than academic papers for school. I wasn't even aware of this field until I stumbled across the position being advertised on my college's career development Web site during my senior year. I thought it sounded like a perfect match to my interests. I knew I did not want to "do science" as a career, but I wanted to keep my hand in it. I had been told many times that I was good at conveying technical and scientific information for the layperson. Technology transfer allows me to be a bridge between scientists and businesspeople.

Date Started Business: October, 2002

How Started: I made the transition from full-time office employee to at-home contractor by simply asking my employer. He was very receptive, as he had been using contractors for quite some time. He also could greatly empathize with me wanting to change geographic locations. The company is located in a rather depressed fishing town, without many opportunities for young, single people.

Brief Description of What You Do: I do Internet-based research, and make calls to interview experts in the industry I am studying. The company I contract for does work for small and large businesses, national laboratories and universities—any entity that's developed a technology and wants to learn how they can profit from it. I put the pieces together and come up with a view on what is happening in a market, what the current state of the art is, and what needs are not currently being met.

I also get a feel for how a company could best approach the market—which strategies have worked before for other people. Clients' expectations tend to vary greatly. Some want to get very involved and provide very useful feedback. Others take a hands-off approach, and are simply curious if we find the same stuff that their in-house people have found. They want the third-party feedback to confirm they're on the right track.

For example, the last project I completed was for a new non-toxic way to control the pecan nut case bearer moth in pecan crops. During my research, I called pest control consultants, pecan growers, presidents of pecan growers' associations, and editors of relevant trade publications. I found out what would make people want to buy this technology. I found growers would not pay extra for the environmentally friendly aspect of this technology. I also found out that there was really only one way to introduce this technology to growers. It became evident that my client would have to work through the pecan growers' associations to get their message across. If these organizations didn't find merit in this technology, it'd be dead in the water.

For every project we contact three targets. We find at least three companies that say they're interested in taking the next step towards deal-making. We initiate the contact, and use our gathered information to make a case for the technology. Our focus is on making money for the customer. We offer follow-up support to our formal report. So I don't just create academic-type papers that sit on a shelf. They are tools in the total package to help our customers make knowledgeable decisions and contacts in the industry.

Specific Challenges: It's difficult to be disciplined! Plus, living by myself, it gets lonely working from home all day. I have some interaction with office co-workers through e-mail and *Groove*, a collaborative workspace program, but it's just not the same as face-to-face contact. I keep a part-time job at a coffeehouse to have some structured working environment in my life. It's a great break from being in my head all day, working at a computer. The part-time job also offers health insurance, which is a huge boost.

Income Potential: $30,000-$65,000. So far, business has been really good, and I've gotten work every time I've asked for it. Income right now is simply a matter of how much I want to work. Presently, a 48-hour project pays $2000. As a full-time employee, I was expected to do three of these per month. So the potential is there for $6,000 a month. I choose to work less and have more free time to do things around the city, travel, and pursue hobbies.

Advice: Look to see if a potential employer has anyone who works from home. The possibility of switching to a contractor position held a big appeal to me when deciding to accept their job offer after graduation. I had a potential escape route if that area of the country didn't work out for me.

Necessary Background/Experience/Expertise/Qualities: Being able to make people want to talk to you is key. Calling people is sometimes difficult. Everyone has busy schedules, and talking to a complete stranger isn't high on their list of priorities. Natural curiosity is another vital quality. This job is all about learning. I jump into unfamiliar fields, and need to quickly learn the basics in order to ask intelligent questions.

Suggested Strategy to Pursue This Field: A background in any of the sciences is helpful. I didn't have any formal education about business and marketing, but I've done just fine. It seems that other technology transfer consulting companies are more demanding in terms of seeking people with MBAs. I've found that my liberal arts education has served me well.

●   ●   ●

Themes:

Smaller Market
Former Journalist
Slow Economy Startup

Name: Barbara Elmore

City: Waco, Texas (County population: 215,000. City of Waco: 115,000)

Background: 29 years in the print journalism business; BA degree in journalism

Date started business: April 2002

Positioning: I began by offering creative commercial writing to all kinds of businesses. I later narrowed my search to certain types of businesses, such as realtors, and expanded my message to include more kinds of writing as well as proofreading and editing.

Specific challenges: Going from a full-time management job with good pay and benefits to, as a colleague said, "walking a tightrope without a net." Other challenges: Waco is not a big-city market. A few large companies operate here, but most are medium and smaller. Many employ out-of-town ad agencies.

Strategy: To break into the smaller market and overcome a less-than-robust economy, I set my rates lower than someone with my experience normally would. Also, as mentioned, I took on any word-related work: copywriting, editing and proofreading. Finally, I emphasize quick project turnaround. In the newspaper business, you produce a big new product every day. That deadline mentality works to my advantage here.

Writers in smaller markets might consider doing what I did—expanding my offering to include other writing-related services (a strategy that's landed me more clients). I have recently expanded my cold-call message to include technical writing, and while I haven't tackled that so far, I do detect interest and I am hopeful that will open up a new avenue to me. I would suggest it as a way to fatten your customer list if you have the skills.

My Story: As a journalism major in college, I went directly from cap and gown to a newsroom job, writing headlines and editing copy on the news desk of an afternoon newspaper, the *Waco Times-Herald*. I was in the office by seven each morning. I hung around with guys who chain-smoked and ate boiled eggs and chili mid-morning at a place across the street from the newspaper office. Over the years, I worked as a reporter, section editor, editor of a weekly newspaper and finally, managing editor of the *Waco Tribune-Herald*.

In late 2001, after being in the same job for 16 years, I read *The Well-Fed Writer* and thought about how to accomplish the same thing in Waco, a much smaller market than Atlanta. I even e-mailed Peter to ask him what he thought. He was encouraging.

On Friday, March 29, 2002, I packed up my last cardboard box and left my second-floor office. Two weeks later, I got my first writing job without making any calls. A friend who knew what I was doing recommended me. It didn't hurt that I also knew the editor of the publication seeking a writer. That one job brought me many others—same customer, different departments.

Even though that job came serendipitously, I could not have gone anywhere without making the cold calls. How many? I don't know. After 500 calls, I lost count.

In December 2002, when work began to slow down a bit, I created a Web site, which is now up and is getting some interest. I also joined the local Chamber of Commerce and attend the networking events it hosts. They are especially attentive to new members.

As I write this, it's been almost a year since I left my well-paid job as a newspaper executive. I haven't matched my salary yet, but I'm sure I will. Meanwhile, I am doing quite well. I have reached my short-term goal: working for myself, doing it my way, and having more time to do what I want to do.

Web site: www.wordscene.com

•   •   •

Themes:
Smaller Market
Nationwide Prospecting
Specialized Niche
Former Journalist
High-Tech Focus

Name: Casey Hibbard, Compelling Cases, Inc.

City: Santa Fe, New Mexico (population: 60,000)

Date Started Business: October, 2001

Specific Niche: Simply put, I tell my clients' success stories. Compelling Cases is a full-service case study development firm that, right now, consists of me and some writing and design contractors. Basically, my clients hire me to interview their satisfied customers. Then, I write a compelling case study or extended testimonial that my clients use in sales, marketing and PR—ultimately to build credibility with prospects, partners and investors.

Right now, this is a marketing staple of smart technology companies that have to prove the return on investment of using their products or services, BUT I believe case studies can work for just about any business-to-business company, and even nonprofit organizations. The best part is, I only have to talk to my clients' *happy* customers!

Background: Before going to the "other" side and becoming a marketing writer, I was a general assignment and business/technology reporter for newspapers. I have a degree in Communications, and spent two years as an editor and project manager for a division of the University of California, Davis.

Specific Challenges: The first hurdle was repackaging myself into my new "brand." Going 100 percent with this niche basically required starting a whole new business—a new name, Web site, business cards and completely new marketing strategies. For three years, I had marketed myself as an all-purpose commercial writer. To fully seize this niche the way I envisioned required a full overhaul.

Another hurdle was the lack of awareness in the general public and marketing arena about case studies. Blank stares from people at cocktail parties or networking events quickly made me realize just how specialized my writing field is. Other writers were shocked that I would focus on such a narrow area. Yet, their expressions of doubt only fueled my determination. I strongly believed in my idea and was convinced that there were quite a few companies out there that needed what I offered. I just had to find them.

Strategy: My strategy can be summed up in two words: targeted marketing. First, there are two types of companies out there—those who know what case studies are and need them, and those who don't. I chose to go after the companies that already do case studies or that might need to do them in the near future. I put all my resources toward connecting with this group—attending technology-related events and seminars, reading and writing articles for technology publications, studying prospective companies online, and finally cold calling via phone, personalized letter or e-mail. I chose to market myself nationally in order to reach as broad an audience as possible.

Income Potential: This can vary regionally, but the average two-page case study that includes interviewing and managing the approval process with the end customer brings in $500 to $700 each. Realistic monthly income once established ranges from $4K to $6K, based on a fairly full workload.

My Story: As a general FLCW, I noticed an intriguing trend—the more I specialized, the more my business snowballed. I began devising ways to specialize more and more. First, I did mostly Web site copy, then leveraged my technology writing background by working mostly with technology companies.

After a while, tech-industry clients were increasingly asking for case studies. Personally, I loved the positive "success story" aspect of the work and this was clearly an area of growing need for tech companies. I realized I enjoyed this niche enough to focus on it exclusively.

Though I still continued doing some other copywriting for old clients, I had to be strict with myself and not take on new non-case study clients. Though the extra money in the short-term was attractive, writing brochures wasn't going to grow my case study business. I started referring that type of work to other writers.

As I began educating my clients and the marketing community about my business, the response was tremendous. They supported me and began referring me to others. To combat the lack of awareness about case studies, I revised my elevator speech repeatedly until people understood. I began getting new clients at a faster rate than ever before and it keeps accelerating. It was exciting to have the chance to interview organizations like Domino's Pizza, Steinway & Sons and the Orlando Magic.

The day I realized my business was truly successful was when I announced to my clients that I'd be relocating to another state (husband's job change)—and it didn't matter! I had a business that worked perfectly in a virtual model, as well as a strong base of loyal clients.

Advice: Don't be afraid to specialize in a specific writing niche, if you feel like there's a big enough market for your specialty. It works because you create a mental "hook" with prospects that makes you stand out.

Necessary Background/Experience/Expertise/Qualities: Beyond the qualities needed to be a general copywriter, case study writing requires a few specific skills. 1) Most importantly, you can't be afraid to write about technology. You don't have to understand the bits and bytes behind technology, but you do need to understand what it does and how it benefits users or end customers. 2) An ability to focus on one type of writing and not get bored. If you love the diversity of doing different marketing materials, this may not be for you.

Suggested Strategy to Pursue This Field: Begin doing case studies along with regular copywriting to build your experience base, then specialize after you have a solid portfolio.

Web site: www.compelling-cases.com

• • •

Themes:

Specialized Niche
Nationwide Prospecting
No College Degree
Part-Time Business Startup
Creative Business-Building

Name: Scott P. DeMenter

City: Menasha, Wisconsin, though I market my services to professionals in the death care industry all across the United States.

Date Started Business: 1999

Background: When I began my freelance copywriting business, I was in my mid-twenties, had dropped out of college, and had only written for a few national magazines. Then I came across Bob Bly's book, *Secrets of a Freelance Writer* and began reading everything I could about copywriting, advertising, marketing, public relations, and starting a freelance business.

To gain experience, I volunteered to write copy for a number of local nonprofits. I then approached several magazines I had previously written for and asked them if I could write advertising copy *pro bono* for their direct mail subscription offers. After a year, with a small portfolio under my arm, I began to search for a niche where my copywriting samples wouldn't get me laughed out the door. I found it right under my nose.

Specific Niche: To gain health benefits and a steady paycheck, I had accepted a job working as the superintendent of a local cemetery. After taking a closer look at the marketing needs of that cemetery, and soon the death care industry in general, I decided this was the perfect niche. It was focused, recession-proof and virtually devoid of competitors. Even with my pathetic portfolio, my cemetery background gave me the foot in the door that no other copywriter could, or would, challenge. I became the big fish in a little pond.

Because there was initially so little competition in the death care industry, I was able to offer a very broad assortment of copywriting services. But in the past few years, competition has increased dramatically. This has forced me to concentrate my offerings on the basics of copywriting: ad copy, brochure copy, sales letter copy and Web site content. By narrowing my focus to a limited number of services, I became seen as an expert in those fields.

Brief Description of What You Do: Because I work primarily with cemeteries and funeral homes—small, often family-owned businesses— I do a lot of handholding. There are no marketing managers in these businesses. The person I work with is normally also the owner. This means that I must help them uncover their needs and goals and determine their budget. They often have no idea what a copywriter can do for their business until I explain it to them in detail.

This type of involvement is quite time-consuming, and because my clients' businesses and budgets are small, they may not be able to provide me with repeat business for several years. Consequently, I must consistently prospect for new clients by running classified ads in the trade publications every month.

Specific Challenges: Naturally, my lack of experience, lack of a college degree and lack of a great portfolio were a challenge to me. But the greatest challenge by far was my need to simultaneously work full-time as a cemetery superintendent and run a freelance copywriting business. This meant my clients usually received my home answering machine instead of me. It was a poor first impression and poor customer service.

But because my job at the cemetery was flexible, I was often able to come in late or leave early. This was a tough way to build a business into a full-time venture, but with enough persistence and sacrifice, it can be done by anyone. Although, if I had it to do it over again, I'd take a second or third shift job to give my business a more professional image.

Strategy: Although having no initial competition seemed like a positive, the downside was that my prospects weren't really familiar with the type of services I provided. This meant educating them about the benefits of hiring a copywriter. By far the most effective tactic was writing articles on marketing and advertising for the death care industry's trade publications. Each article included my photo, Web site address, phone number and a brief description of my business. In lieu of payment, I requested a free classified ad in the issue in which my article would appear. Reprints of those articles were then posted on my Web site and used in the information packages I sent out to inquiring prospects.

Advice: It's not enough just to be able to string words together. You must understand the marketing challenges your customers face and how marketing communications can specifically help them achieve their business goals. Understand how your copywriting services can enhance their brand image, increase sales, and position them properly in the marketplace. The more consultative advice you can give your clients, the more valuable you will be to them.

Build value into your services with little extras. Offer free advice, quick turnaround times, and more than you promised to deliver. Remember that all your clients want are solutions to their problems and positive feelings. Help them to attain these things and you will have repeat customers, great word of mouth and easy access to referrals.

Necessary Background/Experience/Expertise/Qualities: Writing ability is simply the price of admission into this field. To be successful, you must understand how copywriting fits into the bigger marketing picture. You don't need a college degree to get this information, just read every marketing book you can get your hands on and everything about the industry you're specializing in. If you're going to succeed as a freelance copywriter, you must love what you do, love your customers and love the process of building your own business. If you don't, you won't have the desire to persevere on those days when everything seems to be going wrong (and believe me, you'll have plenty!).

Suggested Strategy for Success: Reading would be my number one piece of advice. It not only provides you with the information necessary to succeed, reading also makes you a better writer. The next best thing is going out into the real world and doing it. If you're like me, you'll look foolish at first, fail miserably over and over again, and eventually discover that your trial by fire was the best thing that could've happened to you. When success finally does come, you won't take it for granted.

Web site: www.DeMenter.com

• • •

Name: Heather McCarron Allard

City: Providence, Rhode Island

Background: BA degree in Humanities. Two writing courses in college, but ZERO formal writing experience. Ten years in retail sales and marketing, with large consumer product companies—cosmetics, sneakers and toys. Jobs involved selling, customer service, training and preparing training materials. Exited in 2000 and now have two daughters.

Date Started Business: January 2002. Possibly the first New Year's resolution I stuck to.

What Preparations Did You Make For Self-Employment? I followed *The Well-Fed Writer* like a prescription for success. As an at-home mom, I have to be doubly prepared—because plans can change instantly. I started my business cheaply, and took advantage of lots of freebies, like 250 free business cards from **www.vistaprint.com**. I crafted a primitive web page with *Microsoft FrontPage*. I spent a few hours typing up cold call/e-mail letters and telephone scripts. I sent out five offers to do *pro bono* work to build my portfolio—three companies bit and one hired me.

Position: I started out offering basic copywriting services—brochures, press releases, etc.—but started to enjoy the more creative stuff like Web content, taglines and ad copy. Using the Providence *Book of Lists*, I targeted graphic and Web designers. I got a few sweet pieces for my portfolio and positioned myself as a creative copywriter.

Specific Challenges: I stay home with my children, so free time is virtually non-existent and I have to make the most of every moment. I sometimes feel out of the loop, with a vocabulary reduced to "poo poo" and "binky".

Then there's the dilemma of *to tell or not to tell* clients that I'm an at-home mom. I'll be on the phone with clients and my kids will laugh or yell. Some clients say, *How old?* and I know they have children. Other are turned off.

Solutions/Strategies: Every day, I ask, *What one thing can I do to keep things rolling?* and then I do it. It might be a call, an e-mail or checking out a client's Web site. It's really worked for me—using every minute has built my business.

If I sense a client's skepticism about me working from home with kids, I spell out the advantages: low overhead means better rates. I have regular babysitters and can be flexible with meetings, conference calls and e-mails. Having children means being doubly disciplined and I take pride in meeting deadlines and "nailing" jobs on the first try. I'm professional and truthful with clients, knowing they might choose not to do business with me. If people think a woman can't raise children AND work, I probably wouldn't want to work for them anyway.

I did more e-mail cold calling than telephone calling. With daughters playing, dog barking, and TV on, it's hard to sound as professional on the phone. And the clients I was pitching to preferred e-mail anyway.

My Story: After being an at-home mom for years, I wanted to contribute to our family income—and keep my sanity. My husband and I are against daycare, so I had to find a home-based biz. I love writing and when I saw Peter's book on a writing Web site, it felt like a fit. After reading it cover to cover, I began my checklist.

Advice: Mothers are amongst the least valued people in our society. It's easy to think you have nothing to offer the business world. But mothers forget that motherhood is like running a business. There are countless motherhood skills that transfer to your freelance copywriting business. As mothers, it's important to have a schedule, yet remain flexible—to be an organized improviser. Ditto with a copywriting business. You might have three projects you're working on, when, suddenly, a new client calls with a one-week deadline.

Being a mother means hearing the word *No* all day. Same with cold calling and countless negative responses. You thicken your skin, reframe the situation and know someone *will* say *Yes*! And finally, mothers know raising children takes patience and hard work. It's the daily little things that build a healthy, successful child OR copywriting business. To make anything happen, believe in yourself—even when others tell you it's impossible. Hang inspirational stuff in your writing area—anything that gets you over your self-doubt hurdle. I taped a Chinese fortune to my monitor that read, *Many a false step is made by standing still.* Kitschy, but it works when the phones are silent and the voices in your head aren't.

Most Proud of: Within ten months, I wrote a full-page ad for *Brand Week* magazine—a national trade magazine for advertising and marketing executives. My ad appeared in the "Marketers of the Year" issue, and I earned $100 per hour. Thousands read my ad and my dream became a firm reality. I'd come from writing several *pro bono* pieces to this amazing success. I'd proven to everyone—even myself—that I could do it, that I could build something from nothing. My sense of fulfillment was overwhelming.

Average Hours Worked and Monthly Income: I work an average of 40 to 50 hours per month and earn about $2100.

• • •

Themes:

Ex-Agency Copywriter/Creative Director
Highly Motivated Self-Starter
Works Solely Through Middlemen
Averages Close to $200K Annually

Name: Jill Shtulman

City: Chicago, Illinois

Background: I started off as a copywriter in the old Montgomery Ward catalog support department. Then I segued into agency positions—copywriter at Tatham, senior copywriter at Rapp Collins Marcoa, and finally, vice president and associate creative director at Rapp Collins.

Date Started Business: August, 1989

Positioning: I focused on direct marketing and print advertising (brochures, ad campaigns, inserts) with a concentration in financial, insurance and publishing sectors.

Specific Challenges: My challenges were few. I had already spent many years in advertising positions and as a result, I had built a substantial network of contacts. Moreover, I did moonlighting for five years prior to starting my business, so I didn't need to "hit the ground running." My personality—a decisive and structured self-starter—was ideal for freelancing. The only challenge was competing against a very talented group of Chicago-based competitors.

My Story: Just two days after I became financially vested at my agency, I quit to form JSA Creative Services LLC. I had been moonlighting for five years, and had carefully studied what my competitors were doing right—and wrong. So I put together a plan. The first prong of the plan was to concentrate in sectors where the work was consistent and plentiful. Financial institutions had large direct marketing budgets and mailed in all economic climates; as a result, 60 percent of my efforts went into that arena.

Instead of working with the clients myself—as most freelancers do—I used third parties to do the prospecting work for me. In other words, I went to small marketing agencies, printers, database companies, design firms and other complementary businesses. I became part of their team; they marked up what I wrote. It was a win-win situation. I worked on Fortune 500 company assignments, yet didn't need to spend hours of my day sitting in meetings and foraging for business.

I also began courting the "bastard stepchild" of larger companies. For instance, Hallmark greeting cards were handled by a large agency, but Hallmark holiday ornaments was a division that was up for grabs. It did not have the funding of its more lucrative sister. As a result, I was able to work with them for years.

I networked a lot at the beginning, through associations and professional contacts. For a big city, Chicago is still a "who you know" town. Most importantly, as my business grew, I used the Internet as a prospecting tool. Through targeted e-mails to the membership base of direct marketing associations in other cities, I was able to gain national clients. An article about me in The Wall Street Journal added to my credibility; I could not have bought that kind of exposure.

As I move forward, I want my business to be totally portable, so that I can work anywhere at any time. Since 75 percent of JSA Creative Services LLC is now nationally-based, I have made great strides in achieving that goal.

Advice: Before you go out on your own, NETWORK. It's very important to have a solid contact base before making that jump. Experience counts a lot in this business, so make sure you get lots of it. Concentrate on lucrative sectors; fashion may be "sexy", but sectors like financial are the best funded. Above all else, always give the client a little more that what he or she asks for. Remember, the client is paying you, not the other way around.

What I'm Most Proud Of: I'm most proud of building strong and solid relationships with the third parties (as stated above). Most writers spend only half their time writing; the other half (or more) is spent growing their business or in lengthy meetings. By choosing to concentrate on writing and foregoing the glory of dealing directly with big-name clients, I've been able to take on more writing assignments than most writers could.

Success: Since 1989, my income has never dipped below six-figures, and is usually in the $200K range. Since expenses are low (home-based business), I consider that to be successful.

Web site: www.jsacreative.com

•   •   •

Themes:

Magazine Publishing Refugee
Serendipity Experiences
Uses Intern for Marketing
Builds Relationships First

Name: Kennerly Clay

City: Philadelphia, Pennsylvania

Background: Several years in magazine publishing (promotions, distribution/circulation, editorial); Non-profit (event planning, fundraising, grant writing, press kits); technology writing and script writing for CD-ROM training programs; web content development.

Got laid off twice in two years. Said, *That's it.*

Date Started Business: March, 2001.

Positioning: A "generalist" whose eclectic background lends itself to writing on a wide variety of subjects.

Specific Challenges: While I had the benefit of being married and having six months of unemployment compensation as a cushion, I felt I was starting from scratch. Several moves and layoffs meant a minimal local network. My cold calls were VERY cold. Nobody had ever heard of me anywhere. 9/11 really hurt—I barely had one job a month and I doubted the thickness of my skin.

Strategy: I followed the directions in *TWFW* and started making phone calls. I was counting on being able to generate enough business in six months (when my unemployment would run out) to get going as a freelancer.

My Story: The only start-up expense was letterhead and business cards. I'd already built my Web site and had several portfolios. I wrote out my cold call script, grabbed the Yellow Pages, started with ad agencies and design firms and then called everybody else who could use a writer. By May, I landed my first couple of clients. I continued to make phone calls through-out the summer, but learned quickly that things just die in July and August.

I was still getting a few new clients, plus phone calls and appointments. And whenever I followed up on materials sent, I always got an encouraging response. This activity kept me going until January, when I landed a big client, resulting in a flurry of activity that lasted for six months.

Spring 2002 saw a number of breakthroughs. I cold-called a technology consulting company a second time after having already left a message. The president answered and I couldn't have called him at a more perfect moment: He was sitting at his desk staring blankly at his Web content, wondering how he was going to rewrite the whole thing. Not only that, but he needed a brochure and some other marketing materials down the road. We met and he asked me to work on several jobs right away AND handle the design end of things. From then on, I gained confidence in my ability to outsource certain types of work, and to offer my clients A to Z (copy, graphics, printing) services.

I've also found that the internal administrative tasks—including database calling, various forms of marketing, Web site updates, etc.—can really pull energy and focus away from jobs I'm working on and new work coming in. By chance, I found a fantastic intern who came to work with such enthusiasm and willingness to learn, I can't imagine how I got along without her before.

She manages my contacts (using a script similar to the one I borrowed from *TWFW*). She writes the headlines and copy for my postcard mailers. She has written several ads for my business and placed them in a local media newspaper, plus she tracks all of my marketing efforts. She even re-wrote my web content and developed my new tagline. I've also made a point of giving her opportunities, to write articles for one of my clients, for example. Her contribution is invaluable and I recently hired her for eight hours a week (she was previously unpaid). We're both delighted.

Advice:
- Get an accountant. Learn Quickbooks or a similar accounting program.
- Network with corporate types at events and conferences. Join a group that can bring you some exposure and potential clients.
- Keep all the complimentary e-mails and notes you receive from clients. When you're feeling inadequate, review them and remind yourself of your value.
- Get a Web site in your name or business name and post your samples online. Your e-mail address should be **yourname@yourdomain.com**— linked to your site.
- No homemade business cards. Reeks of amateur.

- Your Web site should look as clean and professional as your stationery. If you can't do it really well yourself, pay someone to do it better.

- Re-read *TWFW*. I found I was only ready for certain information in the beginning. Six months later I was ready for more.

- Ask for referrals after the first job you do for a client. Send a letter and a brief questionnaire, asking for names, numbers, etc. of people that might be interested in my services. Post testimonials on your site.

- Call old clients to say hi and that you hope their business is doing well. Don't just assume that because you haven't done anything for them in six months that they don't want or need you anymore.

- Be honest. Be real. Make friends. I never pretend to be an expert on things I know little about. The best client relationships are those that have evolved into casual, good-humored interactions, though, in truth, that's how they started, too!

Web site: www.eclecticcontent.com

• • •

Themes:

Ex-Ad Agency Account Exec
Ex-Dot-Commer
Minimal Portfolio
Lucky Out of the Gate
Flourishing in Hi-Jobless City

Name: Jennifer Lynham

City: North Bend, Washington (30 miles east of Seattle)

Background: Seven years as an Account Executive at large advertising agencies in New York City and Portland, Oregon. I always loved the writing part of the job, which included doing creative strategies, competitive reports, white papers, even legalese and some ten-second radio tags. As I moved up the corporate ladder, my job became more schmoozing and less writing…no thanks.

Between quitting the agency job and starting my own deal, I moved up to Seattle with the boyfriend, now my husband. Shortly after settling in, I got an offer to be the content director for a Web site startup based in Nashville.

I did that for several months until it (of course) flopped. They stopped paying me on January 3, 2001; I ordered *The Well-Fed Writer* on January 4; and by January 12 I had my first gig.

Positioning: General copywriting.

Specific Challenges: Lack of professional portfolio. I had lots of *pro bono* stuff, useless content from the dot-not, and a few internal documents from my corporate days.

I'm very bad on the phone because I use a lot of visual cues to gauge communication flow. I panic if there's any white noise during a phone conversation, and tend to fill up the space with self-defeating babble.

Strategy: In this downsizing economy, I've found that by positioning myself as a "two-fer," a copywriter who can also manage projects; it allows me to get jobs that maybe purely creative types wouldn't be qualified for (or would want, for that matter...)

My Story: I got my first lead to a paying job about ten minutes after finishing *The Well-Fed Writer*. I put the book down and typed "Public Relations Agencies" into USWestDex.com. I started with the last page, and the first real live person I reached actually agreed to meet with me that Friday at 9:00 a.m. to review my work, even though she didn't have any projects at the moment.

At 7:30 that morning, she called to cancel because she had just landed a humungous *Microsoft* project and couldn't spare the time. I reminded her that I used to work on *Microsoft*'s brand image advertising and she said, *Oh, great!! If you can commit to this project for the next month, you're hired. Come in at 9:00 and help me with this beast.*

It went fabulously. For a month we worked our tails off, I learned a ton, and made over $6,000—not bad for my first assignment! And I got an impressive 60-page *Microsoft* document for my portfolio, which was really important to have at the beginning; it's hard to bill yourself as a real, professional writer around Seattle without having at least one *Microsoft* project under the belt.

What You'd Do Differently: Not spend so much time on administration. When I first started, I spent many hours formatting my call lists, trying to design my own marketing materials (I have ZERO design skills), and painstakingly researching companies before I called. It's good to take a gander at a Web site before you dial, but I was spending ten minutes or more per company, only to hear 75 percent of the time that they didn't even use freelancers.

What I'm Most Proud Of: I'm proud that in my third year of business I continue to flourish in the city with the second-highest unemployment rate in the nation. I think this is happening because I love to write anything and everything, and I have the flexibility and willingness to see forest-for-the-trees opportunities that others might run away from. For example, I took an ongoing gig at a big agency here as a proofreader. When their full time copywriter got overloaded, I was right there to offer my writing expertise. $12,000 and many assignments later, I wonder if I would've gotten in had I shunned the lowly task of proofreading.

Ditto with an editing job for a huge wireless company. The rate was lower than my usual, but I got to work at home, and it was a guaranteed 40-hour week paycheck. Plus, I added "instructional design" and "wireless" to my portfolio. My advice would be not to lower your standards, but be open to any and all kinds of writing-related assignments because you never know where they'll lead.

I'm also proud that I've been able to use my writing skills to contribute to my community. I won the Snoqualmie Valley Chamber of Commerce's "Best New Business of the Year," in part for writing editorials about issues concerning local businesses, and in part because of the many communiqués I wrote on behalf of the chamber to the City Council and the Mayor. The officials' response to this first-time-ever outreach has been quite overwhelming.

I also write regularly for www.PetShelter.org, a Web site devoted to animal welfare, and have crafted several brochures and articles about various pet-related issues that matter to me. My advice is to use your wordsmithing gift to influence and educate people about your passions. It keeps you balanced and allows you to make a real difference using words, your most powerful and unique tool.

One more proud thing: my Web site. I designed it myself a couple years ago, to teach myself HTML. It was okay, and it got me some jobs after I sent people to it, but it didn't look ultra-professional. About eight months ago, I hired a designer to help me smooth it out, and I've gotten about $10,000 worth of assignments in the last six months because people randomly found me on the Web and liked my site. The hardest thing I've ever written was my own site, but it was well worth the time and money.

Web site: www.lynhamink.com

●　　●　　●

Themes:
Ex-Journalist/Ex-PR Guy
Worked Network Extensively
Cold-Calling Advocate
Healthcare Orientation

Name: Mike Reardon

City: Southampton, Massachusetts (population, 5,500)

Date Started: February, 2002.

Story: In April 2001, I was laid off after eight months at a Boston area public relations firm that handles high-tech clients. The high-tech bubble had burst. Our clients were cutting back on their outside public relations budgets and/or taking their PR in-house. I worried about the future, but was also relieved. I hated the corporate culture.

For the rest of 2001, I looked for work, collected unemployment and did some freelance writing and PR work. Since I couldn't find a job and the freelance work was going well, at the end of 2001, I decided to go solo as a freelance writer and PR consultant.

Positioning: The first thing I did before jumping in as a freelancer was to decide where my strengths lay as a writer (I viewed the PR consultant part as simply an adjunct to writing). I had been a newspaper reporter for ten years and in that time had covered several types of stories, including politics, healthcare, business development and the arts. I also worked for about two years as a communications director for the mayor of a mid-sized Massachusetts city. I decided I would advertise myself as a writing specialist in politics, medicine, social services, and the arts. In the meantime, I was not about to turn down any work, regardless of my business niche.

Strategy: The next question was, where to begin? I had an extensive list of contacts through my years as a reporter and in politics, so I started there. I called or e-mailed these people, told them about my business and asked that they please keep me in mind should they need writing or public relations help. In addition to getting work directly from some of these folks, several of them referred me on to others.

I wrote a press release announcing the launch of my business and sent it to local papers and a regional business journal. The business journal ran my release as a brief and from that I was hired by my steadiest client to date—a hospital south of Boston.

Cold calling has also been a great way to generate business. Because I very much enjoy medical writing, I have been concentrating on this aspect of the business. My first year in business, I cold-called several hospitals and health care facilities around the Boston area and landed several lucrative projects (one close to $5,000). As someone with experience as a writer, I was fortunate to have writing samples to send potential clients.

Many of my clients are repeat customers—a freelance writer's dream. Projected revenue is $60,000 to $75,000 a year within the next two years.

What I Like: Much of the writing I've done for hospitals and healthcare facilities has been interesting. For instance, I've written several feature stories for hospital newsletters and Web sites on medical procedures, new equipment and business developments. I have also written press releases, brochures, executive profiles, trade journal articles, and other projects for a variety of businesses and organizations. I'll take on just about any writing assignment, unless it's too technical or involves special expertise beyond my scope.

Challenges: It sounds strange, given my years as a newspaper reporter and public relations professional, but one challenge I had to face as a commercial freelancer was my fear of cold-calling strangers. So, for you introverts out there, I'm here to tell you that I know it's not easy for many of us to make those calls. I still struggle with it, but I'm getting more confident.

When faced with the looming task of cold calling, I employed a couple of strategies. First, I'd designate a day or two each week and spend the bulk of that time making calls. This way, I'd scheduled this specific activity into my work week. No excuses. This is what you're doing today.

I then compiled calling lists by category. One day it might be hospitals and medical facilities. Another day, arts organizations and business groups. The more calls I made the more confident and relaxed I became. Not interested? Thank you for your time. Have a nice day. Goodbye. Next. If I got voice mail, I'd leave a message and call again in a few days if I didn't get a call back.

Advice: Don't just blindly make calls. It's extremely important to call the right person. Use company Web sites to find names and contact information of communications directors, or marketing and public relations executives.

Determine from clients exactly what they're looking for on a project. Most communications, marketing and public relations directors are overworked and often give the writer only a brief description of what they want. This can lead to trouble when you turn in something that's not what they were expecting (it's happened to me, I'm not proud to admit). If there's any doubt in your mind what you should be writing, spend more time talking with the client until the assignment is crystal clear.

Most Proud Of: Continuing to build confidence in myself and my ability as a writer, despite slow times and setbacks. It's a step-by-step process and now I can't even imagine working for an employer ever again.

Web site: www.writeimage.biz

•   •   •

Themes:

Ex-PR/Marketer/Journalist
Thriving in Competitive Market
Crafted Career to Fit Dreams

PB: Peter contacted me first in December 2002 and it was one excerpt from his e-mail that raised both my eyebrows. It's all about your expectations and his are obviously high. He wrote: I am a freelance journalist, comedian and corporate writer, living in NYC. I have recently started my own business and it's going well. The going rate in NYC is $100-$150 per hour and I'm averaging 25-30 hours per week with the corporate gigs, which gives me a good amount of time to pursue creative activities. For me, the biggest challenge is filling the pipeline and minimizing downtime between projects. *Nice problem, eh?*

Name: Peter D. Hyman

City: New York City

Date Started: December, 2001

Positioning: I offer a variety of corporate writing services, including Web site copy, speechwriting, capabilities packages and marketing analysis strategy documents. My positioning is that, having spent time in both the world of journalism and corporate communications (and still actively writing as a freelance journalist), I offer something from both sides.

Specific Challenges: Main challenge was and is maintaining the pipeline and minimizing downtime between clients.

Strategy: Having worked in PR/marketing for three years in NYC, my market became my web of contacts. I continue to break into companies by using personal connections to get in front of the marketing decision makers. An age-old strategy, but one that works.

My Story: My business grew out of necessity and frustration. I got laid off from a corporate communications job in late 2001, spent a good deal of time in 2002 just doing journalistic writing and some other creative pursuits (comedy, screenplays, etc) and was looking for a full time job. I realized that a full time job would not give me time to do the creative work I wanted and, moreover, that agency life was not what I wanted. I determined there was a market for corporate writing as a consultant, created a business and started doing it.

Advice: There are a hundred quotes from great thinkers who can summarize this more eloquently that I can, but the best advice is to put yourself in a situation where you have to dare to fail...and don't be afraid of your own imagination. My business grew out of need, out of being unemployed. I would not have voluntarily gone to that place, but being in that place allowed my creative intuition to form a business that combines my skills and what I want professionally out of life.

What I'm Most Proud Of: Well, making a good living in NYC and being able to write/perform those other things that I feel passionate about (like my first book, *The Reluctant Metrosexual: Dispatches from an Almost Hip Life*, released in July 2004—**www.pdhyman.com**).

Web site: www.pdhcommunications.com (Copywriting)

•   •   •

Themes:
Small Town Life By Choice
Married Couple/Both Commercial Writers
Tech Writing/Magazine Editing Backgrounds
Crafting Life on Their Terms

PB: Michael and Wendy live what would appear to be a mighty idyllic life in picture-postcard Woodstock, New York. They are living proof that you can set your business and life terms and the world will follow. These two actively sought out a small town, having made the decision to not work for employers/clients who required an onsite presence. But they're quick to remind you that THE main reason they chose this lifestyle was not for the money, but to free up their time to pursue other interests. Wendy has just become a certified yoga instructor, and Michael's at work on his third novel. In this interview with Michael (Wendy was tied up with a client), he shares some good advice on prospecting, working as a couple and building the dream according to your "specs."

Names: Michael Belfiore and Wendy Kagan

City: Woodstock, New York (2 hours from New York City)

What's Woodstock like?

It's a very artistic community—tons of musicians, artists, writers and aging hippies. Like New York City, there are plenty of interesting, creatively driven people but without the noise, pollution, crime, lack of space and outrageous cost of living. We're right at the foot of the Catskills in the midst of heavily forested lands. Nice place.

Your respective backgrounds?

Mine was theater (translation: I did a lot of temping). I got into freelancing as a tech writer—i.e., temping at a higher pay scale. Wendy earned an MA in English from Columbia University—which still impresses me to no end—and that led to editing for magazines. We met in New York at a magazine, fell in love and realized a few things: I didn't want to work onsite anymore—typical with tech writing—and Wendy didn't want to live in the city anymore. Around that time, a commercial writer I knew passed some overflow work to me. I not only enjoyed it, but also realized that this kind of writing was more conducive to working at home.

How hard was the transition from tech writer to commercial writer?

It was challenging, but in a good way. The standards for commercial writing tend to be much higher than for tech writing—the people who hire me actually read what I'm writing! With tech writing, they didn't seem to care what I wrote as long as it was formatted right. It was frustrating because I wanted people to appreciate what I wrote. So for me, commercial writing has more job satisfaction.

All this got us thinking about a move to a smaller town with higher quality of life and a client base that's okay with dealing with us remotely. We still meet with clients—the face-to-face is crucial in building strong relationships. In fact, I really enjoy the occasional client meeting—makes me feel connected to the working world. That said, I have regular clients with whom I occasionally meet (often in NYC, 100 miles away) as well as plenty I've never met face-to-face, and they're fine with that.

How have you gone about landing your business?

Getting established can be tough in the beginning, but I used your cold calling system with good success: As predicted, one in four or five wanted me to send info or follow up somehow. I always encourage people starting out to cold call. It works. Yes, it is hard to pick up the phone and talk to a stranger, but personally, I find it empowering when people not only don't hang up on you, but actually take you seriously as a professional.

Starting out, it was easier to work with middleman clients (in my case, mostly PR firms), who are often shorthanded. And though, in my experience, they've tended to pay less than an end-user, for that reason, they're more likely to take a chance on less experienced writers.

And while cold calling was a great way for us to get the business going, frankly, for us, referrals and networking really built it and kept it going. One current client is a graphic design firm that does work for a company a friend works at. The friend was one of several folks I called up early on and asked for referrals to anyone in PR.

I'd call up the referrals and say, *Jane Brown from ABC Company thought you might be interested in hearing from me.* One guy responded, *Oh, ABC—we do tons of work with them—send me your stuff.* At that point, I hadn't done work for ABC, though I'm guessing he assumed I had. Sort of an "implied referral." Wendy's biggest client is a company where a cousin of hers works. Over time, she's picked up more and more work from them as the word has spread through a lot of different departments.

As married work partners, do you work separately? Collaborate?

Both—by playing to each other's strengths and weaknesses. Wendy's really good at finely crafting the language (i.e. ad copy) where space is limited and it has to be brief and compelling, but not as good at the detailed technical concepts. I can sell a technical product while explaining what it is. That's where we work separately. But if one of us is swamped, we can help the other with the pieces of their project that we'd be best at doing. This process makes us stretch our respective skills and helps us grow as writers. I also enjoy and am better at the cold calling and marketing and I'm also the Web site/tech guy (and that's come in handy a few times in some scary moments!).

What's it like working together?

We're incredibly fortunate in that we love being around each other. Sure, we have our moments, but we're great officemates, and, in fact, we don't work as well when we're apart. And we're in one room—not even a divider between us! As for advice, try to separate the business and the personal. Get out of work mode when dinner rolls around and talk about something else.

How have you positioned yourselves?

We learned from the dotcom crash to not tie ourselves to any one field. Because we've learned about a lot of fields, we've been able to do work for clients in banking, finance, security, travel, technology, consumer electronics, and food. Wendy has focused mainly in travel and food, with her biggest travel client paying her $2 a word for the more flowery travel destination-related writing.

How have you dealt with the ebb and flow?

It can be tough, but just keep it in perspective. I have a tendency to generalize my experience. When everything's cranking, I'm thinking, *Wow, I'm something!* But when things are down, I'm thinking, *Maybe I should get a job.* When things slow down, get out and enjoy it and when you're slammed, know that it's only temporary.

Any other advice?

Build your relationships out of generosity and it will always come back to you. That means remembering that your fellow writers aren't just competitors, they're colleagues. Deal with them from that generous spirit as well. Help someone out. And ask for help. You'll probably get it, because often those people asked someone for help way back when and got it, and now, they're "paying it forward."

What are you most proud of in this process?

I'm proud to have made this work, both business- and lifestyle-wise. We have a great life. And every year, our income goes up 10 or 20 percent. This year, we're on target to make six figures. Remember, you're limited only by your own efforts.

Web site: www.belfioreandkagan.com

Appendix C

Here, at greater length, are the details of the project I landed at the party mentioned in Chapter 12 ("The Well-Networked Writer"). This isn't necessarily a "typical" (whatever that means) scenario, just one I feel has much to offer in the learning department. Enjoy.

So, there we were, at the snack table at the party. While I never probe too deeply in social settings, in this case, I didn't have to. As discussed, he owned a small commercial and residential security company (let's call it ABC Security) and when he found out what I did, he shared that he'd been working, somewhat unsuccessfully, on a brochure for his company. His 20-person business had been growing for ten years almost strictly by referral and on the foundation of one long-time "anchor" client, but he and his salespeople had no printed material to give to a prospect—none.

While it clearly needed to get done, he had neither the inclination, time nor in-house expertise to do it himself. Nor a big budget to hire an agency or graphic design firm to do it. *Well*, I said, *that's what I do. And I've got the creative network in place to help you handle the whole job, from start to finish.*

Not Writing, Problem-Solving

Was I offering copywriting services? Nope—I was offering a solution to a pressing problem. Don't forget that. Clients don't want copywriting services or a brochure. They want you to solve their problems. Here's what we did…

In the initial meeting, I determined that he actually had four different markets, each with their own needs and "hot buttons." While a residential consumer, say, was concerned

241

with things like peace of mind and professionalism, a building contractor would focus more on costs, timely completion, etc. One brochure couldn't possibly speak effectively to all four audiences. No wonder he was having trouble writing it. But four brochures sounds awfully expensive, right? Not necessarily. This is where a little knowledge of printing and the digital production process comes in mighty handy.

Creative Solutions

My favorite graphic designer created one four-color "shell" of the brochure: all the graphic elements minus the copy. It was an 11" x 21" page—an 11" x 17" section, which, when folded in half, yielded four 8.5" x 11" surfaces plus an extra half-page (roughly 4") flap on the right that folded in.

We printed 5000 shells and once we finalized and laid out the content for the four different brochures, we ran the shells back through the press, "overprinting" four unique versions of black text on each set of 1250 pieces. *Voila!* Four different versions of the brochure done very cost-effectively. The cost to print the four-color shell: about $2200. The cost to print the four versions of the black text was an additional $600. (*Note: These numbers are for illustrative purposes only. Printing prices vary widely by supplier.*)

Yes, we did sacrifice some creative possibilities by having to limit the text to black (as opposed to reversed-out text or some other cool graphic text effect), but if you're working with a talented designer, chances are you can minimize those concessions. Had a graphic design firm handled the project, we reminded the client, the total cost would likely have been twice what he paid. Competent freelancers just make good economic sense for any businessperson.

Maximizing the Flap

On the front side of the extra 4" flap, I suggested we come up with a list of the "The 10 Questions You Need to Ask of Any Security Provider (And Why!)." These questions would "pull the curtain back" on my client's industry. This can be a pretty savvy marketing strategy that ends up accomplishing several things:

WIN BROWNIE POINTS BY EDUCATING. By sharing useful "inside" information about an industry and how it works, we established his company as the "expert." The unspoken message: *Yes, we'd love your business, but regardless of who you ultimately hire, make sure you make a sound decision that works on all levels.* And by spilling the industry's beans, you demonstrate that you have nothing to hide, that you're one of the "good guys" and that you're in the game for long haul—all strong selling points.

HIGHLIGHT COMPANY BENEFITS. At the same time we offered a "behind-the-scenes" look at the business through these questions, the answers we provided naturally highlighted the benefits of doing business with his company. A few example questions:

1. **Are your systems serviceable by other security companies?**
   The #1 question to ask. Avoid companies with "proprietary" systems (not the way ABC Security works) that tie you to their servicing. If you're unhappy with that service, your only option is to replace the equipment.

2. **How long have you been in business?** *This industry has extremely high turnover. Look closely at any company in business for less than three years. ABC Security? Operating continuously since 1993.*

INJECT DOUBT ABOUT COMPETITORS. By being clear and specific about the ideal scenario for the consumer (i.e., how my client's company did it), the reader can't help but question what they know (or *think* they know) about the competition. And because you've picked your questions carefully, highlighting the advantages your client's firm has over their competitors—advantages that clearly benefit the consumer—your client can't help but look good.

Incidentally, why not come up with your own list of "The 10 Questions You Should Ask of Any Copywriter" and highlight the qualities a good one should possess?

Using Questionnaires

To expedite the process of collecting information about these four audiences, I had the client complete a questionnaire (similar to the one discussed in Chapter Two) designed to yield the raw material for the final content. The first two questions were:

1. *What do you feel is the USP (Unique Selling Proposition) of ABC Security?*

2. *What points about security in general and ABC Security in particular could be used for all four brochures? In other words, what are the ideas that could communicate to all your audiences?*

First, I wanted to get a sense of what made ABC Security stand out in the marketplace. This USP could form the foundation of an overall theme for the piece. Secondly, I needed to get an overall sense of the industry in order to zero in on the copy blocks that could be common to all four versions of the brochure.

These first questions were followed up by specific inquiries about each of the different audiences so I could begin forming the right language to speak most effectively to them in each of the individual pieces:

"Audience" Questionnaires:

1. *Describe this audience in a few lines (for my benefit).*

2. *What does this audience look for in a security firm?*

3. *What are the "hot buttons" for this audience?*

4. *What about ABC Security and how you operate would appeal to this audience?*

5. *What have you heard from existing clients of this audience type about doing business with ABC Security? (i.e., "Our customers tell us...")*

6. *What sort of logistical, nuts-and-bolts details does this audience want and need to know? Anything else that should be added for this audience?*

Lessons Learned—Things to Do Again

BE OPEN. Work can come from anywhere. Keep the antennae up.

TEAM UP. Join forces with other pros (i.e., graphic designers) for "turnkey" solutions. My client didn't have a plan for executing this project. By coming to him with a soup-to-nuts solution, we helped him get a pressing challenge off his plate and as such, made it easy for him to do business with us.

THINK SMALL. As discussed in Chapter Seven, there's a huge untapped market of small- to medium-sized companies, largely ignored, most of which need plenty of materials and often have the budgets to hire freelancers.

BE A PROBLEM-SOLVER, NOT JUST A WRITER. Be a benefit, NOT a feature. It's about raising your value in the eyes of the client from a writer to a consultant.

BE KNOWLEDGEABLE. Learn a little about all aspects of the process (in this case, printing). It led to a creative solution, a happy customer and a nice fee.

LISTEN. Pay attention to the client—don't decide you know what's best.

USE QUESTIONNAIRES. When appropriate, use them to quantify content parameters when you suspect the client may try to dump way too much on you in an attempt to "cover their bases."

Lessons Learned—Things To Do Differently

NICE TRY. We envisioned large chunks of copy common to all versions, meaning minimal unique verbiage. Yet while we did have "common copy," it wasn't always in the same place, and as such, couldn't be part of a fixed generic shell.

More unique verbiage meant more time. I was able to bill for a few extra hours at the end after explaining the challenges (and because the project had long "dead zones," which required more "gear-back-up" time), but you never want to go back to a client and ask for more hours unless the client "changed the deal" somehow.

KEEP IT MOVING. While having the client fill out the questionnaires reduced my research hours and saved him money, it took the timetable out of my hands. And as president, his duties couldn't help but intrude. Result: long delays. On the plus side, I got richer answers to my questions than had he been answering off-the-cuff. The ideal solution? Give him the questions to ponder and set a specific time to interview him, which would have kept the project moving on my schedule, not his. And that would've been serving *him* by getting the project done and in his hands that much sooner.

SALT WITH THAT? In retrospect, I would've added more time for editing. All in all, I probably ate five hours or so, a good chunk of them on editing. After all, we're talking four versions with edits here. Live and learn.

Appendix D

Business Structures, Taxes, Retirement and Insurance

DISCLAIMER: *The following is provided for informational purposes only and should not be considered a substitute for professional advice on business structures, tax planning, retirement options and insurance plans. Please consult your own accountant, attorney, financial planner or insurance agent.*

Not being an expert in tax issues, business structure, retirement plans and other financial matters related to business startup, I decided to find a good book on the subject. I found that book: *J.K. Lasser's Taxes Made Easy For Your Home-Based Business* by Gary W. Carter, a professor at the University of Minnesota (**www.thetaxguy.com**). I contacted Gary, and he agreed to submit a chapter to my book.

Gary's book is an excellent primer for anyone considering starting their own home-based business or already has, but wants to make sure they've structured things in the manner most optimal for their situation and circumstances. Assuming very little on the part of the reader, Gary has crafted a comprehensive guide that not only covers all the important bases but does so in an engaging, easy-to-digest manner. It should occupy an important spot on your bookshelf (next to *The Well-Fed Writer* series, of course...). Check it out.

A Few Caveats...

I. This section is simply a brief overview of the issues relating to the setup of a home-based business from the business structure, tax, retirement and insurance angles. Gary's detailed book nicely fleshes out the first three (for health insurance resources, see the links at the end of the insurance section).

247

2. Much of the discussion about business structure centers around limiting personal liability that results from potential lawsuits. While this will always be a factor, in truth, one-person writing shops will rarely—if ever—encounter a lawsuit (in over ten years in the business, I've never encountered it nor heard of any other writer having such a problem). Not to say you shouldn't cover the base, just that it's an unlikely scenario.

3. While this info (and Gary's book) provides the nitty-gritty of starting a business, I urge you to hire your own financial professionals—accountant, financial planner, attorney, etc.—to clarify specific issues or to handle the actual legal/logistical setup.

   I hire an accountant to do my taxes each year. I collect all my receipts and spend about 4 to 5 hours on my own dividing them up into expense categories so I'm ready when we sit down. I'm in and out of the accountant's office in less than two hours and for less than $200. Why anyone would want to handle tax preparation himself is totally beyond me. The money you pay a good accountant will be a pittance compared to the time, money and hassle they'll save you. Remember, your time is worth anywhere from about $60 to $100+ an hour, right?

4. Finally, you don't have to incorporate. True business novices have e-mailed me, asking if this is a required first step. There may be advantages to doing so, but all you need to start operating as a business is a business license. Take it away, Gary…

Well-Fed Business Structures

For tax purposes, a business is "that which occupies the time, attention, and labor of man for the purpose of a livelihood or profit." It need not be full-time, you could be engaged in several businesses at once and it does not presume you're actually earning an income, or generating any revenue at all—only that you're trying (in contrast to a hobby, where the primary goal is fun rather than profit).

Sole Proprietorships

Any unincorporated business owned entirely by one individual, regardless of the number of employees. It's the simplest form of business and has the advantage of low-cost formation, operation and termination. Contact your state, city or county Department of Revenue to find out about sales tax (service businesses like writing don't have to worry about sales tax, which applies to tangible products) and other filing requirements.

Because, a sole proprietorship is not an entity separate from the individual proprietor, 1) any income or loss from the proprietorship is combined with income and deductions from other sources on Form 1040, and 2) the owner has unlimited liability for debts and claims against the business.

Partnerships

A partnership is an association of two or more persons to carry on a business, with each contributing money, property, labor or skill and expecting to share in the profits and losses. The four entities that are treated as partnerships for tax purposes are: general partnerships, limited partnerships, limited liability partnerships (LLPs), and limited liability companies (LLCs) having more than one member.

Like a sole proprietorship, a partnership is not considered a separate entity for computing income tax, but acts as a conduit through which incomes and deductions are passed to the partners. As partnerships can be an extremely complex way to conduct business from a tax standpoint—and probably not the best business structure for writers—get an accountant involved early if you're contemplating one.

Corporations

Establishing a corporation involves submitting articles of incorporation to the Secretary of State of the state in which you want to incorporate. Because it's a simple process and one an attorney will charge big bucks to handle (PB Note: I paid an attorney $450 ten years ago), you might want to do it yourself (roughly $100 to $150 for the miscellaneous standard filing fees). The Secretary of State's office will typically send you an Articles of Incorporation package that allows you to fill in the blanks, pay a fee, and *voila!*—you're a corporation.

C CORPORATION

When you form a regular corporation (a C Corporation), you form a separate tax-paying entity, with income earned taxed at corporate rates. Taxation is on two levels. Earnings paid to the owner (shareholder) are taxed once at the corporate level and once paid out as dividends, are taxed again at the shareholder (personal) level. As such, for small businesses, and especially one-man operations, there aren't many advantages to incorporating as a C corporation.

S Corporation

An S corporation has the same corporate characteristics as a C: it's a legal entity chartered under state law, separate and distinct from its shareholders and officers. The big difference is that income of the S corporation is taxed only to the shareholders of the corporation rather than to the corporation itself.

While structuring your business as an S corporation is complex from a tax standpoint, it offers the advantages of a single level of taxation at the shareholder level with limited liability for corporate shareholders. Another potential advantage is the ability of S shareholders to avoid employment taxes on their share of corporate income above a reasonable wage. To elaborate, all income from a sole proprietorship, partnership, and LLC is subject to self-employment tax. S corporation income is not subject to self-employment tax if it is not paid in the form of wages to shareholders. However, the IRS keeps a close eye on S corporations that understate wages to shareholders in order to avoid this tax.

The IRS projects S corporations to be the fastest growing type of business tax entity through 2005, despite the fact that LLCs now offer an arguably more attractive option for small businesses (an LLC is simpler for a single business owner and generally provides the same advantages as an S).

Limited Liability Companies (LLCs)

An ideal financial structure for a business entity would provide limited liability for its owners, a single level of taxation, maximum flexibility in dividing profits and losses and uncomplicated rules for tax compliance. The LLC provides most of these attributes.

Consider This...

Limited liability is probably the chief reason most businesses incorporate and it does offer more protection than sole proprietorships or partnerships. However, given the myriad possibilities for liability to find you even within a corporate structure, if limiting liability is your main goal of incorporating, you might be better advised to save the accounting and attorney's fees and instead, purchase additional business liability insurance (which protects an owner against personal claims of mismanagement or malpractice).

The Home Office Deduction

As of 1999, home office deductions are available to more people than they've been for over two decades. Through proper tax planning, virtually anyone who runs a home-based business can legitimately claim home-office deductions without fear of an IRS audit.

Definitions

According to the tax laws, you can't deduct expenses for the business use of your home unless you use a portion of your home on a *regular* and *exclusive* basis:

1. As the *principal* place of any business in which you are engaged

2. As a place of business where clients or customers meet and deal with you; or

3. (in the case of a separate structure—like a garage—which is not attached to your house) In a use that is *connected* with any business in which you engage.

Exclusive means the portion of your home used for business can't be used for any other non-business purpose (i.e., to qualify, your home office can't be your dining room table). However, no rule says exclusive business use of your home office must be limited to one business or even to your principal business. You can manage more than one business from your home office and still satisfy the exclusivity test.

Expenses—Limited

The only expenses limited by the tax laws (Section 280A) are those related directly or indirectly to the use of your home office that *wouldn't* otherwise be deductible: gas, water, sewer, heat, electricity, garbage pickup, homeowners insurance, cleaning, direct repairs to your home, and depreciation (allocable to your home office). Those deductions are limited to no more than the net income from the home business. Expenses that exceed the income can be rolled over to subsequent years.

Expenses—Not Limited

Expenses that are deductible *regardless* of their business connection are not subject to the limitation. They include the portions of your property taxes, mortgage interest and casualty loss allocated to your home office (also phone expenses, office furniture depreciation, supplies). These can all be deducted even if you're showing a loss from the business.

Depreciating Personal Property

You can depreciate personal property used in connection with your home-based business, including, but not limited to, the following: computers, peripherals, copiers, fax machines, desks, chairs, lamps, files, safes, appliances, carpets, telephones, books, etc. Consult *Section 179* of the IRS code for specific guidelines.

Deduction For Health Insurance

As a business owner in a sole proprietorship or partnership, you can deduct from your gross income a percentage of the amount you pay during the year for health insurance for yourself, your spouse, and your dependents. From 1999 through 2001, that percentage was 60 percent. That increased to 70 percent for 2002, and became 100 percent for 2003 and beyond.

With S corporations and partnerships, the amount paid for health insurance of a more than a 2 percent shareholder or partner is included in shareholder's or partner's gross income as a fringe benefit, but the shareholder or partner can deduct the cost under the same rules as sole proprietors.

Planes, Trains and (Especially) Automobiles

There are two main categories of deductions for being on the road for business: 1) *travel away from home* and, 2) *transportation. Travel away from home* means you're out of town long enough to require a rest—generally overnight. In this case, allowable deductions include all meals, lodging, other living expenses and all transportation costs for getting there and back.

Transportation means local excursions around town or trips out of town completed within one day, and allowable deductions include only the expenses related to getting to and from your destination (including automobile expenses, tolls, parking, and taxi/bus fares), but not meals or lodging. If your home office qualifies as your principal place of business, you can deduct daily transportation expenses incurred in going between your home and another work location in the same trade or business. For instance, freelance writers going to meet with clients at their office for a work purpose can deduct the expenses of traveling to and from that office.

THE STANDARD MILEAGE ALLOWANCE

For either travel scenario—travel away from home or transportation—in the interest of simplicity, most people opt for a standard mileage allowance offered by the government rather than keeping track of all automobile-related expenses separately. Simply keep track of your mileage on trips and multiply by the standard mileage allowance, which for 2004 is 37.5 cents per mile. For current rates, visit www.irs.gov (look under "News Room").

PER DIEMS

The government allows you to deduct a standard per diem for meals and incidental expenses in lieu of what you actually spend. **www.policyworks. gov/perdiem** provides all the rates in all counties of all states in the country. The rates are broken down into two categories, meals and incidental expenses (M&IE) and lodging. As a self-employed person, you can only deduct 50 percent of your meal expenses.

MEALS AND ENTERTAINMENT

Taxpayers have always tried to push meals and entertainment deductions to the limit and the IRS has always been tugging back the other way. M/E expenses must be *ordinary* and *necessary* and must meet one of the following two tests:

1. They must be directly related to the active conduct of your business, or

2. They must precede or follow a substantial and *bona fide* business discussion and be associated with the active conduct of your business.

Buying lunch or dinner for an existing client (to cement a relationship and/or discuss projects) or prospect (from whom you hope to earn business) qualifies as legitimate.

Self-Employment Tax

Self-employment (SE) tax is what you pay as a self-employed individual to finance your coverage under the Social Security system. The tax is based on your net earnings from self-employment, and the combined rate is 15.3 percent (12.4 for Social Security and 2.9 percent for Medicare). While the maximum amount of earnings from self-employment subject to the Social Security part is $87,900 (2004), all your net earnings from self-employment are subject to the Medicare part (2.9 percent). While the dollar limit goes up just about every year, the rate has been the same since 1989.

This tax may be a real eye-popper for some people the first year they have income from their small business. As an employee, your employer generally pays half of your Social Security tax and withholds the other half from your paycheck. As a self-employed person, you're on your own for the whole bill.

Your combined obligation for SE tax and income tax on self-employment income should be paid in quarterly estimated payments. The good news is that the tax is computed on net earnings from self-employment, which is your self-employment income reduced by the allowable business deductions for income tax.

Federal Estimated Tax Payments

Even though your final tax liability cannot be determined until you file your income tax return at the end of the year, the government wants you to pay your taxes in installments throughout the year, using Form 1040-ES. This requires you to estimate the amount of tax you expect to owe for the year, after subtracting tax credits and tax withheld by employers. If you don't send in enough each quarter by the due date, you might be charged a penalty, even though you are due a refund when you file your tax return. Corporations, as well as individuals, are required to make estimated tax payments.

Figuring the Payments

The simplest and safest way to figure the payments for your individual return is to take the tax liability from your previous year's return, subtract the tax you expect to be withheld during the current year on wages for you (and your spouse if filing jointly) and use the difference for your total estimated tax payments. One-fourth of the total should be sent in by the due date for each quarter. Check the IRS web site or with your tax professional for payment due dates for your particular business structure.

Retirement Plans

Someday, we all want to put our feet up and chill out. Or at least have that option. Through a retirement plan, you get tax advantages for setting aside the money for those much-anticipated days of leisure.

Both sole proprietorships and partnerships can set up a simplified employee pension (SEP) plan, a Keogh plan or a savings incentive match plan, known as the SIMPLE retirement plan. A small or one-person corporation that wants to avoid complexities can also establish a SEP or SIMPLE plan (applies to both C and S corporations).

Contributions to these plans are deductible, and the earnings on them remain tax-free until you receive distributions from the plan in later years. Generally, a 10 percent penalty applies for early withdrawals before age 59½, but there are exceptions.

Simplified Employee Pensions (SEP)

A SEP is a written plan that allows you to make contributions directly to an individual retirement arrangement (SEP-IRA) that is owned by you, and separate accounts owned by each of your employees. Beginning in 2002, you could deduct as much as 25 percent of your net earnings from self-employment (up from 15 percent prior) up to a maximum of $205,000 of self-employment income (2004)

Keogh Plans

Although setting up a Keogh plan is more involved, they provide greater benefits than a SEP. A Keogh (also called qualified or H.R. 10 plan) allows greater contributions to the plan than a SEP. While contributions to a SEP are limited to 25 percent of participant's compensation (with other caveats), contributions to a Keogh can be 100 percent of compensation in some cases.

You can get help setting up and administering a Keogh from banks, mutual fund providers, insurance companies and trade or professional organizations. They act as plan providers and can offer IRS-approved plans.

The Savings Incentive Match Plan for Employees (SIMPLE)

The SIMPLE plan was authorized by the Small Business Job Protection Act of 1996. The idea was that by making the rules much simpler than those of other qualified plans, small business owners would be encouraged to adopt retirement plans. A SIMPLE plan can be established as an IRA or as part of a Section 401(k) plan. In 2004, an individual can put up to $9,000 in a SIMPLE retirement plan, and it'll top out at $10,000 in 2005.

The Traditional IRA

Whether an employee or self-employed, you can set up and make contributions to a deductible IRA if you received taxable compensation during the year and were under 70½ at the end of the year. While the limit is $3000 through 2004, it increases to $4000 for 2005 through 2007 and $5000 for 2008 and beyond. If you or your spouse were actively participating in an employer's retirement plan, the amount of your deductible contributions to an IRA depends on your adjusted gross income. Consult a financial services professional for the guidelines.

The Roth IRA

1997 saw the introduction of the Roth IRA, offering a retirement vehicle where contributions were not deductible (as they are with the traditional IRA), but all earnings accumulate tax-free *and* qualified distributions are completely non-taxable. Distributions are qualified if they're made after the account holder is 59½, deceased, disabled or is paying expenses (up to $10,000) in connection with a first-time home purchase (and provided the Roth IRA has existed for at least five years). Contribution limits are the same as for traditional IRAs.

Contributions for both traditional and Roth IRAs can be made up until April 15th of the following year.

For the following reports and others, contact the IRS at (800) TAX-FORM. Or download from the Internet at **www.irs.gov**. *For forms and instructions by fax, dial 703-368-9694 to read IRS Tax Fax.*

Publication 910: Guide to Free Tax Services

Publication 334: Tax Guide For Small Business

Publication 541: Partnerships

Publication 535: Business Expenses

Publication 550: Investment Income and Expenses

Publication 587: Business Use of Your Home

Publication 463: Travel, Entertainment, Gift and Car Expenses

Publication 1542: Per Diem Rates

Publication 946: How to Depreciate Property

Publication 560: Retirement Plans for the Self-Employed

Publication 590: Individual Retirement Arrangements (IRAs)

Publication 533: Self-Employment Tax

Publication 505: Tax Withholding and Estimated Tax

Publication 583: Starting a Business and Keeping Records

Instructions for Form 1120S (Tax Requirements for S Corporations)

•   •   •

(PB Note: I wrote the preface for the following section on health insurance, which includes attributed information as noted. It's followed by a list of resources compiled by me along with a brief discussion of business liability insurance I wrote as well.)

Health Insurance

Health insurance is one of those sacred perks of traditional employment that often keep someone in a job they hate, making it harder to make the break to self-employment. In my humble opinion, it should only be a serious sticking point if you're a single parent, or married with a family and your spouse is also self-employed. In those cases, premiums might easily run $500 a month or more. If you're married and your spouse is employed, you'll likely fall under his or her employer's policy. If you're single and childless, yes, you'll have to get a policy but even if your premiums run $250 a month, is a $3000 annual outlay a good enough reason to NOT be living the life you really want?

You're Already Paying

Heck, in most cases, as an employee, you're already paying part of your health insurance premiums. Though, when it comes right out of your paycheck every month, it seems painless. As a freelancer, you can also have your premiums automatically deducted from checking every month, which will approach the "invisibility" of the deduction you get through an employer.

FYI, I am covered through an HMO, Kaiser Permanente. Good organization, national coverage. With Kaiser, you're bundled together with a larger group of subscribers and it's your group's total usage during the year that determines your premiums and how much they increase annually (and know they *will* increase every year; it's just a question of amount). Of course, the group arrangement has its pros and cons. As someone who rarely uses it, I'm essentially subsidizing those who use it a lot, but on the flip side, should I suddenly need to increase my use dramatically, my individual premiums won't go through the roof as a result.

Hunt 'N Click

No insurance guru am I so I put my mouse to work. The following health insurance overview was adapted from info found on **www.life-line.org,** the site for the *Life and Health Insurance Foundation for Education* (LIFE) and a great site for all the lowdown on health insurance options (plus other types of insurance as well). I contacted the nice folks at LIFE and they happily granted me permission to use the piece.

●   ●   ●

Health Insurance Overview (www.life-line.org)

Health care is changing rapidly. While twenty-five years ago, nearly all Americans had indemnity insurance (allowing the user to go to any doctor, hospital, or other health provider), today, more than half of all Americans who have insurance are enrolled in some kind of managed care plan, a more structured way of both providing health services and paying for them. The initial impetus for managed care was a desire to contain costs. Increases in health-care costs had far outpaced increases in inflation throughout the '80s and into the '90s.

Today there is a full range of health insurance choices: In terms of cost and greatest patient freedom of choice, traditional indemnity plans are at one end of the spectrum (most expensive, most choice) and Health Maintenance Organizations (HMOs) are at the other (least expensive, least choice). Between the two are point-of-service (POS) plans and preferred provider organizations (PPOs), which are hybrids of indemnity plans and HMOs. POS, PPO and HMO plans are all known collectively as "managed care."

Indemnity Plans

With an indemnity plan (sometimes called fee-for-service), you can use any medical provider. You, or they, send the bill to the insurance company, which pays part of the cost. Usually you have a deductible, which is the amount of the covered expenses you must pay each year before the insurer starts to reimburse you.

Once you meet the deductible, most indemnity plans pay a percentage of what they consider the *usual and customary* charge for covered services. The insurer generally pays 80 percent of the usual and customary costs and you pay the other 20 percent, which is known as coinsurance. If the provider charges more than the usual and customary rates, you will have to pay both the coinsurance and the excess charges.

Policies typically have an out-of-pocket maximum. This means that once your covered expenses reach a certain amount in a given calendar year, the insurer will pay the usual and customary fee for covered benefits in full, and you no longer pay the coinsurance. (If your doctor bills you more than the usual customary charge, you may still have to pay a portion of the bill.)

There also may be lifetime limits on benefits paid under the policy. Most experts recommend that you look for a policy with a lifetime limit of at least $1 million. Anything less may prove to be inadequate.

Managed Care

Managed care plans generally provide comprehensive health services to their members and offer financial incentives for patients to use the providers who belong to the plan. There are three major types of managed care plans: preferred provider organizations (PPOs), point-of-service (POS) plans and health maintenance organizations (HMOs).

PPO (PREFERRED PROVIDER ORGANIZATION)

A PPO is the form of managed care closest to an indemnity plan. A PPO negotiates discounts with doctors, hospitals, and other providers of care who will accept lower fees from the insurer for their services. As a result, the premiums are lower because some of the provider payments will be discounted.

If you go to a doctor within the PPO network, you will pay a co-payment (a set amount you pay for certain services, say, $10 for a doctor, or $5 for a prescription). In addition, your coinsurance will be based on the negotiated discounted charges for PPO members. For example, the insurer may reimburse you for 90 percent of the cost if you go to a provider within the network and less if you choose a provider outside the network (plus, when using outside providers, you may have to pay the difference between what the provider charges and what the plan will recognize as a reasonable charge).

PPOs allow members to make self-referrals: plan members can refer themselves to doctors of their choice, including specialists inside and outside the network (though members may incur higher co-payments for using out-of-network providers).

POS (POINT-OF-SERVICE)

Many HMOs offer plan members the option to self-direct care, as one would under an indemnity or PPO plan, rather than get referrals from primary care physicians. An HMO with this opt-out provision is known as a point-of-service (POS) plan. Whether the plan functions like an HMO or an indemnity plan depends on whether plan members use their primary care physician or self direct their care at the "point of service."

For example, when medical care is needed, the plan member has up to three choices, depending on the particular health plan. The plan member can choose to go through his or her primary care physician, in which case services will be covered under HMO guidelines (i.e., usually a co-payment will be required).

Alternatively, the plan member can access care through a PPO provider and the services will be covered under in-network PPO rules (i.e., usually a co-payment and coinsurance will be required). Lastly, if the plan member chooses to obtain services from a provider outside the HMO and PPO networks, the services will be reimbursed according to out-of-network rules (i.e., usually a co-payment and higher coinsurance charge will be required).

HMO (HEALTH MAINTENANCE ORGANIZATION)

HMOs are the oldest form of managed care plan. In an HMO, instead of paying for each service that you receive separately, your coverage is paid in advance. This is called prepaid care. For a set monthly fee, HMOs offer members a range of health benefits, including preventive care, but typically your primary care physician must authorize care.

HMOs will give you a list of doctors from which to choose a primary care physician. This doctor coordinates your care, which means that generally you must contact him or her to be referred to any specialist. Typically, with most HMOs there is a co-payment for office visits, hospitalizations, and other health services.

Information Resources

For more information on health insurance (as well as life and disability insurance), visit **www.life-line.org**.

For a good glossary on insurance vernacular, visit: **www.medicalplans4less.com**

To find a health insurance agent in your area, visit: **www.insurancenearyou.com**.

Provider Resources

Fractured Atlas (www.fracturedatlas.org)

For roughly $75/month for an individual in most any state, Fractured Atlas (a New York-based organization with a mission to provide support and resources for artists across the spectrum) can provide a basic, no-frills health insurance plan.

National Writers Union (www.nwu.org)

The NWU offers a health plan to members living in the state of New York, and a dental-vision-life insurance package to members everywhere. These plans are administered by Alicare. Contacts: **nwuinfo@alicare.com** (800) 725-9213 (NWU/Alicare Help line)

American Society of Journalists and Authors (www.asja.org)

ASJA offers insurance to their members through Fractured Atlas and other sources. Visit their website for more details.

Working Today (www.workingtoday.org)

If you live and work in the New York City area, check out Working Today for access to a group HMO plan along with a bunch of other juicy resources for the self-employed.

Business Liability Insurance

DISCLAIMER: *The following should not be considered professional advice on the relative merits of purchasing business liability insurance. Please consult an insurance industry professional for specific advice and recommendations.*

I've gotten enough emails on the subject of business liability insurance that I thought I'd address it in a cursory overview. Business liability insurance—available through the same insurance agent who sells you auto and homeowners policies—is similar to homeowners insurance, but for a business. It covers such issues as defamation of character, advertising insurance (your ad promises one thing, but you deliver something different and have to make it up to customers), slips and falls (visitor/clients on your business premises), etc. Contact your agent for a full description of coverage. According to my agent at State Farm, a BLI policy will run roughly $375 to 600 a year.

Long Shots

If you have a business office outside your home, BLI is pretty much imperative, just as homeowners insurance would be for a home. If you have a home office, as most of us do, it's your call. I don't have it and most home-based freelancers I know don't. Point is, most of the things it covers are, plain and simple, just not likely to happen to the average freelancer. And yes, I'm sure your attorney could come up with any number of horror scenarios (remember, that's their job) but the fact is, they're long shots of biblical proportions. In my ten years of doing this, I've never known or heard of anyone who had a problem that BLI would have prevented. That said, do your own due diligence.

And FYI, there's also something called professional liability insurance, which is really more for larger companies and higher-risk professions. I talked to a colleague who looked into it several years back, found the application to be exhaustively onerous and the premiums prohibitively expense (many, many thousands of dollars a year). Simply not worth it and not necessary for what we do.

Homeowners Plus?

Again according to my agent, for those who work out of their home, there exists the possibility of adding an "endorsement" to your existing homeowners policy to cover certain aspects of business operation. State Farm actually has a program that addresses this called, *Business in the Home* (wildly original…) that could end up saving you money over a traditional BLI policy, perhaps making it a good and economical solution.

Appendix E

The following is a not-necessarily very scientific compilation of resources for writers. By definition, it is the farthest thing from exhaustive, and while every one of them isn't necessarily exclusively geared toward commercial writers, they were all recommended by successful FLCWs as being of value. Find a more comprehensive list of writing resources at **www.wellfedwriter.com** ("Links").

Writing/Marketing Books

The Copywriter's Handbook by Bob Bly
  A classic on the how-to of business writing.

Selling Your Services by Bob Bly
  Great insights on giving quotes—especially high ones—and justifying prices, along with the psychology of winning clients.

Hey Whipple, Squeeze This: A Guide to Creating Great Ads by Luke Sullivan
  Wonderful book with gems on every page to help you improve not just ads, but anything you write.

Guerilla Marketing by Jay Conrad Levinson
Guerilla Publicity by Jay Conrad Levinson
Guerilla Marketing for Writers by Levinson, Freshman & Larsen
  A trio of standouts on creative marketing and publicity strategies

Marketing Strategies for Writers by Michael Sedge
Mostly geared to magazine writers but with enough fabulously entertaining lessons on being outrageously bold that ANY writer looking to profit from their writing can benefit.

1001 Ways to Market Your Services, Even if you Hate to Sell by Rick Crandall
A fun and wildly juicy marketing "thought-starter" with yes, 1001 one to two paragraph examples. **www.ForPeopleWhoHateToSell.com**

Marketing Your Services: For People Who Hate to Sell by Rick Crandall
Delves into greater detail on many marketing topics, plus examples.

Get Clients Now! by C.J. Hayden
Bestseller by business coach C.J. Hayden for consultants, coaches, salespeople, and anyone who markets a service business.

Cold Calling for Women: Opening Doors & Closing Sales by Wendy Weiss

How to be Your Own Publicist by Jessica Hatchigan
Do-it-yourself playbook shares insider secrets for scoring positive publicity

The 22 Immutable Laws of Marketing: Violate Them At Your Own Risk by Al Reis & Jack Trout (authors of *Positioning*)

Wizard of Ads: Turning Words Into Magic and Dreamers in Millionaires by Roy Williams
Challenging insights for anyone who communicates for a living.

Ogilvy on Advertising by David Ogilvy (THE classic work on advertising)

Direct Marketing by Howard Nash ("the bible of direct marketing")

Atlas Shrugged by Ayn Rand
The classic novel about business and economics as it relates to the way the world works.

Purple Cow by Seth Godin
Strategies for differentiating your offering from the competition.

"The Business Side of Creativity" by Cameron Foote (**www.creativebusiness.com**)
The largest-selling "how-to" book on setting up a freelance creative business.

Cold Calling Techniques That Really Work! by Stephan Schiffman
  Proven techniques for reaching decision-makers and making appointments (and pitches).

Zing: Five Steps and 101 Tips for Creativity on Command by Sam Harrison
  A great guide to jumpstart your creative juices.

Don't Make Me Think by Steve Krug
  (Says one reader: "If you read just one book on web usability, make it this one.") **www.sensible.com/index.html**

Web Word Wizardry by Rachel McAlpine
  A must-have how-to for web content writing

Ready, Aim Specialize: Create Your Own Writing Specialty and Make More Money by Kelly James-Enger
  For magazine freelancers (many still do a bit of that…)

The E-Myth Revisited: Why Most Small Businesses Don't Work and What to Do About It. by Michael Gerber;
  If you've never run your own business (and even if you have), READ THIS BOOK.

References

Simpson's Contemporary Quotations: The Most Notable Quotes Since 1950 by James B. Simpson

Words That Sell: The Thesaurus to Help You Promote Your Products, Services, and Ideas by Richard Bayan

The Synonym Finder by J.I. Rodale
  PB: This nearly 1400-page beauty is, hands-down, the most often used reference book on my shelf. Arranged like a dictionary for easy use.

Woe Is I: The Grammarphobe's Guide to Better English in Plain English by Patricia T. O'Conner
  Very practical and delightfully written

The Associated Press Stylebook and Libel Manual, from Addison Wesley

Newton's Telecom Dictionary An informative and entertaining reference for anyone who writes for the telecomm industry.

The Grammar Hotline at Georgia State University's Center for Writing and Research. 404-651-2906 and writing@gsu.edu.
   Perhaps schools in other markets have similar.

Writing/Marketing Web Sites

www.writersweekly.com The FREE Marketing E-mag for Writers, published by freelance writing maven Angela Adair-Hoy.

www.writing-world.com (formerly **Inkspot.com**) The Writer's Resource—One of THE premier and most respected sites for writers: articles, links, resources, and networking.

www.yudkin.com Published! and Creative Marketing Solutions, both by 20-year veteran freelancer Marcia Yudkin, offer dozens of useful articles on making a living as a freelance writer. Subscribe to her Marketing Minute at **www.yudkin.com/markmin.htm**.

www.worldwidefreelance.com A great resource for freelance writers with a fully-searchable database of markets from North America and around the world.

www.bly.com The site of THE guy who launched it all—the original commercial writer and author (or co-author) of 55+ books on writing and business. Great articles, tips, resources.

www.writersmanual.com "The bragging zone for writers worldwide."

www.writingformoney.com The Internet newsletter that shows you how to make money and live a great life as a freelance writer.

www.writingfordollars.com Find current markets that pay; how to market what you write and earn more; tips for entering high paying markets; and interviews with successful writing professionals.

www.writersdigest.com *Writer's Digest*, one of the world's leading magazines for writers.

www.writers-editors.com Where editors, businesses, and creative directors can locate writers, copy editors, proofreaders, ad copywriters, ghostwriters and PR help.

www.creativebusiness.com Run by Cameron Foote, author of *The Business Side of Creativity*. 100+ downloadable articles and forms (many free) to help freelance writers.

www.writermag.com *The Writer*, one of the world's leading magazines for writers.

www.writedirections.com Classes, how-to articles, writing resources, coaching/consulting and free newsletters loaded with tips, tool, and leads!

www.writingcareer.com E-media publishers of the writing trade.

www.dobkin.com The home of "Marketing Master" Jeffrey Dobkin, author of *How To Market a Product for Under $500*. Excellent (and free) articles on various aspects of the marketing process.

www.abraham.com Actionable strategies from marketing guru Jay Abraham to "grow your business beyond anything you ever expected or even hoped."

www.cargillsells.com Gill Cargill, a top sales training professional, and according to one reader, "a fabulous resource for anyone who needs to market his or her business."

http://bartleby.com/141/ The Elements of Style (now it's online!).

http://dictionary.reference.com Dictionary.com.

www.absolutewrite.com (Both free and premium versions).

Online Copywriting Resources

www.useit.com/papers/webwriting/ Jakob Neilson is a guru in the field of web usability. This page on his site has links to numerous articles, books and guides.

www.nickusborne.com Articles, newsletter, link to Web writing book.

www.excessvoice.com/index.htm Nick Usborne's Excess Voice site and newsletter for online copywriters.

www.marketingwonk.com/lists/icopywriting/ I-Copywriting Discussion List.

www.gerrymcgovern.com Gerry McGovern, web content guru.

www.highrankings.com/seo-writing.htm The Nitty-gritty of Writing for the Search Engines. An e-book showing how to write optimized copy.

www.highrankings.com/forum/index.php?showforum=15 High Rankings Forum Section on Web Copywriting.

Writing/Marketing E-Newsletters

Bob Bly's Direct Response Letter (Monthly)
Editor: Bob Bly
Website: **http://www.bly.com**
Focus: Copywriting

eNewsletter Journal (Monthly)
Editor: Meryl K. Evans
Website: **http://www.internetviz.com**
Focus: E-mail Newsletters (Ezines)

The Marketing Minute (Weekly)
Editor: Marcia Yudkin
Website: **http://www.yudkin.com/markmin.htm**
Focus: General Marketing With an Emphasis on Writing

Marketing Sherpa [E-mail Sherpa] (Weekly)
Managing Editor: Anne Holland
Website: **http://www.marketingsherpa.com**
Focus: Marketing Know-how/Case Studies

MarketingProfs Today (Weekly)
Editor: Ann Handley
Website: **http://www.marketingprofs.com**
Focus: General Marketing Tips from Industry Experts

The Publicity Hound's Tips of the Week (Weekly)
Editor: Joan Steward
Website: **http://www.publicityhound.com**
Focus: Effective Public Relations

Publish for Profits (Bi-weekly)
Editor: Alexandria K. Brown (a.k.a. The Ezine Queen)
Website: **http://www.ezinequeen.com**
Focus: Publishing Ezines

Straight from the Horse's Mouth (Weekly)
Editor: Harmony Major
Website: **http://www.harmonymajor.com**
Focus: Internet Marketing

TargetX's E-mail Minute (Weekly)
Editor: None listed
Website: **http://www.targetx.com**
Focus: E-mail Marketing

The Well-Fed E-Pub (Monthly)
Editor: Peter Bowerman
Website: **http://www.wellfedwriter.com**
Focus: Copywriting/Marketing

WordBiz Report (Weekly)
Editor: Debbie Weil
Website: **http://www.wordbiz.com**
Focus: Business Writing

Writers Groups

A short list of regional and national writing/business organizations. Some may be more commercial in nature than others. PLEASE remember: Every group has a different profile and "vibe." Respect their right to NOT accept everyone if, in their estimation and for whatever reason, it's just not a fit. Remember, you can always start your own group.

Chicago
IWOC (Independent Writers of Chicago): **www.iwoc.org**
CADM (Chicago Association of Direct Marketing): **www.cadm.org**

Ohio
Downtown Writers (Columbus-based): **www.downtownwriters.com**

Washington, DC
Washington Independent Writers: **www.washwriter.org**

Austin, TX
The Writing Mafia—contact Tom Myer at **tom@tripledogdaremedia.com**. (Tom adds: "Any commercial writer elsewhere in the country wanting to start their own WM after our model is welcome to contact me, and we'll get you started.")

Tampa Bay, FL
Bay Area Professional Writers Guild (Google for site, as it may change)

New Jersey
New Jersey Creatives: **www.njcreatives.org**

Professional Writers Alliance (PWA) of Mercer County:
www.pwawriters.org

Communications, Advertising and Marketing Association:
www.njcama.org

Atlanta
The Freelance Forum: **www.freelanceforum.org**

Creativity Atlanta: **www.atlantaadclub.org**

Seattle
Freelance Seattle: **www.freelance-seattle.net**
(two-branch listserv: discussions/project postings

Seattle Writergrrls: **www.seattlewritergrrls.org** not purely commercial,
but good for keeping the creative side of our jobs fresh.

Los Angeles
Contact Dave Tandet at **david@frontlinewriting.com**. Dave is part of
a small, spirited and growing group of commercial freelancers.

Nationwide (find local chapters)
IABC—International Assoc. of Business Communicators: **www.iabc.com**

PRSA—Public Relations Society of America—**www.prsa.org**

BMA—Business Marketing Association—**www.marketing.org**

BNI—Business Network International—**www.bni.com**

NOWA - Network of Writers and Artists—**www.nowa.org**

EFA—Editorial Freelancers Association—**http://the-efa.org**

STC—Society For Technical Communication—**www.stc.org**

Well-Fed Chat Rooms

U.S.

To Subscribe:

1. Send e-mail to **wellfed_writers-subscribe@yahoogroups.com** with no subject or body.

   OR

2. Go to **http://groups.yahoo.com/group/wellfed_writers/join** (you'll be prompted to create a Yahoo account).

U.K.

Visit **www.wordmeister.co.uk/ukwfw.html** to sign up.

At-Home-Mom Links

www.WAHM.com
The Online Magazine For Work-At-Home Moms

www.bizymoms.com
Who Says We Can't Have It All? Be A Work-At-Home Mom!

www.momwriters.com
For Those Facing The Challenge Of Writing With Children Underfoot

www.hbwm.com
Committed To Bringing Working Moms Closer To Their Children

www.momsnetwork.com
Helping Moms Succeed—One Of The Original Sites For Work-At-Home Moms

www.homeworkingmom.com
A Mom's First Step to Working at Home

www.athomemothers.com
Complete Support for the At-Home Motherhood Lifestyle

Appendix F

Why am I devoting a section of this book to self-publishing? For one simple reason: Self-publishing has absolutely been well-fed writing for me. For nearly three years, *TWFW* supported me full-time. Yes, I took on a decent number of writing jobs and stayed in the flow of commercial writing, but I didn't need the commercial work to make ends meet. Now, we're not talking about "picking-out-chateaux-in-the-South-of-France" kind of money, but the book provided enough to pay all the bills (including two book printings a year), fund my savings program and take a few nice vacations a year.

Thanks to the Internet, self-publishing has become a more viable direction than ever before. And given how hard it is to land a publisher and how long it takes to get your book in print once you do (18 to 24 months on average), many are going the self-pub route.

• • •

Sometime back—I'll never forget the day—I was checking my e-mail and I got another book order notification. On my Web site, a little data-capture mechanism asks for name, e-mail addy (to build a reader's list) and the source where the ordering party heard about the book. The buyer's answer? *Everywhere!* Music to an author's ears.

Multiple Impressions

I kept hearing different iterations of the same basic theme. One woman wrote: *I first heard about your book on writersdigest.com, then on writerswrite.com and finally on writersweekly.com. I figured I needed to check it out.* What does that tell us? That people need multiple impressions before they take action. Useful information.

273

It all started with my book and me. No big publishing house, agent, publicist or juicy promotion/marketing budget. And virtually no mainstream media coverage. Yet, I still landed three major book club endorsements, including Book-of-the-Month Club, plus reviews from (historically self-pub-averse) *Library Journal* and *Booklist*. And several book awards. All the while selling over 30,000 copies in 3.5 years (FYI, that's good for *any* book, but especially for a niche offering like mine). How did I do it? By tapping the Internet, which allows you to zero in on your audiences with bulls-eye accuracy.

Exponential Efficiency

In the hugely competitive scramble for attention in the book world, the Net can be the great equalizer for the little guy. Let's take *The Well-Fed Writer* as an example. Okay, so who's my audience? I chose to focus on three: writers of all stripes, at-home moms and home-based business seekers.

GO TO YOUR MARKET

To sell books, you need reviews, which you get by going where your various target communities hang out. Scour the Internet for Web sites, associations, newsletters, newsgroups and other writers of related books. At these sites, find the "Contact Us" link and make your pitch by e-mail. And repeat the process, over and over—400+ times in my case. Try any URLs that sound right for your topic. In my case: writers.com, writing.com, freelancewriting.com, athomemoms.com, homebusiness.com, etc.

YOUR WEB SITE

Mandatory. Period. It's the linchpin of any Internet marketing push. Always add your URL to your e-mail signature (you never know where interest will come from). And by e-mailing press releases to the media, complete with URL, you give them instantaneous click-thru access to your site and all the things they need to make their job easier (like author pics, cover art, reviews, interview clips, etc.) which in turn makes it easier for them to say *Yes!*

Go visit my site when you get a moment (**www.wellfedwriter.com**). Not the last word in Web sites, but it might give you some ideas.

The Marketing Boomerang

Do enough marketing and you'll experience the delightful phenomenon I call the marketing boomerang. First, you're contacting people to get reviews, interviews, mentions and articles. Keep at it and they'll be contacting you to get a review copy. And ultimately, you'll see reviews from entities that never even contacted you; they just got the book on their own and did a review.

Send Lots of Books

Unless your books are VERY expensive, send out LOTS of review copies—even if you suspect the requestor is a mooch. In my case, for about $4 (book, mailer, press kit and media mail postage), I invest in the very best form of advertising: the book itself.

Your Official Publication Date

Put three-plus months between your official publication date (the date you're officially releasing the book) and your bound book date (the date you actually have printed books in your possession). It's perfectly okay to sell your books on your own site prior to your official publication date. The 90-day cushion gives you plenty of time to build awareness in the traditional media and in your grass roots Internet communities.

Mainstream Media?

Given that I didn't have a mainstream topic (like dieting, relationships, self-help, personal finance, sex, etc.), I've not pursued the mainstream media, which is fickle and addicted to finding the next hot thing. The only exception is when I travel to a city to a do a seminar or signing; then, my book and message are more newsworthy. Even a small article in the daily can fill up a seminar.

To get the attention of members of the media, contact them personally for best results. And when sending press releases, focus not on your book, but *the angle represented by your book.* Media people don't care that you wrote a book. All they want to know is, *What's in it for my readers?*

Book Clubs

You won't make much money with book clubs, but the promotional weight of becoming a *Book-of-the-Month Club* selection is incalculable. Check *Literary Marketplace* in the library for a complete listing of book clubs.

Shortcut to Big Library Sales

A key to library sales and enhanced credibility in general is to land reviews in such prestigious publications as *Booklist, Library Journal, Publishers Weekly, ForeWord magazine,* and *Kirkus Reviews.* They want review copies (galleys are okay) 90 to 120 days prior to your official publishing date. Once the book's officially out, it's too late. And because these pubs only review 10 to 15 percent of books submitted, librarians rely heavily on them to screen new books, often ordering all books reviewed.

How can you increase your odds of getting reviewed? Well, besides writing a really good book that appeals to a broad enough audience, *don't* skimp on your cover. Over 100,000 books get printed each year. The people considering titles for purchase, distribution or review just *look* for reasons to cull the herd and the cover is a no-brainer. Spend the money to get yours professionally designed (DON'T hire your cousin who's artistic…).

Push for the Bookstores?
Start by getting listed with the databases of the big wholesalers: Ingram (for bookstores) and Baker & Taylor (for libraries). Once you've done that, anyone can walk into a bookstore or library and order the book. But before expending a lot of energy trying to get your books in the bookstores—through the different chains' small press review processes—make sure you've established a strong and enduring demand for it. If you don't, you'll end up with a ton of returns up to a year later, in any condition, for a full refund. No fun.

If you've created a demand that drives enough people into enough Barnes & Nobles or Borders asking for the book, I promise you, they'll find you and start stocking the book.

Be a Goodwill Machine
Answer all your reader e-mail. I promise you, they'll be blown away that they got an answer at all. Give them some real attention and I promise, you'll have a friend for life and they'll tell others. Getting a reputation as a nice, generous and accessible author is a good thing.

Hire a Consultant
As a naïve first-time, self-publishing author, one of the best things I did was hire a professional publishing consultant with 40 years in the industry. Now, I offer the same mentoring services (see the *Mentoring* link at **www. wellfedwriter.com**).

Hire Out Distribution
If someone does a good job, I believe in acknowledging him or her, so yes, this is a plug. BookMasters, Inc. in Ohio printed my books and is handling all fulfillment functions, from the one-book buyer to the Ingrams, B&Ts, and Amazons of the world. They do all shipping, invoicing and revenue collection. They do this very well, so let them. You've got enough to mess with.

Keep It Up
Always be looking for more contacts in your target communities. And remember: You can't do it all. Pick and choose your battles.

On a Lighter Note...

Here's an article I wrote some time back for the *PMA Newsletter*, published monthly by Publisher's Marketing Association, the largest independent publishing association in the country (**www.pma-online.com**), and an organization well worth joining if you've decided to venture into self-publishing (along with SPAN: Small Publishers Association of North America—**www.spannet.org**). While I was clearly having a few chuckles here, it underscores the potential profitability of self-publishing. I firmly maintain that our former president would have made far more money self-publishing.

•   •   •

HAIL TO SELF-PUBLISHING

Dear President Clinton,

Congratulations on your recent record-setting, big-bucks advance for your upcoming memoirs. $10 million, huh? Bet that'll put a few legal bills and hefty Westchester county mortgages behind you. Good for you. Though I must confess, when I read that you'd given Knopf the nod to publish your recollections, I couldn't help but ponder lost opportunities.

No, not the legacy thing. Yes, I know you'd have preferred to be remembered for greater foreign policy triumphs than showing Castro where he could stick his cigars. No, I'm talking about missed opportunities to make three or four times the money off your "sure-thing" title. One word: self-publishing. Now, before you laugh and say, *My pride and joy needs to be lovingly administered to by professionals every inch of the way,* hear me out.

Sure, you deserve the royal treatment, but which would you rather have? One big name publishing company sucking up to you and paying you $10 million? Or the entire wholesaling and retailing segments of the industry sucking up to you and eventually paying you many times that?

Get real. *You* need a big-name publisher to sell your book? You gotta be kidding. *You* are a publisher's and bookseller's dream. Fascinating people are exactly what sell books. And regardless of what people think of you, you're *The Ultimate Fascinating Person.* Short of not writing the thing, there's no way you couldn't sell millions. In your case, Knopf is a very expensive and monumentally unnecessary accessory.

What do you need them for? To print your book? Please. Give me your fax number—I'll shoot you a list of 20 printers just waiting to beat their price.

I've got freelance ghostwriters, photographers, graphic designers and typesetters out the wazoo waiting to craft your book into something that would make Michelangelo weep tears of joy.

To "ensure comprehensive distribution" of the title? Right. How they could say that with a straight face is beyond me. See those lines blinking on your phone? Ingram and Baker & Taylor, the two biggest book wholesalers, are holding for you on lines two and three, just waiting to cut deals to position the book for placement in every bookstore and library in the country. Barnes & Noble and Borders are on lines four and five, rehearsing their "whatever-they-offer-you-we'll-beat-it" speeches. They've even been burning the midnight oil trying to figure out how to bypass the wholesalers.

For publicity and media relations? Sheesh. Let me paint you a picture. Right now, every book editor for every newspaper in the country has left a standing order with the mail room to immediately hand-carry your review copy to his desk the second it arrives. Their orders are clear: *Peek and your head goes on stake in the lobby as a warning to the others.*

Oprah and Jerry and Geraldo and Katie and Matt and Regis and Kelly and Rosie and Rush and Larry and Charlie and Bill and Ted and Diane and Jay and David and Conan and The View and Fresh Air and a zillion others are skittering around drooling, panting, heaving and wetting themselves over the prospect of even five minutes with you. They've threatened their minions with hideous agonizing eternal torment if they don't land you first and fast.

I'm guessing they'll price it around $30. What're those greedy bums offering you, $3-4 tops? Okay, figure $2-3 each for printing, press kits, etc. That's $27 left. You'll give up an absolute max of 50% to the distribution network and I'm being gloomy here (I can hear their howls of protest now—"MUCH lower!!")

That's roughly 13 bucks a pop, net. Times what? 5-6 million copies easy? We're talking $65-75 million. I'm telling you, big guy, you're leaving some serious cheese on the table. Put me in, coach. Gimme a shot here. I'll do it for a buck a book. Whattayasay?

•   •   •

Look for **The Well-Fed Self-Publisher:** *How to Turn One Book Into a Full-Time Living* coming in late 2005/early 2006. Want to be notified of its release? E-mail me at **peter@wellfedwriter.com**.

Index